THE SHAPING OF THE SWEDISH HEALTH SYSTEM

THE SHAPING OF THE SWEDISH HEALTH SYSTEM

Edited by

Arnold J. Heidenheimer
and Nils Elvander

with the assistance of Charly Hultén

ST. MARTIN'S PRESS   NEW YORK

© 1980 Arnold J. Heidenheimer and Nils Elvander
All rights reserved. For information write:
St. Martin's Press, Inc., 175 Fifth Avenue, New York, N.Y. 10010
Printed in Great Britain
First published in the United States in 1980

Library of Congress Cataloging in Publication Data

Heidenheimer, Arnold J
    The shaping of the Swedish health system.

    Includes index.
    1. Medical policy — Sweden — Congresses.   2. Medical
care — Sweden — Congresses.   3. Medicine, State —
Sweden — Congresses.   I. Elvander, Nils.   II. Hultén,
Charly.   III. Title. [DNLM: 1. State medicine —
Sweden — Congresses.   2. National health programs —
Sweden — Congresses.   W275 GS8 S52 1978]
RA395.S8H44 1980   362.1'0948   80-12410
ISBN 0-312-71627-3

Typeset in Great Britain by
Pintail Studios Limited, Ringwood, Hants.
Printed by Biddles Limited, Guildford, Surrey.

CONTENTS

THE SHAPING OF THE SWEDISH HEALTH SYSTEM

INTRODUCTION

The conception which guides this book is to present a contextual analysis of Swedish health care policy in historical and comparative perspective. The literature on this subject is rather fragmentary. Swedish scholars of social medicine and sociology have focused on current problems in health care delivery and consumption. Some non-Swedish social scientists have studied various aspects of the Swedish health system in a comparative perspective. But nobody, apart from Odin Anderson, has tried to relate an analysis of the emergence of the system to political analysis of the problems confronting it today. This book attempts to fill this gap, thereby serving a public of Scandinavian social and medical scientists, politicians, and health administrators, as well as the many foreign scholars who are interested in the Swedish health system.

Noting that 'foreign writers about the Swedish scene have often relied heavily on official documents and statements', Assar Lindbeck has concluded that this tendency has caused 'the picture of Swedish economic and social policy abroad to be less interesting than it really is'.[1] This judgement might apply to some publications about the Swedish health system, but we trust not to this volume. Many of our contributors, and perhaps especially the non-Swedish ones, have supplemented official sources with unofficial ones by utilising the records of interest organisations, information gained in interviews, as well as other sources of printed and oral information.

Most of the chapters in this book have a strong historical dimension. One reason for this is that social scientists have ventured to investigate where their historian and medical colleagues have not been inclined to tread. Another, more positive, reason is that many of the authors share the perspective that much of what is most politically interesting about the Swedish policy can only be appreciated in a longer-term perspective. Recent international studies have placed Sweden's health system ahead of other European ones in terms of measures of quantitative development, and even concluded that, 'At current growth rates, Swedish health manpower will rapidly exceed levels that other countries would consider an oversupply.'[2] But before political and social scientists can contribute to an explanation of how Sweden achieved this position, they should become more aware of how and why Sweden ranked so very differently in such comparisons during preceding eras.

Because they seek to open up new ground, most of these studies are deliberately exploratory and suggestive and do not attempt to be definitive. The comparative chapters, particularly those by Ole Berg on the modernisation of medical care in Sweden and Norway, by Hirobumi Ito on health insurance in Sweden and Denmark, and by Odin Anderson and James W. Björkman on equity in health care in Sweden, Britain and the USA, should provide the basis and stimulus for more extensive and probing comparative studies in the future.

A decision-making approach to medical politics and policies is predominant in many chapters. This is partly because most of the authors are political scientists. There is, however, no theoretical or methodological uniformity among the authors. There is a wide range between the theoretical 'solutions' in Ingemar Ståhl's chapter on the growth of health care in Sweden, or the quantitative analysis of the *remiss* procedure by Bo Bjurulf and Urban Swahn, and the historical and qualitative analyses in several of the other chapters. But we have encouraged all contributors to address inter-related sets of questions, so as to try to identify the factors which caused the Swedish health system to develop into its present shape.

Our efforts to create a common pattern of problem identification were advanced through a symposium on Swedish health policy, which was arranged by us in Sigtuna, Sweden, in August 1978. All the contributors to this book participated in the conference; the chapters have emerged from their conference papers. The rest of the audience, some 30 people, were mostly medical educators and health administrators. The symposium was a stimulating confrontation between an international group of social scientists, on the one hand, and the 'practitioners' of Swedish health care and medical education on the other. The discussions in Sigtuna have influenced the content of this book in many ways.

The chapters are ordered in a chronological and systematic sequence, beginning with the historical and comparative studies by Ole Berg and Hirobumi Ito. In the second part, Bo Bjurulf and Urban Swahn, and Uncas Serner deal with the decision-making process and the development of health legislation. Then follow two papers by Arnold Heidenheimer, and Mack Carder and Bendix Klingeberg, on the role of the medical profession in health policy reforms after 1945. The economic problems of health care today are discussed in the fourth section by the economists Jan-Erik Spek and Ingemar Ståhl. Finally, a comparison of Swedish health care utilisation with that in Britain and the United States is presented by Odin Anderson and James W. Björkman.

Acknowledgements

The research results presented in this volume were facilitated by the assistance of numerous institutions and individuals who extended support to the project, the editors and the authors.

The editors would like to express appreciation for the encouragement and advice provided by Swedish medical colleagues, such as Bror Rexed, former director-general of the Board of Health; Björn Smedby, of Uppsala University; and Bo Hjern, of the Swedish Medical Association. They would also like to acknowledge grants from the Swedish Medical and Social Science Research Councils which supported the Sigtuna conference, and for additional support from these councils and Washington University, which helped to provide editorial assistance.

We would also like to say how indebted we are particularly to Charly Hultén, who not only helped us to prepare and organise the Sigtuna conference, but also provided indispensable assistance in improving several of the manuscripts. Additional valuable editorial assistance was provided by Carol Skalnick Leff in St Louis.

Ole Berg would like to thank Carol Leff for editorial improvements, and Arthur Engel, James W. Björkman and Stephen J. Kunitz, for helpful comments on earlier drafts.

Bo Bjurulf and Urban Swahn express appreciation for financial support from the Bank of Sweden Tercentenary Foundation.

Mack Carder and Bendix Klingeberg acknowledge financial support from the Swedish Institute and Washington University.

Arnold J. Heidenheimer expresses appreciation to the Swedish Institute for financial support, to the Universities of Bergen and Stockholm for inviting him to give seminars relating to the research, and to students at Washington University whose interest encouraged both his own work and that of Messrs Carder, Ito and Klingeberg.

Hirobumi Ito expresses appreciation for stimulus and advice from Arnold J. Heidenheimer and Erik Holst, to Arthur Engel for help with utilising historical materials, and to the Swedish Institute for financial assistance.

All the authors and editors express appreciation for the constructive criticism and appreciative response of those Swedish medical educators and administrators who participated in the Sigtuna conference.

We are particularly appreciative of the manner in which the presentations and comments by Edgar Borgenhammer, Henric Hultin, Egon Jonsson, Martin Holmdahl and Gunnar Ström cast valuable new and critical light on some of the topics dealt with here. Earlier, valuable assistance for our endeavours was provided by Rolf Ejvegård, Nils-Gustav Hildeman and Gunnar Wennström, among others.

Notes

1. Assar Lindbeck, *Swedish Economic Policy* (University of California Press, Berkeley, 1974), p. xi.

2. Jan Blanpain, *et al.*, *National Health Insurance and Health Resources: The European Experience* (Harvard University Press, Cambridge, Mass., 1978), p. 264.

A BASIC ORIENTATION

Geographic Rudiments

One feature of Sweden that may not be immediately apparent to the foreign reader, but which is essential to an understanding of Swedish public policy, is how unevenly the country is populated. While her economy is heavily industrial, large areas of Sweden are basically rural, with vast reaches to the north and west hardly populated at all.

Thirty per cent of Sweden's 8.2 million people live in her three major cities (Stockholm, pop. 1.4 million; Gothenburg, 700,000; Malmö, 460,000). Eight other towns have populations of 100,000 or more. The remainder of the population, roughly 5 million people, is thinly spread over the country's 450,000 square miles (an area greater than Italy, Switzerland and Austria combined).

This has obvious implications with respect to the provision of social services — particularly in a strongly egalitarian ideological context — and these underlie much of the discussion in the ensuing chapters.

Local Government: *Län*, *Landsting*, *Kommun* and *Stad*

Swedish county administrative districts (*län*) are the supreme units of regional administration of the central government. Since 1971, each *län* has been ruled by a county administrative board (*länsstyrelse*), chaired by the provincial governor (*landshövding*), who is appointed by the government. The boards answer directly to the government, whereas other regional organs of the central government fall under one or another of the central administrative organs. Five of the ten members of these lay boards are appointed by the government, and five by the respective county council (see below). Once the sole representatives of the Crown in each province, the county administrative boards have come to play more the role of co-ordinators of central government policy at the regional level. They can also exert supervisory control over social and physical planning undertaken at the local level.

The county councils (*landsting*) are directly elected bodies, whose geographical sphere of authority coincides (with a few exceptions) with *län* boundaries. The county council is the organ of local autonomy over *län*-wide services, mainly health and medical care (which accounts for roughly 85 per cent of county council budgets), but also social services, public transportation and regional planning. In administrative terms

11

county councils have the character of an independent secondary level of local government in that they encompass several municipalities. Their authority shall not, however, infringe upon constitutionally guaranteed municipal sovereignty.

Finally, the primary level of local government is the municipality (*kommun*). Rapid urbanisation, with consequent depopulation of rural areas, together with an increase in assigned functions, necessitated a basic restructuring of local government, which has been undertaken successively in post-war years. A series of basic reforms in the 1950s and 1960s reduced the number of municipalities from 2,498 in 1951 to 277 in 1979. Consequently, most municipalities now include several communities plus the surrounding hinterland within their bounds. Roughly half have more than 20,000 inhabitants (but only 35 have more than 50,000). Legislation passed in 1965 standardised the status of municipalities, removing the former distinction between towns (*städer*) and rural or 'unincorporated' areas.

The municipalities of Gothenburg, Malmö and the island of Gotland, referred to here as county boroughs, combine county council and municipal functions. In metropolitan Stockholm the county council has taken over some municipal functions.

County councils and municipalities co-operate through two powerful nationwide organisations: the County Council Federation (*Svenska Landstingsförbundet*) and the Federation of Municipalities (*Svenska Kommunförbundet*). (The Swedish Association of Towns (*Svenska Stadsförbundet*) was absorbed into the latter organisation in 1968.)

The Social Insurance Funds

There is a social insurance fund (*försäkringskassa*, *sjukkassa*) in each county council and county borough. The funds represent regional branches of the National Health Insurance Service. There are over 550 local offices throughout Sweden.

Having grown out of voluntary associations founded in the late 1800s, the social insurance funds are something of a juridical anomaly in Swedish public administration today. Membership (coverage) is now obligatory for all residents, most fees being paid by employers. The funds administer such essential features of the 'welfare state' as health insurance, social security, old age pensions, sickness pensions and compensation, rent supplements, etc. Nevertheless, they have not been integrated into the central administration, but are governed locally by boards appointed jointly by the respective county councils and the government. However, statutory laws and decrees issued by the central government and government agencies regulate much of their work.

The National Health Insurance Service is under the supervision of the National Social Insurance Board (*Riksförsäkringsverket*), an organ of the central government, to which individuals may also appeal against decisions made by the local funds.

Two Corps of Publicly Employed Medical Officers

District medical officers (*provinsialläkare* prior to 1963, and *distriktsläkare* since then) constitute the 'first line of defence' in the Swedish system of public health and medical care. Working in community health centres (*läkarstationer*), they handle roughly 35 per cent of all outpatient visits. (About half of these cases are subsequently referred to hospital outpatient clinics and 15 per cent to private practitioners.) Responsibility for primary care and the district medical officer organisation was transferred from the central government to the county councils in 1963.

In conjunction with this change of administration a network of supervisory public health officers, county medical officers (*länsläkare*), was set up under central government (*län*) auspices in 1962.

It should be noted that hospital doctors as well as DMOs are publicly employed (full time); no more than 15 per cent of Sweden's physicians are in private practice.

Socialstyrelsen + Medicinalstyrelsen = Socialstyrelsen

The National Board of Social Welfare (*Socialstyrelsen*) and the National Board of Health (*Medicinalstyrelsen*) were amalgamated in 1968 to form the National Board of Health and Welfare (*Socialstyrelsen*). Thus, the word 'health' has disappeared from the Swedish, but not the English, nomenclature.

Some Common Swedish Acronyms

LO = the Swedish Trade Union Confederation
SACO/SR = the Swedish Confederation of Professional Associations
SAF = the Swedish Employers' Confederation
SYLF = the Association of Junior Physicians
TCO = the Swedish Central Organisation of Salaried Employees

For a succinct description of the Swedish law-making process and the role of commissions of inquiry, see Chapter 3 (p. 75 ff.).

Part One:

THE DEVELOPMENT OF SWEDISH HEALTH INSTITUTIONS IN THE SCANDINAVIAN CONTEXT

1 THE MODERNISATION OF MEDICAL CARE IN SWEDEN AND NORWAY

Ole Berg

As I define it, a health care system encompasses all health-oriented activities performed by those other than the ill person himself. Thus viewed, such a system is likely to be extremely heterogeneous. In contemporary Scandinavia it includes physicians, dentists, clinical psychologists, pharmacists and different kinds of paramedical personnel, as well as the only half-heartedly accepted 'alternative' practitioners such as homeopaths, chiropractors and acupuncturists. It also covers the even less accepted zone therapists and iridologists, and finally the surviving, but only partially 'visible', varied group of folk practitioners. In pre-modern Scandinavia there existed a number of groups of health workers between the physician and the genuine folk practitioner: surgeons, feldshers, barber-surgeons and the like, the dreaded executioners, and finally the so-called *circumforanei* – many of whom were swindlers.

The kinds of medicine practised by the different groups of health practitioners can be grouped into three broad categories:

1. Animistic medicine, which is performed by folk practitioners. It is not wholly animistic, but also contains elements of empirical medicine, particularly in more recent times.
2. Dogmatic medicine is the type of medicine practised by homeopaths, herb doctors, humoral therapists, chiropractors and the like. Some versions of dogmatic medicine may have much in common with scientific medicine, while others, as in the case of some types of religious medicine, may resemble folk medicine.
3. Scientific medicine is the medicine practised by the organised medical profession since roughly the third quarter of the nineteenth century. Medicine before this time was mainly pre-scientific and had much in common with what I term dogmatic medicine.

In a very general way, one can say that what distinguishes the three kinds of medicine, in theory and practice, is their different degrees of 'intellectualisation'. Animistic medicine is the least intellectualised,

17

Table 1.1: A Schematic Characterisation of Three Types of Medicine

	Animistic medicine	Dogmatic medicine	Scientific medicine
Conception of nature of disease	To be sick is to be possessed by evil spirits, or sickness demons.	Each school its own conception; but disease often seen as non-specific (i.e., the whole organism sick).	Specifiable malfunction or syndrome of malfunctions in the human organism.
View of etiological agents and causal mechanisms in disease	Vaguely specified because evil spirits should not be talked about. The breath, bite or embrace of elves, trolls and the like could cause disease as could evil persons, animals, contact with the dead, etc.	Relatively specified in some schools (e.g. chiropractic); little specified in most schools. But often fixed and rigid general views of the causes of disease; some schools characterised by predilection for one type of cause (chiropractic).	Specified in ever greater detail, and increasingly in biochemical or biophysical terms.
Type of therapeutic intervention	Lure or force the sickness demons out of the patient and back to the place they came from (often far north or a particular place in nature). Some of the means used for this purpose, even if magically conceived, had a clear empirical background.	Relatively specific in most schools, but each school's repertoire often restricted to one therapy (chiropractic, zone therapy, acupuncture). Some schools characterised by one therapeutic principle (homeopathy, allopathy, partly also macrobiotics and humoral therapy).	Very specific; increasingly quantitatively calculated.

Source of knowledge	Inspiration, revelation or special experience; tradition; some trial-and-error.	Partly research and experimentation, but much knowledge is fixed and static and can be traced back to the revered founder of the school (chiropractic, homeopathy, zone therapy).	Systematic (basic) research and experimentation. The empirical (non-theoretical) element of diminishing importance.
(Intergenerational) Transfer of knowledge	Folk practitioners taught their successors, often their own children, but self-education also important. The 'black books' and, later, medical literature also played some role.	Varies from relatively extensive formal education (chiropractic particularly) to mere self-education.	Extensive formal theoretical and practical training. Increasing amount of specialised follow-up training.

scientific medicine the most intellectualised. In Table 1.1 I have tried to spell out in some detail what this implies.

If we take degree of intellectualisation as a measure of the degree of modernisation, animistic (and empirical) medicine becomes the archetypal pre-modern, or traditional, medicine, and scientific medicine the typical modern version. Dogmatic medicine may then be called either semi-traditional or semi-modern. Thus the shift of a health care system from a situation where traditional medicine dominates to one where modern medicine becomes increasingly dominant may be designated health care modernisation, or health care detraditionalisation.[1] My first objective in this chapter is to try to give an account of these processes as they unfolded in the neighbouring countries of Sweden and Norway.

Because scientific medical knowledge is always provisional, a health care system based on scientific medicine must also be in constant flux. This means that we may speak of a modernisation process *within* the most modern part of health care, an intra-scientific medical modernisation. To understand this process, it is necessary to grasp the basic logic of modern medicine. As space does not permit detailed discussion of this argument here, I shall only dogmatically present some assertions about it.

Most scientific medicine is reductionist in orientation: it seeks to understand psychological and biological phenomena (health and ill-health) in terms of chemical and physical principles. This leads to a growing specialisation or fragmentation, and technologisation of medicine. Specialisation and technologisation again create a need for medical teamwork and for the physical concentration of medical resources; in practice this means the institutionalisation of health care. A corollary of institutionalisation is paramedical expansion. But since medical progress also gives rise to new medico-technical tasks and leads to the routinisation of some medical work, the paramedical expansion may take on the character of an explosion.

On the basis of this argument one may define different stages or phases of intra-scientific medical modernisation. I shall identify four such phases, each of them epitomised by a 'typical doctor'; Phases One and Two by the general practitioner — practising first in the home of his patients, later in his office — Phase Three by the specialist, and Phase Four by the subspecialist (see Table 1.2).

The second objective of this chapter is to try to shed some light on the intra-scientific transformations of the health care systems of the two Scandinavian countries. I shall focus on the shift from Phase Two

Table 1.2: A Four-phase Model of Intra-scientific Health Care Modernisation

		Phase 1	Phase 2	Phase 3	Phase 4
Primary characteristics	Typical doctor	General practitioner	General practitioner	Specialist	Subspecialist
	Principal site of practice	Patient's home	Doctor's office	Hospital, clinic (or doctor affiliated with hospital)	Medical centre (or doctor affiliated with centre)
	Doctor's orientation (reference group)	Patient and community orientation	Patient orient., but growing profession orientation	Profession orientation (national)	Subprofession orientation (international)
Secondary characteristics	Typical paramedical personnel	General purpose nurse	General purpose nurse	Erosion of general nursing; emergence of semi- and subprofessions. (Beginning paramedical hierarchy)	Demise of general nursing; specialised paraprof. dominant. (Paramedical hierarchy)
	Ratio Paramed./MD		Small (<1)	Rapidly increasing ($\geqslant 1$)	
	Ratio Health admin./practising MD		Insignificant	Slowly increasing	

(office-based GP) to Phase Three (specialist, usually hospital-based). The emphasis in this chapter will be on the *description* of the medical modernisation processes. In the final section of the chapter I will offer some tentative explanations for my most important findings.

Health Care Modernisation and Detraditionalisation

The size of a health care system need not, of course, be constant in relation to population size. To chart the health care modernisation process in a country, one must do more than gauge the growth of scientific medicine; one must also look at the fate of traditional medicine.

Longitudinal health care utilisation data would yield the most direct measures of the modernisation process. Since such data do not exist, we have to make do with health care provider data. Unfortunately, even these data are incomplete and, as far as traditional healers are concerned, almost wholly impressionistic. The following discussion, therefore, must at times be somewhat conjectural.

The Emergence and Growth of a Medical Health Care System

Despite the increasing importance of 'sub-medical' occupational groups in postwar years, the principal provider of scientific health care is still the medical doctor. For this reason, I shall here employ only physician data as a quantitative measure of health care expansion.[2]

The number of physicians in Norway and Sweden was very low until the nineteenth century — around 250 in Sweden and 150 in Norway in the early 1800s. Doctors in Sweden were mostly Swedes. They had also, since the beginning of the nineteenth century, been educated at Swedish universities and the Serafimer Hospital in Stockholm — though many completed their medical training abroad. Doctors practising in Norway on the other hand, were more often than not Danes or Germans. All of them had received their education abroad, mainly in Copenhagen. The first Norwegian university, in Christiania (Oslo), was not founded until 1811, and the first three professors of medicine were not appointed until 1814.

But these doctors cannot be considered practitioners of scientific medicine. Practical medicine was still dominated by Arabic interpretations of Hippocratic and Galenic humoralism. But while pre-scientific medicine had many of the characteristics of what I have called dogmatic medicine, it also contained important empirical, even experimental, elements.

During this pre-scientific era, medicine was not a unified profession. It was split into two often competing groups – the academically trained physicians ('internists') and the craft-trained barber-surgeons. In the beginning the latter dominated, but by the middle of the nineteenth century surgery had become integrated into an increasingly scientific medicine. In Sweden, by the turn of the eighteenth century, almost two out of three doctors were medical graduates. Somewhat less than 30 per cent of these also held a surgical degree.[3] The situation was probably not very different in Norway.

In spite of Sweden's much longer medical tradition, it does not appear that Swedish doctors were generally better trained in the pre-scientific period than were Norwegian doctors. Norwegian medicine was at this time part of Danish medicine, and Danish medicine was at about the same level as that in Sweden – though undoubtedly at a lower level than in Germany, Holland, France and Italy.

Let us now turn to the data – not completely reliable though they are.

As is shown in Table 1.3, Norway and Sweden each had a couple of hundred doctors at the start of the nineteenth century. This gives a population-to-doctor ratio of well over 8,000 for Sweden and somewhat less than 6,000 for Norway. Ostensibly, formal health care must have been a real alternative only for very few people. Table 1.4 shows that these people lived predominantly in the few small cities, and that this continued to be the case up until the fourth quarter of the nineteenth century in Norway and until the beginning of the twentieth century in Sweden. Thus, while the rural population-to-doctor ratio stayed above 30,000 in Norway until the 1830s and above 40,000 in Sweden until the late 1830s, urban rates hovered around 1,000 in Norway and somewhat below 1,500 in Sweden. The very poor communications systems in rural Scandinavia throughout most of the nineteenth century further underline these dramatic variations in doctor availability. Town and country were entirely different worlds with respect to health care. Whereas the towns may already have had a doctor-dominated health care system from the late eighteenth century, this was not true in rural areas until the late nineteenth or early twentieth century.

The physician population did of course grow during the nineteenth century, but the increase was mainly in absolute terms. In relative terms the Swedish physician population remained constant from 1805 to 1880, while the Norwegian physician population increased somewhat up until 1850 and then remained the same for two decades. Since the

Table 1.3: The Growth of the Professional Health Care Systems in Sweden and Norway, 1805–1975

Year	Physicians		Population per Physician		Ratio Change Since Previous Registration (%)		Relative Physician Density Sweden/ Norway (%)
	Sweden	Norway	Sweden	Norway	Sweden	Norway	
1805	281		8,445				
1814		160		5,634			
1834		152		7,690		-36.5	
1850	463		7,500		11.2		
1854	424	315	7,735	4,594	-3.1	40.3	58
1860	445	334	8,674	4,808	-12.1	-4.7	55
1870	560	415	7,445	4,277	14.2	11.0	57
1880	555	565	8,227	3,368	-10.5	21.5	41
1890	806	696	5,937	2,875	27.8	14.6	48
1900	1,131	890	4,542	2,517	23.5	12.5	55
1910	1,247	1,266	4,428	2,012	2.5	20.0	46
1920	1,634	1,346	3,614	1,969	18.4	2.1	54
1930	2,239	1,826	2,743	1,586	24.1	19.5	58
1940	3,024	2,472	2,107	1,261	23.2	20.5	60
1950	4,890	3,397	1,440	985	31.7	21.9	68
1955	5,700	3,901	1,279	914	11.2	7.2	71
1960	7,130	4,260	1,053	884	17.7	3.2	84
1965	8,520	4,950	917	796	12.9	10.0	87
1970	10,560	5,685	763	684	16.8	14.1	90
1975	13,750	7,302	595	550	22.0	19.6	93

Sources: Sweden before 1860: H. Bergstrand, 'Läkarekåren och provincialläkareväsendet' in W. Kock (ed.), *Medicinalväsendet i Sverige, 1813–1962* (Nordiska Bokhandelns Förlag, Stockholm, 1963), pp. 108, 112. Sweden after 1860: *Allmän hälso- och sjukvårdsstatistik* (Central Bureau of Statistics, Stockholm).
Norway before 1860: I. Kobro, 'Fra ca 1800 til vår tid' in I. Reichborn-Kjennerud, *Medisinens historie* (Gröndahl, Oslo, 1936), p. 289. Norway after 1860: *Medicinalforholdene og sundhetstilstanden/Helsestatistik* (Central Bureau of Statistics, Oslo).

1870s and 1880s, growth has been rapid and steady, with the number of inhabitants per doctor currently approaching 500 in both countries.

Rural–urban differences in doctor density shrank in both countries up to about 1910. Since then, it has remained relatively constant in Sweden, at least up to 1940, while it has actually increased somewhat in Norway. Unfortunately, we do not have separate urban and rural data for the postwar period. Norwegian data for 1970 do, however,

Table 1.4: The Growth of the Professional Health Care Systems in Rural and Urban Areas, 1818–1940

Year	Physicians Rural		Physicians Urban		Population per Physician Rural		Population per Physician Urban	
	Sweden	Norway	Sweden	Norway	Sweden	Norway	Sweden	Norway
1818		21		c. 140		40,000		c. 675
1827	71	24				40,210		
1833		31		121		33,500		1,075
1840					39,930			
1849/50	112	95				13,000		
1855	120	108		c. 210		12,000		c. 960
1860	136		309		25,183		1,408	
1865	175	129				11,130		
1875	210	170				8,710		
1880	192		363		20,182		1,900	
1885	197	218				6,900		
1890	216	238				6,425		
1900	267	384	864	516	15,101	4,200	1,278	1,224
1910	453	484	794	614	9,172	3,514	1,722	1,125
1920	477	496	1,157	728	8,723	3,750	1,506	1,085
1930	627	794	1,612	917	6,612	2,534	1,238	875
1940	742	1,025	2,282	1,332	5,378	2,199	1,043	678

Sources: Sweden: *Allmän hälso- och sjukvårdstatistik*. (Pre-1900 figures are uncertain. They are based on data about public physicians.)
Norway; 1818–1900: 'Indstilling fra Den kongelige lægekommision af 1898' in *Stortingsforhandlinger*, 1911, third part b, p. 102.
1910–1940: Calculated on the basis of distribution of physicians by municipal or public health district as given in *Medicinalforholdene og sundhetstilstanden*.

show that the variations between town and country remain substantial; this is so even if we look at primary care physicians alone.

Tables 1.3 and 1.4 show that the decisive and stable growth of medical health care, particularly in rural areas; started much earlier in Norway than in Sweden. Norway also appears to have kept her lead for a considerable period of time. In 1860 Sweden's physician density was merely 55 per cent of that of Norway. It remained roughly at that level until the 1920s; it was 54 per cent in 1920. Since then, however, Sweden has consistently gained on her western neighbour, and is now about to overtake both Norway and the Nordic pioneer, Denmark.

The doctor figures discussed above suggest that both Sweden and Norway acquired extensive and rather readily available health care systems in the course of the twentieth century. But to determine to what degree this expansion can be equated with thoroughgoing modernisation, we must also have at least a rough overview of the size of the non-scientific health sector.

The Marginalisation and Transformation of the Non-scientific Health Care System

Not surprisingly, there is no systematic quantitative documentation about the size and composition of the non-scientific health sector, not even in more recent years. Official authorities in both countries have alternately tried to suppress and ignore this sector. Before we proceed to the sketchy data, these suppressive activities deserve attention.

In Sweden these activities go back to 1688, when the *Collegium Medicum* was granted the privilege of controlling and punishing all unacceptable practice of the art of medicine ('obehörligt utövande av läkarkonsten'). The Norwegian history of restrictive legislation begins formally in 1794, when a so-called 'anti-quack law' was enacted. In Sweden the laws of 1688 remained in force until the twentieth century. The first law against quackery was passed in 1915 and revised in 1960. In both cases, the changes went in the direction of greater restriction. In Norway the anti-quack law was *liberalised* in 1871, but made more restrictive again in 1936. A new attempt to further tighten up the law in the early 1950s came to nought.[4]

Today's laws are not particularly strict. Rather than outlaw quackery in general (as in Iceland and Finland), they merely specify what non-doctors may not do. Thus quacks are forbidden to treat certain diseases (contagious diseases, venereal diseases, cancer, diabetes, epilepsy); to use diagnostic or therapeutic techniques like anaesthesia, surgery or radiology; to bear the title of doctor, physician or the like; or to make exaggerated claims in advertising their services. There are few significant differences between the two laws, but the Norwegian law appears to be slightly stricter than the Swedish. Both the present and the previous laws have been laxly enforced in both countries; lawsuits are ordinarily brought against quacks only when their patients have died or been severely injured as a consequence of illegal treatment.

Although we do not know exactly how extensive the traditional health care system was during the eighteenth and nineteenth centuries, it was doubtless very large. Hardly a village lacked a healer ('en klok'). C. H. Tillhagen describes the Swedish situation as follows:

There were wise men or women in virtually every parish, frequently even more than one. From Indals-Liden in Medelpad it is reported that there were eight wise men in the late nineteenth century. . . . Information from other sources support the assumption that in the good old days the 'wise' men were quite numerous, perhaps more numerous in relation to the size of the population than are today's [1950] doctors.[5]

There is no reason to doubt that the situation was similar in Norway.[6]

Thus it seems evident that in rural areas health care must have been dominated by an extensive system of traditional medicine until the present century. Traditional healers were not absent from the cities either, though they hardly dominated there. One of the most renowned Norwegian folk practitioners, Mor (Mother) Sæther, practised with great success in Christiania (Oslo) from about 1830 until her death in 1851, in spite of strong opposition from the medical faculty and a number of lawsuits brought against her.

We have seen that the scientific health care system has expanded tremendously in the course of this century. We would expect that the traditional system has contracted, though perhaps not to the same extent. Ethnologist Elisabet Wijkström concludes, on the basis of interviews with elderly Swedes, that people increasingly began to see doctors in the two decades after 1910.[7] Reports from public doctors confirm her conclusion. In a 1951 statement to the National Board of Health, a doctor with 24 years of practice in a northern Swedish district conveyed his impression that quackery was in significant decline in his area.[8]

Margareta Bowallius, also an ethnologist, has studied a sample of the annual reports of the Swedish provincial doctors for the years 1900, 1947 and 1962.[9] Her studies substantiate the impression that traditional medicine has lost considerable ground. Quacks are mentioned much less frequently in the later reports. In the draft bill for the Swedish anti-quack law of 1915 the National Board of Health states that the public doctors' annual reports for 1911 contained references to 150 quacks.[10] A similar estimate made by the Board on the basis of the county doctors' annual reports for the year 1951 listed 44 'wise' men and women ('kloka gubbar och gummor'); in addition, there were 15 specialised folk practitioners.[11] A large number, however, fall somewhere between folk medicine and dogmatic medicine — many of these come close to being swindlers.

The Norwegian quackery commission of 1953 collected information from the county doctors about the prevalence of healers of various sorts.[12] On the basis of this information, I have classified about 50 as traditional healers, most of them from Trøndelag and northern Norway. Another 40 fall into the grey area between traditional and dogmatic medicine.[13]

There is reason to doubt whether public doctors' reports give a complete picture of the magnitude of the non-scientific sector, particularly the traditional part. Nevertheless, these reports do lend strong support to my contention that traditional health care is of clearly diminishing importance. It is equally obvious, however, that non-scientific health care is not at all on the verge of disappearance.

This is especially true in that dogmatic medicine, mainly a twentieth-century phenomenon in northern Scandinavia, appears to have grown in importance, becoming significant mostly after the Second World War, and particularly after 1960. The vitality of dogmatic medicine is reflected in the existence of formal organisations for homeopathic, chiropractic and naprapathic medicine, but also in patterns of health care consumption and public attitudes. A 1975 Swedish study reported that 1.5 per cent of the adult population had seen a chiropractor, homeopath or other healer during the last three months.[14] A survey in Norway in 1976 showed that 19 per cent of all adults had at least once seen an 'alternative' doctor; 10 per cent had seen an herbalist, 6 per cent a homeopath.[15]

These fragmentary data, suggesting a persistent though peripheral role for non-scientific medicine, are further buttressed by indications of increasing public interest in dogmatic medicine. The 1976 Norwegian survey showed that 79 per cent believe in herbal medicine and 47 per cent in homeopathic methods: 43 per cent believe in special healing abilities and 33 per cent in religious healing. The popular weekly press both capitalises on and encourages such attitudes by featuring reports about 'alternative medicine', which is also promoted through several new specialised magazines and popular books. Non-scientific drugs are sold in large and growing quantities. It should also be mentioned that a few doctors in both countries have taken up some of the techniques and methods of dogmatic medicine. This has probably contributed greatly to the increasing status and credibility enjoyed by practitioners of 'alternative' or dogmatic medicine.

It is not possible, on the basis of the material I have surveyed, to determine which of the two countries has a larger non-scientific sector. But it is interesting that the structure of that sector has changed so drastically in both countries. The dogmatic doctor has to a large extent replaced the folk practitioner. We might thus say that the shrinking non-scientific sector has been modernised along with the medical sector as a whole.

In closing this discussion I would also like to stress the indubitable fact that non-scientific health care has shifted its geographical focus. Traditional medicine was primarily a rural and parochial phenomenon. It had 'roots'. Dogmatic medicine, like scientific medicine, is much more an urban and cosmopolitan phenomenon; it lacks spatial roots. Most dogmatic doctors practise in the big cities, particularly the better trained among them.

Modernisation Within the Scientific Health Care Sector

Since scientific medicine is inherently dynamic, the scientific health care sector is in a state of permanent transition. In Table 1.2 I have tried to characterise the main aspects of this transition by dividing up the development in this century into four phases, each characterised by a 'typical' doctor. The dividing lines between the phases are of course not easy to draw. While one type of doctor dominates, the next is already well established, and representatives of the phase thereafter have also appeared on the scene. The 'phasing-out' of each type of doctor also takes time. Intra-scientific modernisation, therefore, produces an increasingly heterogeneous medical profession. It may be noted in passing that this heterogeneity is of a vertical type; modernisation breeds stratification. At the bottom of the medical authority and status ladder one finds the 'oldest' doctor, the GP, while at the top one finds the subspecialist.

In this section we shall focus only on one transition, namely the one from the office-based GP (Phase 2) to the specialist (Phase 3). This transition is a crucial one. It marks a decisive step in the retreat of doctors from society — or, to put it differently, in their 'desocialisation'. I shall try to spell out what this means.

The GP is oriented towards the whole person. All health problems belong to his professional domain. His catchment area can therefore be small. He can live close to his patients, in the same milieu. The GP will therefore tend to develop what I have termed a community and patient orientation (cf. Table 1.2). This orientation will ordinarily be more pronounced in the case of the house-calling doctor (Phase 1) than in the case of the office-based doctor (Phase 2).

When the doctor starts specialising, a range of factors operate to distance him from this previous close relationship with his patients. Specialisation entails a narrowing of focus, the development of a special interest, for example, in a particular therapeutic technique rather than in the patient as a whole. The specialist will generally see patients less frequently and will thus require a much larger catchment area in which to exercise his skill. Finally, dependence on technology draws the specialist away from the small office and into the hospital — the wholly medical world. All these factors attenuate the doctor–patient relationship and instead direct the specialist towards a profession-orientation in which his peers are the primary reference group.

To examine this important transition, it would be useful to examine some data. As such data are not yet available, however, except for more recent years, I shall instead make use of data about hospital physicians. This recourse is not ideal for my purpose, because not all specialists are hospital-based, and neither are all hospital physicians specialists; some, for example, are residents, or 'pre-specialists', whereas others are not only specialists but subspecialists. Yet data about the percentage of doctors associated with hospitals do throw some light both on a crucial aspect of the transition with which we are dealing and on the character of the intra-scientific modernisation process generally.

Institutionalisation

Not long after the consolidation of the scientific health care system in nineteenth-century Sweden and Norway, the internal transformation of these systems started. Medicine was split up into an increasing number of specialties (horizontal fragmentation), and doctors started their 'retreat' from society; they entered institutions. As Table 1.5 shows, well over one-tenth of all doctors were already based at hospitals in the year 1900.

In subsequent decades, the absolute and relative growth in the

Table 1.5: Hospital Physicians, Sweden and Norway, 1860–1975

	Sweden Somatic	Sweden Psychiatric	Norway Somatic	Norway Psychiatric	Hospital Physicians as % of all Physicians — Sweden Somatic	Sweden Psychiatric	Norway Somatic	Norway Psychiatric
1860	53	9			12			
1880	105	19			19			
1900	158	31	111		14		12	
1920	352	71			22			
1925	492	76			26	4		
1930	649	98	411		29	4	23	
1935	808	144			31	5		
1940	1,134	160			38	5		
1946	1,710	177	855		43	4	30	
1950	2,060	239			42	5		
1955	2,182	231	1,158		38	4	30	
1960	3,787	501	1,479		53	7	35	
1965	4,407	610	2,062	131	52	7	42	3
1970	5,599	718	2,490	165	53	7	47	3
1974/75	7,450		3,257	225	56		49	3

Sources: Sweden, 1860–1920: H. Bergstrand, 'Läkarekåren och provinciälläkareväsendet', in W. Kock (ed.), *Medicinalväsendet i Sverige, 1813–1962* (Nordiska Bokhandelns Förlag, Stockholm, 1963), pp. 107–57; 1925–74: *Allmän hälso- och sjukvårdstatistik*. (The figures from before 1920 do not include physicians at cottage hospitals or polyclinics.)
  Norway, 1900–60: 'Innstilling om sykehusordningen', (Norwegian Department of Social Affairs, 1963), p. 9; 1965–75: *Helsestatistikk*.

hospital physician population was high and steady. The hospitals' share of the total physician population increased by 5 to 10 per cent per decade in Sweden and a little less in Norway. By the outbreak of the Second World War, more than 40 per cent of all Swedish doctors and about 30 per cent of all Norwegian doctors were associated with hospitals. Sweden reached the 50 per cent mark in the late 1950s, Norway a decade later. Thus, one might say that Sweden entered Phase 3 of the intra-scientific health care modernisation process in the course of the 1950s and Norway in the course of the 1960s. But if we also take account of non-hospital specialists, we can date the advent of Phase 3 back another decade or so. Then we may say that Phases 1 and 2 roughly belong to the prewar years and Phase 3 to the postwar years.

In most recent years the institutionalisation trend seems to have flattened out (this does not show in the tables), but I contend that this is deceptive. What we are perhaps witnessing now is the semi-institutionalisation of primary care. Solo practice is increasingly being replaced by group practice, as in publicly owned community health centres. Such centres may be fairly large, amounting to small clinics in fact – with catchment areas of up to 50,000 in Sweden and 20,000 in Norway. Doctors affiliated with such centres can and will increasingly be specialists.

We saw in the previous section that the modernisation of the total health care system got under way earlier in Norway than in Sweden. We also saw that Norway kept her edge over Sweden until fairly recently. Now it seems that the internal modernisation of the scientific health care system started earlier in Sweden than in Norway. It also seems that in this respect Sweden retains, and even increases, her lead over Norway. I shall return to the reasons for this reversal.

We have seen that health care viewed as a whole was modernised much later in rural than in urban areas in both countries. It is in some sense meaningless to ask whether rural areas are also lagging behind with regard to intra-scientific health care modernisation. As already pointed out, specialists cannot be distributed like general practitioners; the former need much larger catchment areas. In so far as specialists become attached to institutions, they are of course even more difficult to distribute evenly across the land, and the more so, the bigger the institutions to which they are affiliated. Thus, Phase 4 doctors, subspecialists, will be more of a central and metropolitan phenomenon than Phase 3 doctors, specialists, and the latter more of a central and metropolitan phenomenon than Phase 2 and 1 doctors, GPs. It is true that specialists and institutions are not intended to service only those who live close by them; they exist for the benefit of all within their catchment area. However, it might be argued that the improvement in health care brought about through specialised and subspecialised institutional services benefits those who live in the vicinity of a hospital more than those who live far away from it. This argument carries particular weight for the peripheral areas of the western and northern parts of Norway, where communication systems are especially poor. Thus, one can say in a way that modern medicine has a built-in centralising thrust, making it relatively less attractive to live in outlying areas.

Some Tentative Interpretations

Space does not allow me to elaborate the provisional explanatory model that I will now employ. I shall therefore simply indicate the main elements of this model. Basically, I see the health care modernisation process as a product of a successful and self-reinforcing internal medical development: the content of medicine largely *implies* a certain organisational design for the health services system. But the logic of modern medicine is not an iron logic. Political, economic and cultural factors may exert some modifying influence. In addition, and perhaps more important, such non-medical factors will affect the *speed* of the modernisation process. In comparing the modernisation processes of several countries, or regions within one country, non-medical factors are of great importance.[16]

Modernisation and Detraditionalisation

We have seen that the health care system of the two countries was far from fully scientific throughout most of the nineteenth century. We have also seen that there was no pronounced medical-scientific expansion until the fourth quarter of that century. Further, it appears that once the growth of the scientific sector had started, it remained high and fairly steady ever since. This pattern of growth is the first feature of health care modernisation to account for.

The paucity of physicians in nineteenth-century Sweden and Norway is hardly surprising. Up until the last three decades of the 1800s, practical medicine was mainly holistically oriented, and none too effective. Actually the most able folk practitioners, those who were mainly empirically oriented, compared quite well with the average doctor.[17] It is a small wonder then that factors other than formal medical competence had a major, and mostly negative, impact on the demand for physicians.

One such non-medical factor was of course *money*. In the subsistence economy of rural areas, very few were able to pay what doctors demanded. Both countries lacked a substantial landed aristocracy. Sweden had a small upper class, Norway only a few individual semi-aristocrats (landed gentry and mine and milling magnates) in the south-east.[18] In addition, both countries had only few public officials spread across the land. Thus it was primarily in the small cities, which comprised less than 10 per cent of the population in the early 1800s, that it was economically feasible for doctors to establish a practice.

Another factor that undoubtedly retarded the expansion of the medical care system was *cultural*. Indeed, in some respects this factor may have been of greater direct importance than economic scarcity. After all, pre-scientific doctors represented the culture of the most privileged social strata. There existed therefore a tremendous cultural gap between doctors and ordinary people, which created distance, mutual scepticism and to some extent hostility.

Doctors, of course, generally reacted negatively towards the rather primitive way of life of the uneducated common people; in particular, the lack of notions of hygiene among rural people is a recurring theme in the public doctors' annual reports to the central health authorities.[19] Ordinary people, for their part, found doctors arrogant and very difficult to relate to in any meaningful way.[20]

Folk practitioners had an edge over their well-educated rivals both as regards money and culture. They ordinarily charged moderate fees and they were a part of the culture of their patients. If we are to define the socio-economic status of the ordinary healer more precisely, we would probably have to place him among the rather poor. The healer very seldom succeeded in rising to the level of the small freehold farmer.[21] Although fear of the healer's powers could occasionally generate hostility,[22] people seemed to have been generally satisfied with their local healers and were often willing to step into the breach for them if they were threatened by doctors or the police. Thus it is interesting that rural people in Norway disliked the anti-quack law almost from its enactment in 1794. Eventually, in 1863, agrarian politicians in the *Storting* proposed to revise the law; eight years later the government gave in to the demands and a liberalised law was sanctioned.[23] Later, when anti-quack regulations were made more restrictive again, it was especially the rural representatives in both countries who expressed doubt and even opposition.[24]

The supply of doctors was probably nearly adequate in the cities during the nineteenth century. In order to expand their activities, therefore, doctors had to move out into the countryside. But, as we have just seen, doctors were not always very welcome there. To settle down in a rural district as a private practitioner was, of course, out of the question. Doctors could only move out with the aid of the state, as public doctors, and increasingly, the medical profession succeeded in having the state establish public physician posts in rural areas.[25] The number of district medical officer posts in Sweden went up from 71 in 1840 to 267 in 1900; in Norway the number of district physician posts jumped from 27 in 1814 to 152 in 1900. In the present century this expansion has of course continued,[26] with a different impetus; demand for such posts now comes more from the districts and potential patients than from doctors.

But even if doctors could move out of the towns as public employees, they were only partly salaried. To some extent, therefore, they remained dependent on the demand for their services – and they had to face real competition from lay healers. In order to stave off some of this competition, doctors in Norway sometimes felt compelled to resort to the anti-quack law. Thus it was almost invariably doctors who reported quacks to the police. Interestingly, by and large the most able empirically-oriented lay healers were the ones reported.[27]

It should be added that doctors, particularly in Norway, gradually seemed to become more understanding and less arrogant in their attitude towards ordinary people. To some degree they even appear to have tempered their hostility towards at least the better quacks. Thus, in the *Storting* debates about the revision of the Norwegian anti-quack law in the 1860s, a representative who was a physician stated that quacks in practice were 'perfectly tolerated', admitting that he himself had on occasion referred patients to them.[28] Several quacks were also employed by doctors on a regular basis as assistants. Occasionally doctors went so far as to defend quacks in the courtroom.

Undoubtedly, increasing education among ordinary people accounts for some of this change of attitude. But it may also be noted that the more tolerant posture came at a point, towards the close of the nineteenth century, when hostility had become less necessary, because doctors were increasingly able to outperform quacks in strictly medical respects.

The expansion of the scientific health care system in this century is striking. It can be seen as a function of the interaction between a rapid development in medical knowledge and a general increase in the economic capacity of the two countries.

Earlier I pointed out that scientific medicine has a built-in tendency towards centralisation: specialist and institutional services cannot be spread evenly. What is more, specialists attached to highly technologised institutions are the most advanced doctors — the doctors of the present and the future. In an increasingly profession-oriented medical community, they are the ones who will be looked up to and emulated by others, particularly the prospective and newly graduated doctors. Thus medical status concerns are likely in themselves to exert a major centralising influence. Non-specialised low-technology primary care therefore risks being bled for doctors faster than it 'should'. This danger will be especially present if medical manpower is in short supply, as it has been in the two countries for the major part of this century.

For this reason, it is perhaps strange that the distribution of doctors has not become more skewed than it has. Indeed, if we consider primary care physicians separately, they seem to be more evenly distributed today than earlier. One obvious factor is the tremendous migration from rural to urban areas; patients have moved to where the physicians prefer to be. But it is also quite clear than an increasing degree of public regulation has been of great importance: the establishment of more and more district doctor positions, the recent introduction of semi-institutional primary care, a fees policy (under the health insurance systems) which has made it hard for doctors to set up private practice, and a newly instituted control with the establishment of physician posts in hospitals. In 1979 Norway even enacted a provisional law stipulating that doctors must apply to the Directorate of Health Services for permission to open a practice in a central area.

Of these public measures, the first is the traditional and basic one. The others are supplementary, introduced to support and bolster the main policy. The additional efforts have been deemed necessary because emphasis on the creation of more positions for district doctors no longer suffices; these positions are increasingly difficult to fill, turnover has displayed a tendency to rise, and many of the positions are being filled by 'interns' rather than fully licensed doctors.

Despite the tremendous success of scientific medicine in this century, the scientific health care sector has not totally preempted the health care system. There is still a non-scientific sector, now more urban based and dominated by what I have called dogmatic medicine, rather than by traditional folk medicine. While a more intensive analysis is necessary, I believe the changes that have taken place in this sphere can largely be traced back to the content and nature of the various types of medicine and to related changes in popular culture, knowledge and beliefs.

We have seen that there are interesting variations in the speed and pattern of health care modernisation in Sweden and Norway. To explain these variations it is necessary to look first at more general political, economic and cultural developments. I take as my point of departure the different composition of the elites of the two countries.

In Sweden the dominant elite was initially, in the nineteenth century, less interested in modernisation than the Norwegian elite. The modernisation process, then, understandably started first in Norway. But since the Norwegian democratisation process also developed rather rapidly, the modernising elite soon had to take account of the strong traditionalism of the farmers. Acceding to power as early as 1884, the liberal-agrarian party (*Venstre*) was to remain the major governmental party until the socialist accession to power in 1935. Thus, traditionalistic (and fairly egalitarian) forces in Norwegian society were able to exert a decisive influence on the shaping of the modernisation process – and, more generally, on Norwegian political culture.

In Sweden the power elite gradually shifted to a more pro-modernisation stance towards the close of the nineteenth century, and the industrialisation process speeded up. Indeed, Sweden's growth rates began to outstrip Norway's as the two countries entered the twentieth century (see Table 1.6). This rapid growth was possible because the more traditionalistic yeomanry was less politicised than in Norway. By the time Sweden introduced parliamentarism in 1917, industrialisation had been carried so far that much of the strength of the traditionalistic forces had dissipated: the rural population had become (urban) workers. Consequently, Sweden experienced only a very short traditionalistic liberal interlude (Edén (and Branting) 1917–20). Power passed almost directly from the conservative to the socialist modernisers (Branting 1920). Thus, the traditionalistic forces of the political centre did not colour the political culture to the extent they did in Norway.

Even this necessarily brief overview raises a series of highly suggestive contrasts. The Norwegian case represents a relatively smooth and gradual modernisation profile, accommodating traditionalistic elements in its advance. The Swedish case, on the other hand, as is often characteristic of later modernisers, presents a profile of more abrupt and thoroughgoing change, surging ahead of Norway with lesser regard to traditionalist forces.

I present a schematic summary of the relationship between such general modernisation profiles and the development of health care systems in Figure 1.1. This framework, in which the expansion of health care services is conditional on the character and development of modernisation as a whole, helps to shed light on the cross-national

Table 1.6: Indicators of Economic and Cultural Modernisation, Sweden and Norway 1900–1970

		Sweden	Norway	S–N
	1900	39.3	53.4	−14.1
	−10	49.3	53.1	−3.8
Economic modernisation:	−20	56.3	57.9	−1.6
Shift to non-primary sectors	−30	65.3	58.9	6.4
(% of labour force)	−40	69.7(−45)66.5		(3.2)
	−50	79.0	71.0	8.0
	−60	86.2	80.5	5.7

		Sweden	Norway	
Economic	1885–94 to 1905–14	29.6	14.3	GNP per capita 1965
growth	1905–14 to 1925–29	21.1	21.4	(US$)
(average	1925–29 to 1950–54	36.6	29.1	S: 2,713, N: 1,912.
GDP per	1950–54 to 1963–67	40.8	38.0	Reduction factor
capita				(growth), 1865–69/
growth per				1861–69–1965:
decade)				S: 12.64, N: 6.65.

		Sweden	Norway	S–N
	1900	21.5	28.2	−6.7
	−10	24.8	28.9	−4.1
Cultural modernisation	−20	29.5	29.8	−0.3
(indirect measure:	−30	32.5	28.5	4.0
urbanisation)	−40	37.4	28.6	8.8
	−50	46.6	32.3	14.3
	−60	51.6	32.2	19.4

Sources: S. Kuhnle, 'Patterns of Social and Political Modernization', *Sage Contemporary Political Sociology Series*, vol. 1, No. 5 (1975); S. Kuznets, *Economic Growth of Nations* (Harvard University Press, Cambridge, 1971).

differences in health care patterns established earlier in this chapter. The initial Norwegian lead in scientific health care delivery can be seen as a reflection of Norway's more advanced cultural and economic standing in the nineteenth century. As the richer country, Norway offered a stronger economic base for the extension of health care services; as the culturally more developed country, Norway also faced lower cultural barriers to the utilisation of scientific medical services. It is also understandable that, although Swedish health care modernisation started later than the Norwegian, it was faster. This pattern of growth is consistent with the twentieth-century Swedish upsurge in overall modernisation indices.

Figure 1.1: Non-medical Determinants of Medical Manpower Supply

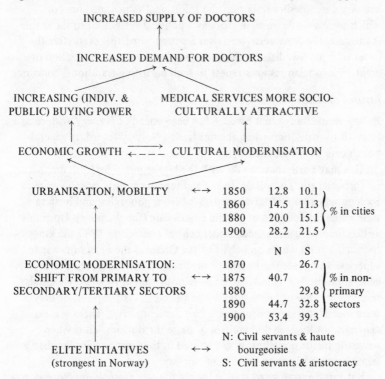

INCREASED SUPPLY OF DOCTORS

INCREASED DEMAND FOR DOCTORS

INCREASING (INDIV. & PUBLIC) BUYING POWER   MEDICAL SERVICES MORE SOCIO-CULTURALLY ATTRACTIVE

ECONOMIC GROWTH ⇄ CULTURAL MODERNISATION

URBANISATION, MOBILITY ←→			
1850	12.8	10.1	
1860	14.5	11.3	% in cities
1880	20.0	15.1	
1900	28.2	21.5	

	N	S	
ECONOMIC MODERNISATION:	1870		26.7
SHIFT FROM PRIMARY TO ←→	1875	40.7	
SECONDARY/TERTIARY SECTORS	1880		29.8
	1890	44.7	32.8
	1900	53.4	39.3

% in non-primary sectors

ELITE INITIATIVES ←→ (strongest in Norway)

N: Civil servants & haute bourgeoisie
S: Civil servants & aristocracy

Source: S. Kuhnle, 'Patterns of Social and Political Modernization', *Sage Contemporary Political Sociology Series*, vol. 1, no. 5 (1975).

The pattern of medical modernisation does not, however, completely mesh with the pattern of economic and cultural modernisation. Thus it is interesting that although Sweden surpassed Norway in economic modernisation in the early 1920s, she did not catch up with her western neighbour in general medical modernisation until the late 1970s. How might this discrepancy be explained? The answer may lie in the degrees of disruption characterising the process in the two countries. We have seen that Norway's transition was smoother and less disruptive of traditional values, while the faster Swedish experience was more abrupt and uneven. It has long been recognised that smoother incremental modernisation may permit the survival of traditional values which do not contradict, and may even reinforce the path to modernisation in some instances. In this regard, I would suggest that commitment to health care, and particularly 'old-fashioned' primary care, meshes well with the traditional values and concerns which were so influential in Norway's political system. In so far as this is the case, the Norwegian lead over Sweden, persisting even after the onset of rapid Swedish development, might be seen as a reflection of greater Norwegian responsiveness to such persisting traditional concerns.

Institutionalisation

It may seem strange that Sweden has been ahead of Norway with regard to institutionalisation when she has trailed Norway regarding general health care developments.

This may partly have to do with the higher *initial* Swedish emphasis on (pre-scientific) hospitals. In the eighteenth century, hospital care in Sweden was administratively separated from poor relief and hospitals were made into centres of general health care (for the poor). Hospitals at this time were also placed under central control: in 1787 the king founded a guild which on behalf of the Order of the Seraphim was to supervise and guide the boards of orphanages, mental asylums and general hospitals.[29] Similar steps were not taken in Norway. Hospitals there were often intimately linked to the work for the poor, or they were special-disease institutions – like the leproseries. There was no central co-ordination and control of these institutions. Thus when *scientific* institutionalisation got started in this century, Sweden had a larger base on which to build than Norway.

But this Swedish head start is hardly the sole reason why Norway has lagged behind in institutionalisation. In this regard, it is interesting that the Swedish institutional lead over Norway increased from 1900 until about 1960. Psychiatric health care is also much more hospital-bound in Sweden.

My view is that this Swedish–Norwegian variation is due to the differences in political culture touched upon above. Given a more unrestrained modernisation orientation in Sweden, it is understandable that hospital-based care – the most modern, the most technical and the most disruptive type of health care – should be accorded higher priority there than in Norway. In this light it is also understandable that the Swedes have been pioneers with respect to the semi-institutionalisation of primary health care. It is furthermore not surprising that while the Swedes have been ardent semi-institutionalisers the Norwegians have been very reluctant ones, and this despite the fact that while the Swedes talk of health centres for 20,000–50,000 people, the Norwegians have in mind centres covering 20,000 people at most. As a final indication of Sweden's more uncompromising modernity orientation, much more of Sweden's primary health care has been carried out in hospitals — on a polyclinical basis — than has been the case in Norway. It is estimated that as much as half of all outpatient care in Sweden is provided by hospital doctors! In Norway, hospital outpatient care is of considerably less importance.

It is also compatible with this picture that Sweden started to cut down on the Norwegian lead in medical professionalisation just as the institutionalisation of health care became important, in the interwar years.

Conclusion

In this chapter I have tried to describe some of the more important aspects of the health care modernisation processes in Sweden and Norway. On the one hand, I have looked at scientific medicine's gradual replacement of other types of medicine — traditional and dogmatic medicine; on the other, I have discussed one of the internal transformations of scientific health care — the shift from a GP-centred to a specialist-centred system. In the final section some tentative explanations for some of the findings were offered.

Both from a descriptive and an explanatory point of view this chapter must be seen as very incomplete and preliminary. The internal developments of the scientific health care system must be described in much greater detail. Thus it is particularly important to map the emergence and growth of the various paramedical occupations and to study the relationship between these groups and the medical profession. From an explanatory viewpoint it is also crucial that the comparative scope be widened. If we are to gain a more realistic and precise impression of how the medical developmental logic interacts with other developmental logics, more nations have to be brought into the analysis.

Notes

1. I use the term 'modernisation' despite the fact that it has been criticised as value-laden and quasi-teleological. I find, however, no good and 'neutral' alternatives.
2. Hirobumi Ito employs a more political and economic approach to the study of health services development in the next chapter.
3. Cf. H. Bergstrand, 'Läkarekåren och provinsialläkareväsendet', in W. Kock (ed.), *Medicinalväsendet i Sverige, 1813–1962* (Nordiska Bokhandelns Förlag, Stockholm, 1963), pp. 108, 112.

4. For details see M. Bowallius, 'Illegal och icke-ortodox läkekonst, I och II' unpublished manuscripts (Institutet för folklivsforskning, Stockholms universitet, 1976, 1978); O. Bö, *Folkemedisin og lærd medisin*, Det norske samlaget, 1972; *Lag om rätt att utöva läkekonsten* (SOU, Stockholm, 1956, p. 29); *Innstilling fra Kvaksalverlovkomitéen* (The Norwegian Department of Social Affairs, Oslo, 1956).

5. C.-H. Tillhagen, *Folklig läkekonst* (Nordiska Museet, Stockholm, 1968).

6. Cf. O. Bö, *Folkemedisin og lærd medisin*; I. Reichborn-Kjennerud, 'Folkemedisin og lægevidenskap' in A. Bugge and S. Steen (eds.), *Norsk kulturhistorie*, vol. 5 (Cappelen, Oslo, 1942), pp. 253–93.

7. E. Wijkström, 'Läkare eller kvacksalvare', unpublished manuscript, Lunds universitet.

8. C.-G. Thomasson, 'Kvacksalveriet i Sverige', *Socialmedicinsk tidskrifts skriftserie*, no. 20.

9. M. Bowallius, 'Illegal och ikke-ortodox läkekonst, II'.

10. 'Kvacksalverilagen', 1915, p. 11.

11. *Lag om rätt att utöva läkekonsten*. See also *Förslag till ny lag om behörighet att utöva läkarkonsten* (SOU, Stockholm, 1942), p. 22.

12. *Innstilling fra kvaksalverlovkomitéen*, vedlegg 1.

13. Ibid.

14. 'Kartläggning av konsumtionsmönstret hos personer som söker vård som erbjuds från personer som bedriver sjukvårdsverksamhet utan att vara medicinalpersonal', report from the county medical officers in Stockholm, Uppsala, Södermanland and Gotland, 1977.

15. D. Bruusgaard and L. Efskind, 'Befolkningens syn på og bruk av folkemedisin', *Tidsskrift for Den norske lægeforening*, vol. 97, no. 27 (1977), pp. 1385–88.

16. In social science research on medicine the approach is usually the reverse: strictly medical factors are not much emphasised, while various social factors, including the role of the medical profession as a pressure group, are seen as dominant. See, e.g., E. Freidson, *Profession of Medicine* (Dodd, Mead, New York, 1972). For a discussion of the political role of Swedish doctors see the chapter, by H. Ito.

17. Cf. O. Bö, *Folkemedisin og lærd medisin*, pp. 34–5.

18. Cf. Ø. Østerud, *Agrarian Structure and Peasant Politics in Scandinavia* (Universitetsforlaget, Oslo, 1978).

19. *Eyr*, the first medical journal in Norway remarked in 1826, somewhat resignedly: 'Seldom or only with great difficulty is the rural doctor so lucky as to win any degree of acceptance. The reason for this must probably be sought in the general distaste for doctors that exists among rural folk (*landalmue*) . . .'

20. The Norwegian medical historian Ingjald Reichborn-Kjennerud says, in his article 'Folkemedisin og lægevidenskap', that around the turn of the eighteenth century the great majority of the people never saw a doctor, and not only for economic reasons: 'People did not have much faith in the doctors of the upper class, or in public officials (*embedsfolk*) generally. Despotism and arbitrariness on the part of public authorities, and recurring complaints from farmers to the king, had created a deep cleavage between public officials and ordinary people. This also adversely affected the relationship between doctors and the sick. Moreover, most physicians were foreigners, many of whom were Danes with little knowledge of Norwegian conditions and the way of thinking of the common man. All this produced antipathy, so even the ablest among the doctors got the worst of it in the competition with barbersurgeons and other healers' (p. 288). The pioneering Norwegian sociologist Eilert Sundt in his book, *Om renligheds-stellet i Norge* (Gyldendal, Oslo, 1975 (1869)), also refers to the lack of rapport between

doctors and ordinary people. Thus the first (unabridged) chapter of his book was originally titled 'The doctors and the common people' (*Lægerne og Almuen*). Sundt is critical of the doctors and tries to show that if they had done more to understand the way of life of their potential patients they would have succeeded much better also as doctors.

21. Cf. C.-H. Tillhagen, *Folklig läkekonst*, pp. 56–67, 93–4; I. Reichborn-Kjennerud, 'Folkemedisin og lægevidenskap', p. 280.

22. Cf. C.-H. Tillhagen, *Folklig läkekonst*, pp. 63–5.

23. Cf. O. Bö, *Folkemedisin og lærd medisin*, Ch. 3.

24. Cf. M. Bowallius, 'Illegal och ikke-ortodox läkekonst, II', p. 5

25. For a more detailed discussion of the Swedish development see section 2 of the next chapter, by H. Ito.

26. In 1940 the number of district physician posts was 364 in Sweden and 342 in Norway. 1960: 599 and 384. 1970: 890 (+133 vacancies) and 509. 1974/5: 1451 (+418 vacancies) and 622.

27. Cf. O. Bö, *Folkemedisin og lærd medisin*.

28. See ibid., p. 137.

29. Cf. W. Kock, 'Lasaretten och den slutna kroppssjukvården', in W. Kock (ed.), *Medicinalväsendet i Sverige, 1813–1962*, pp. 158–242.

2 HEALTH INSURANCE AND MEDICAL SERVICES IN SWEDEN AND DENMARK 1850–1950

Hirobumi Ito

Although West European nations adopted initial health insurance legislation in the decades around 1900, they displayed considerable differences in the nature of the initial programmes, and subsequent rates of development. Sweden differs from both her Scandinavian neighbours in the slower pace of health insurance development during the early twentieth century, but in this chapter we will focus upon the contrasts with Denmark. We will explore particularly the interrelationship between the form and nature of insurance structures, the financing sources they developed, and the structure and growth of the medical profession. Can we clarify to what extent health insurance development explains not only the considerable differences in the size of the medical professions, but also contrasts in how physicians were employed and utilised?

More broadly, I will attempt to show how the different development of the Swedish and Danish systems can be interpreted in terms of trilateral relationships between government authorities, medical associations and sickness funds. From this perspective, it is important to determine not only the circumstances under which these institutions were established or reorganised, but also to develop measures of their growing strength and influence. Thus I have assembled data relating to developments from the middle of the nineteenth to the middle of the twentieth centuries.

Both Denmark (1884) and Sweden (1885) were stimulated by the adoption of the German social policy legislation to appoint commissions to study models of workers' insurance programmes. Soon after, both countries adopted initial health insurance legislation (Denmark 1892, Sweden 1891), but the content of this legislation was different, both from the German model and from each other. Unlike the German laws, the Scandinavian ones provided that health insurance should be made available on a voluntary rather than a compulsory basis. Whereas in Germany the chief financing source was employers' contributions, in both Denmark and Sweden the initial financing support came mainly from the state.

It seems necessary at the outset to confront the assumption that compulsory health insurance is inherently better than voluntary insurance. The significance attached to the choice between voluntary and compulsory systems was evident as far back as the early twentieth century; in his 1912 comparison of German and Danish health insurance programmes, Gibbon explained that he chose these two countries 'because in no other country has insurance against sickness been so widely extended, and because they afford a contrast — insurance in the one being compulsory, in the other voluntary'.[1] He went on to point out, however, that this antithesis was not fully meaningful, in that both programmes were widely extended and successful. This finding has important general significance. Many different aspects determine the quality of health insurance programmes, and the choice between compulsory and voluntary coverage is only one of them.

Above all, compulsory insurance does not always mean broader coverage. Table 2.1, listing the nations which had enacted a compulsory health insurance programme for certain population groups before 1925, shows the proportion of insured persons in the total population in 1925. In the same year, the Danish voluntary health insurance programme outstripped all five of these programmes, with a coverage level of 42.5 per cent of the population, while the Swedish coverage level was a low 13.3 per cent. The establishment of a compulsory health insurance system, therefore, does not necessarily indicate a superior scope of coverage. Initially, many compulsory health insurance programmes covered only limited population groups, and remained static for long periods thereafter. In these cases, compulsory insurance was a political determination which did not demand any significant changes in the society.

Table 2.1: Coverage under Compulsory Health
Insurance Programmes in Germany, Norway,
England, Austria, and Japan in 1925 (percentage of
insured persons in the total population)

Germany	(first law 1883)	32.0%
Norway	(first law 1901)	21.5%
England	(first law 1911)	35.5%
Austria	(first law 1921)	34.3%
Japan	(first law 1922)	3.3%

Source: *Compulsory Sickness Insurance* (International
Labour Office, 1927); Germany, p. 94; Norway, pp. 115–16;
England, pp. 97–8; Austria, pp. 69–70; Japan, p. 11. Some
voluntarily insured persons are included.

This possibility should be carefully examined when different health insurance programmes are compared. Indeed, the scope of coverage may be more significant than its compulsory character in evaluating the efficacy of a health insurance system. After all, the ultimate purpose of any such programme is general public health. Moreover, a broad scope of coverage demands the large-scale mobilisation of financial and health care resources. A significant increase in the insured population requires either social and economic growth or a reorientation of spending priorities, since extended coverage is costly in terms of resources like medical and administrative manpower, facilities and equipment. Expansion, therefore, is more than a political question; social reorganisation is also necessary.

Since this chapter deals only with periods when both Denmark and Sweden had voluntary health insurance programmes, the ideal type of policy-making mechanism is constructed within this context. There are theoretically three groups of main actors: the providers of medical care, the consumers of medical care, and the legislature and central administration. In practice, only organised providers and consumers have potential influence on health insurance policy-making at the national level. Among the various organised providers of medical care, physicians are the most important. Although physician organisations developed hand in hand with other medical professional organisations such as those of nurses, dentists and pharmacists, they were the core of the development. Hence, in this chapter the term 'medical profession' refers only to organised physicians, such as the national medical associations, district medical officers associations, and private practitioners' associations. Consumers in Denmark and Sweden were organised in sickness funds (*sygekasse* in Denmark and *sjukkassa* in Sweden). Thus, in this chapter the term 'sickness funds' is used when referring to the organised consumers. The entire political system is important for the enactment and implementation of health insurance policy. The parliamentary power structure, the political ideology of the government and the bureaucratic structure of the central administration all influence the outcome of health insurance laws and administrative policy. Here these functions are sometimes encapsulated in the single word 'government'.

Health insurance policy is basically determined by co-operation, conflict and negotiation among these three actors; the nature and function of health insurance programmes reflect the balance of power among them. These actors can also be influential in health resource development. This policy-making power structure is shaped by social,

**Figure 2.1: A Hypothetical Diagram of the Voluntary Health Insurance
Policy-making Mechanism**

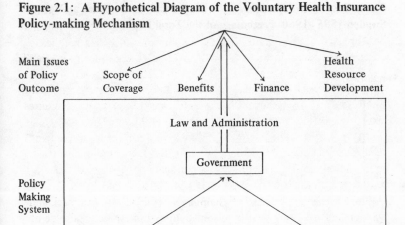

economic and political conditions set in historical context. The general
policy-making mechanism is illustrated in Figure 2.1.

Characteristics of the Danish and Swedish Health Insurance Policy Developments

The first Danish and Swedish health insurance laws, enacted almost
simultaneously, both established voluntary programmes, but there were
great differences between the two systems. In this section, some
important aspects of the different trends and structures of the Danish
and Swedish health insurance programmes are presented.

The Danish voluntary health insurance programme established in
1892, is probably the only case clearly showing the successful
development of a voluntary programme from its early history. The
growth of the scope of coverage is indicative of this Danish success, as
Figure 2.2 demonstrates.

By the early 1930s, the Danish programme came close to full
coverage for the needy population. According to the sickness funds

Figure 2.2: Active Members of Sickness Funds in Denmark and Sweden 1895–1960: Percentage of the Total Population

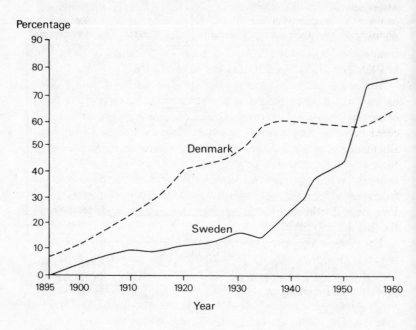

Source: *Statistisk Årbog* (Denmark); *Historisk Statistik för Sverige* (1960), p. 143 (Sweden).

law, well-to-do income groups (defined by law as those having a higher income than that of the average skilled worker) could not be active members of state-subsidised sickness funds, though they could be passive members, making contributions without receiving benefits. With the Health Insurance Law of 1960, well-to-do income groups could be active members under a special tariff.[2]

Compared to Denmark, the Swedish development in the scope of coverage was significantly slower and stagnated until the middle of the 1930s. Apparently the early establishment of a sickness fund did not automatically assure a steady increase of insured persons. As far as the health insurance sector is concerned, Koblik seems correct in saying that '. . . the great spate of welfare legislation did not occur until the 1930s and afterwards'.[3] The new Sickness Funds Law of 1931 sparked a rapid increase in the number of insured, but as this law was not completely implemented until 1938, the increase first registered late in the decade. Another rapid increase was generated in the 1950s by the compulsory National Health Insurance Law of 1947, first implemented in 1955 after several revisions.

Just as the pattern of coverage expansion differed between the two nations, so did the physician–patient relationship in terms of the flow of money for medical treatment. Danish practice reflected the conviction that the physician–patient relationship improves with the elimination of money transfer between them.[4] Hence, in Denmark there was no direct money flow between doctor and patient. The sickness funds made payments based on a tariff negotiated between the federation of local sickness funds and the local medical association. Free medical treatment for sickness fund members was obligatory from the first sickness funds law.

For the Swedish sickness funds, on the other hand, medical benefits were not obligatory until the 1931 law, and only gradually achieved thereafter. By and large there was little contact between the medical profession and the sickness funds until the 1930s, because the Swedish funds chiefly provided *cash benefits*, some of which the patient may have then paid to the physician directly.

The policy-making patterns in Sweden and Denmark were also very different. The initiation of Danish voluntary insurance was strongly influenced by private organisations, sickness funds and the medical profession. As described in detail in following sections, the Danish medical profession played an important role in the establishment of the first Sickness Funds Law of 1892. Ever since, the sickness funds and the medical profession have played the central role in Danish voluntary health insurance policy-making. Voluntarism was successfully practised in Denmark. The role of the government was more to support the private sectors' activities than to interfere in them. The government was welcome to pay (subsidise), but not to say much.

In Sweden until the 1930s the health insurance system as a whole was relatively stagnant; none of the three major actors played a significant role in its development. The reform of the 1930s was undertaken on the government's initiative. Both the sickness funds and the medical profession strengthened at the end of the 1930s by *reacting* to government policy. Even as late as 1947, the government, dominated by the Social Democratic Party, was strong enough to pass the compulsory National Health Insurance Law without effective resistance from the private sector. The contrast between the political quiescence of the Swedish medical profession and the greater activism of its Danish counterpart merits special consideration.

Medical Profession and Health Insurance Issues

Closer attention to the differential roles of the Swedish and Danish medical professions highlights one of the most striking differences in the history of health insurance policies in the two countries: organised medicine's attitude toward health insurance issues. The interest of the Danish medical profession in establishing voluntary health insurance systems co-ordinated with the sickness funds contrasts sharply with the disinterest shown by the Swedish medical profession.

The Danish Medical Association (DMA) was established in 1857. At its core was the local medical practitioners association, which in 1846 had held its first annual gathering at Roskilde. They debated a variety of issues including scientific medical questions, public health and new forms of central health care administration. By 1847, they had already tried to organise the central bureaucracy of the 'Health Board' (*Sundhedskollegium*) more effectively, although this goal was not attained until 1909, with the establishment of a modern administrative bureaucracy, the National Health Board (*Sundhedsstyrelsen*).[5]

During the first meeting of the DMA in 1857, the sickness funds question was high on the agenda, second only to the establishment of the DMA itself. The central question was how to establish a stable and a favourable relationship between the local medical associations and the sickness funds. The Danish medical profession apparently saw that the sickness funds were a potentially promising financial source.

The DMA had strong incentive to discuss this matter during their first meeting in 1857, because that was the year in which the Trade Act was enacted, and it was decided that guilds should be dissolved in January 1861. From the Middle Ages, these craft guilds had been the agency of provision for sickness,[6] and the medical profession was greatly concerned that their sickness funds would be dissolved with the guilds. Fearing the loss of an important financial source as a consequence of the Trade Act, the DMA therefore tried to find ways of preserving the sickness funds. The effectiveness of these efforts is not clear. Many guild sickness funds, however, did persist as voluntary mutual aid organisations after the dissolution of the guild system, gradually coming to take in members from outside of the old guild circle for economic reasons.

A more important development for the Danish medical profession occurred in the late 1860s. Both the number of sickness funds and their membership grew drastically, particularly in the rural areas.[7] The 1870s was a prosperous decade for the Danish sickness funds movement. Local medical associations and sickness funds in Denmark developed hand in hand towards the enactment of the first Sickness Funds Law of 1892.

In view of this close relationship, it is not surprising that two of the most prominent pioneers in sickness funds legislation, L. I. Brandes and T. M. Trautner, were physicians. Brandes was a member of the 1862 and 1866 commissions on sickness funds appointed by the Ministry of the Interior. An activist in the promotion of the sickness funds movement between 1850 and 1870, Brandes himself established a sickness fund in Copenhagen and became its chairman. Trautner had a more direct influence on the 1892 sickness funds law. He was a Superintending Medical Officer (*Stiftsfysikus*) in the Odense diocese and chairman of the DMA between 1883 and 1889. He was also an active member of the Labour Commission of 1885, which produced the 1887 report on which the Sickness Funds Law of 1892 was based. Between about 1880 and 1903 he was quite active in the sickness funds movement. Trautner also established a sickness fund in Odense and occupied several important administrative positions in the federation of regional sickness funds in Odense county.[8] The first Sickness Funds Inspector to be appointed by the Minister of Interior was also a physician: Th. Sørensen, himself an active member of the 1885 Labour Commission.[9]

Even after the enactment of the first Swedish Sickness Funds Law of 1891, Sweden fostered no movements similar to those in Denmark. The Swedish medical profession has historically been wary of nationwide health insurance policy and activities. This contrast with the attitude of the Danish profession was clearly reflected in the types of benefits provided by the sickness funds after the enactment of the first laws.

It is understandable why the Danish medical profession was eager to enact the Sickness Funds Law of 1892. The first law clearly stated that free medical treatment by the GPs for insured persons, as well as for their children under 15 years of age, was compulsory for funds receiving state subsidy (Section 17.1). As Figure 2.3 shows, payments to the GPs constituted a very high proportion of the sickness funds' expenditure

Figure 2.3: Percentage Distribution of Major Benefit Categories in Sickness Funds' Total Expenditure in Denmark 1895–1950

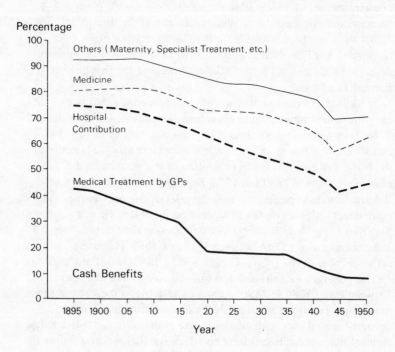

Source: *Statistisk Årbog.*

from the outset. Since 1910, in fact, this type of expenditure has been the largest expenditure item for the Danish sickness funds.

This law guaranteed financial security to a large proportion of Danish private practitioners, and has continued to be an important financial source for them. The terms of payment and the extent of medical treatment were decided through private negotiations between the local medical associations and the federation of local sickness funds. Around 1910, the capitation system was widely used, particularly in the larger urban districts. These arrangements developed without significant state intervention; the state was welcome to pay a subsidy but not to interfere. Under the Danish self-help ethos, such private

Figure 2.4: Percentage Distribution of Major Benefit Categories in Sickness Funds' Total Expenditure in Sweden, 1891–95 to 1946–50

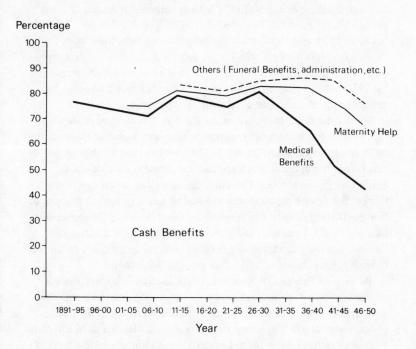

Percentage

Others (Funeral Benefits, administration, etc.)

Maternity Help

Medical Benefits

Cash Benefits

Year

Source: *Historisk Statistik för Sverige* (Statiska Centralbyrå, 1960), p. 143.

activities have always been encouraged, and to this extent the Danish medical profession and sickness funds have interacted closely.[10]

The composition of health insurance benefits in Sweden has been quite different. The Sickness Funds Law of 1891 did not mandate any specific compulsory benefits.[11] Theoretically, the funds could provide benefits both in cash and kind; they were even allowed to provide funeral benefit assistance. However, in the virtual absence of collective negotiations between the medical profession and the sickness funds, more than 70 per cent of the total expenditure was for cash benefits.

The series of Swedish sickness funds laws between 1891 and 1931 can be characterised more accurately as income maintenance insurance in case of illness than as health insurance, since few medical benefits in kind were provided. As one state bureaucrat pointed out in the SMA's journal in 1913,[12] there was virtually no control over whether or not

the insured person received adequate medical care. Medical care in
Sweden was, in general, provided on an individual fee-for-service basis.

It was the Sickness Funds Law of 1931 which first demanded that
funds provide medical benefits to their membership. As this law was
gradually implemented, the composition of benefits changed drastically
between 1931 and 1938; the proportion of cash benefits dropped
rapidly from 80 per cent to 64.9 per cent in those eight years. Emphasis
came to be placed more on benefits in kind than in cash. Nevertheless,
by 1950 only 15 per cent of the sickness funds expenditure was for
general medical care, compared with 35.9 per cent in Denmark.

One of the important reasons for the Swedish medical profession's
lack of interest in the health insurance issue was probably the small
number of private practitioners. In the long run, the number of private
practitioners will depend in large part on the size and economic
conditions of the market. The potential as well as actual size of the
market for private practitioners in Sweden was very limited because of
low population density and modest urbanisation levels (28 per cent in
Denmark v. 15.1 per cent in Sweden in 1880). Private practice in
Sweden was only economically feasible in larger cities. Such conditions
did not favour the growth of a free medical profession.

Because of these unfavourable conditions, Swedish society needed
publicly financed medical officers to combat epidemics and maintain
the nation's health. Hence, in Sweden publicly employed medical
officers were the largest group in the medical profession until the early
twentieth century, whereas in Denmark their numbers were always
small. For a Swedish physician to be a medical officer meant security.
Both state-financed district medical officers (*provinsialläkare*) and
medical officers financed by local government were provided with old
age pensions as civil servants. It is striking and noteworthy how often
they argued about pension increases in their associations right from the
time of their establishment in 1881.[13] They were apparently more
interested in salary and pension increases from the public budget than
in the financial resources of the weakly organised sickness funds.

The situation was quite different in Denmark. In 1871, about 60 per
cent of the active physicians were private practitioners, increasing to 65
per cent in 1880. According to official statistics, private practice
increased rapidly in the middle of the nineteenth century, particularly
in the rural areas. This development corresponds to the previously
described rapid growth of the sickness funds, especially in the rural
areas, from the end of the nineteenth century.

In Denmark the private market for physicians has always been far larger than the public market. Danish society could afford such rapid increases in the number of private practitioners in the last part of the nineteenth century, partly because of the simultaneous rapid growth of the sickness funds. The origin of the widespread and well-organised Danish primary health care system can be traced to the development of the medical profession and sickness funds in this period.

It was also recognised that around 1890 almost all medical officers in Denmark had to engage in private practice in addition to their official functions, but this situation was improved by the 1914 medical officer law which increased medical officers' salaries, and concentrated their functions almost exclusively on public health matters.[14]

In the last half of the nineteenth century, a large part of the Danish medical profession tended to stabilise their financial resources on a private basis, in co-operation with the sickness funds. The Sickness Funds Law of 1892 was established through these efforts. By this law the doctors had achieved two favourable goals which ensured them financial support: compulsory medical treatment by GPs for sickness funds receiving state subsidy, and a relatively high level of state subsidy.

In Sweden, with a large part of the medical profession in public service, there was no similar development. The Danish medical profession as a whole has always been much less dependent on public financing than its Swedish counterpart. Figure 2.5 illustrates the Swedish profession's relative dependence on the public market.

In both countries most hospitals have been public; the number of private beds was less than 5 per cent of the total number. We may say, therefore, that Figure 2.5 comes very close to representing the publicly employed physicians, although some of them − such as university teaching staff and those in public health administration − are not included. Figure 2.5 clearly shows a high and stable proportion of 57.7 to 63.5 per cent in Sweden and a low proportion of 31.1 to 41.9 per cent in Denmark. Accordingly, Swedish physicians were much more dependent on the public market than Danish physicians. The difference is more than 20 per cent of the total population of active physicians.

Another important factor which accounts for the weak influence of the medical profession in the early stages of Swedish health insurance policy was the late development of the Swedish Medical Association, which was only founded in 1903, nearly half a century after the establishment of the DMA, and 17 years after the founding of the Norwegian Medical Association. This delay was probably related to the relatively large proportion of public medical officers. In 1881, provincial and district medical officers founded their own association,

Figure 2.5: Hospital Physicians and Medical Officers in Denmark and Sweden 1920–1950 (Percentage of the Total Number of Active Physicians)

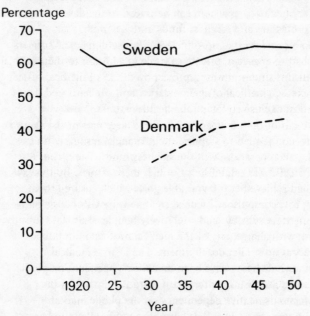

Source: *Allmän Hälso-och Sjukvård* (Sweden), *Befolkningsudvikling og Sundhedsforhold 1901–1960* (Denmark).

and by 1885 about 80 per cent of these physicians were members.[15] As civil servants with both job and old age security, their professional interests inevitably differed from those of private practitioners.

This gulf is not unique to Sweden. According to Fenger, the Danish Medical Officers Association (*Embedslægeforeningen*) has never shown great interest in co-operating with the DMA either. As civil servants, they apparently preferred to keep a distance from the DMA in seeking their own objectives. However, because they were a smaller group, it was not possible for them to impede the early growth of the DMA,[16] as was the case in Sweden.

It would appear that early development of an active medical association depends on the relative importance of private practitioners in the medical profession as a whole. This must be one of the crucial reasons behind the early and rapid development of the DMA. It may also explain why a junior physicians' association was established much earlier in Denmark than in Sweden. The Danish Junior Doctors Association (FayL) was founded in 1905, and by 1907 had earned a status equal to that of the local medical association which had been the single most important organisational unit. Its Swedish counterpart, SYLF, was not established until 1921.

The delay in professional organisation in Sweden undoubtedly had political consequences. As the SMA did not come into existence until 1903, it obviously exerted no influence on the 1891 Sickness Funds Law; nor did the association influence the law of 1910, as it was still too young to exert a significant impact on national affairs. Even the 1931 Sickness Funds Law, so favourable to the Swedish medical profession in providing new sources of finance, was not achieved through the efforts of the SMA; it was the central authorities who took the initiative for this reform. Unified professional awareness seems not to have crystallised until the 1930s in the face of severe unemployment problems for junior physicians. During this decade, the SYLF greatly contributed to the improvement of economic and social conditions for the medical profession, particularly those of assistant physicians.[17]

Despite increasing activism in the 1930s, it can be argued that the SMA did not become well organised until the late 1940s. In 1942, a group of physicians set up a committee to discuss the strengthening of the SMA's organisational structure.[18] Based on the committee's suggestions, new membership regulations were adopted on 13 December 1947, requiring all members to join a local association and at least one national federation of professional organisations – for example, those of the chief physicians, medical officers, private practitioners or military physicians.

This reform, which greatly strengthened the SMA, was coupled with the accession of vigorous and stable new leadership. The prominent Conservative leader Dag Knutson, former chairman of the SYLF, took on the chairmanship of the SMA in 1946, and remained in office until 1962. These two changes can be seen as interrelated factors which had a major impact on a series of conflicts between the SMA and the National Board of Health from the end of the 1940s through the 1950s.

The Growth of the Medical Profession

The high proportion of publicly employed physicians and the late development of the medical association in Sweden were related to another factor. Historically, there were fewer physicians in Sweden than in Denmark or many other Western nations. Whereas the Swedish population between 1869 and 1950 was always 70 to 100 per cent greater than the Danish, the absolute number of physicians in Sweden remained lower than in Denmark as late as 1948. In 1880, for example, with a population of less than two million compared to Sweden's more than four and a half million, Denmark had 250 more physicians. About 1940, Sweden still had 300 fewer physicians to service her six million people than Denmark had for a population of less than four million. Thus, despite consistent growth for each country in both the number of physicians and their proportion to the population, Sweden was slow to catch up in absolute terms.

Table 2.2: Total Population, Active Physicians and Active Physicians per 10,000 Inhabitants in Denmark and Sweden 1860–1960

	DENMARK			SWEDEN		
	Total population in 1,000 (1 July)	Active physicians	Active physicians per 10,000	Total population in 1,000 (31 Dec.)	Active physicians	Active physicians per 10,000
1860	1,611	NA	NA	3,860	445	1.15
1865	1,708	NA	NA	4,114	505	1.23
1870	1,793	NA	NA	4,169	560	1.34
1875	1,894[1]	726[1]	3.83	4,383	549	1.25
1880	1,976	808	4.09	4,566	555	1.22
1885	2,076	866	4.17	4,683	624	1.33
1890	2,179	971	4.46	4,785	806	1.68
1895	2,276	1,142	5.02	4,919	1,002	2.04
1900	2,462[2]	1,350[2]	5.48	5,136	1,131	2.20
1905	2,574	1,452	5.64	5,295	1,198	2.26
1910	2,737	1,631	5.96	5,522	1,247	2.26
1915	2,901	1,733	5.97	5,713	1,385	2.42
1920	3,079	1,918	6.23	5,904	1,634	2.77
1925	3,425	2,134	6.23	6,054	1,917	3.17
1930	3,542	2,485	7.02	6,142	2,234	3.65
1935	3,695	2,851	7.72	6,251	2,639	4.22
1940	3,832	3,332	8.70	6,371	3,024	4.75
1945	4,045	3,995	9.88	6,674	3,850	5.77
1950	4,271	4,441	10.40	7,041	4,890	6.95
1955	4,439	4,963	11.18	7,290	5,700	7.82
1960	4,581	5,650	12.33	7,498	7,130	9.51

1. 1876.   Source: *Statistisk Årsbok.*
2. 1901.
Source: (a) Population: *Statistisk Årbog.*
(b) Physicians: 1876–95, *Medicinal Beretning;*
1901–60, *Befolkningsudvikling og
Sundhedsforhold 1901–60.*

This differential meant a striking difference in doctor/patient ratios. In 1880, there were only 1.22 active physicians per 10,000 population in Sweden, compared with a Danish ratio of 4.09, more than three times higher. In fact, Sweden did not achieve the Danish level of 1880 for more than a half a century, with a ratio of 4.22 in 1935. But by that time, the Danish ratio had mounted to 7.72 (see Table 2.2). Not only has the Danish ratio been consistently higher than the Swedish, but the gap between them actually increased over time until the postwar period. In 1880, the net differential in ratios was 2.87. That early gap persisted and widened, growing to a peak of 4.11 in 1945. Only in 1950, for the first time in 70 years, did the Danish lead begin to shrink; in that year, the difference in ratios decreased to 3.45, continuing to narrow thereafter.

Such a marked difference in historical development demands explanation. The major reason for the low number of Swedish physicians would appear to be the economic difficulties of medical practice. Low population density, low levels of urbanisation, the initially slow rate of economic development and late industrialisation all contributed to undermining the economic base for physician growth. These factors were in turn reflected in the medical training process, for medical students' future socio-economic prospects were a determining factor in the production of trained physicians. Despite the fact that up to 1928 Sweden had three medical schools to Denmark's one, Sweden continued to lag behind Denmark in physician production until the postwar period. The attitude which helped to retard the expansion of the Swedish medical profession is elucidated in statements drawn from the controversy over Swedish doctor supply in the 1930s (see pp. 68–71).

State Involvement in Health Insurance Policy in Denmark and Sweden

Historical experience suggests that voluntary health insurance programmes do not necessarily mean weaker state involvement than compulsory programmes. The compulsory German health insurance programme, for example, was financed not by the state, but by contributions from the insured and their employers. Both the Danish and Swedish voluntary health insurance programmes, on the other hand, had state subsidy. However, the role of state subsidy constitutes one of the most significant differences between the financial structure of the sickness funds in Denmark and Sweden.

Up to about 1930, the proportion of state subsidy in Sweden was significantly lower than in Denmark. Before the 1910 revision, in fact, state subsidy constituted less than 10 per cent of the total income of the sickness funds in Sweden. It was the discrepancy between this low level and the Danish rate of around 30 per cent which apparently prompted Marcus to comment in 1907 that 'the Swedish state subsidy is too little'.[19] Despite a spurt between 1910 and 1915 following the 1910 revision, the Swedish subsidy rate was still less than 15 per cent until 1930. This may account for the fact that the revision did not result in an increase in insured persons (see Figure 2.2).

Under a voluntary health insurance programme, there may in fact be an important correlation between state subsidy and increases in the number of insured persons. Both the level of state subsidy and the number of insured persons only increased rapidly with the 1931 sickness funds reform. The Danish development also supports this hypothesis; a high proportion of state subsidy from the inception of the Danish sickness funds law occurred in tandem with, and must have contributed to, the steady increase of the number of active sickness fund members, with a lower economic burden encouraging people to subscribe to the fund.

State subsidy is inevitably accompanied by a certain degree of state supervision of the health insurance programmes. With a relatively high rate of state subsidy in Denmark, the supervisory central bureaucracy was well organised from 1892 under the name of the Sickness Funds Inspectorate (*Sygekasseinspektoratet*),[20] while the relatively small scale of Swedish health insurance practice before the 1930s demanded neither a demonstrative nor a strong state administrative body. In Sweden the first central administrative agency, the Sickness Funds Bureau (*Sjukkassebyrån*), was established in 1910, almost two decades after the enactment of the first sickness funds law.

Despite its relatively high state subsidy and its well-organised administrative apparatus, the Danish government did not intervene significantly in relations between the medical profession and the sickness funds. According to Gibbon, German authorities interfered more than their Danish counterparts, even though they did not provide any financial support to the sickness funds.[21] This sort of difference is attributable to the differential socio-political structures of these countries. State financial support is not the same thing as state interference or control. In Denmark the 'state should pay but not say' principle was well entrenched. The Swedish government, however, while not providing much financial support until the 1930s, was more active on health insurance matters than the Danish government. The following examples illustrate the differential structures in Denmark and Sweden.

In Denmark, the medical profession and the sickness funds established the so-called Arbitration Chambers (*Enighedskamre*) to handle disputes. Between 1900 and 1902, three such chambers were organised on a completely voluntary basis,[22] one in Copenhagen, one in Jutland and one on a national level. The incorporation of these voluntary organisations into an official legal framework came much later. These three chambers became centralised into the Arbitration Board (*Voldgiftsraad*) on 29 December 1915. The Board consisted of three representatives from the Federation of Central Sickness Funds (*Samvirkende Sygekassecentralforeninger*), three representatives from the Danish Medical Association, and one chairman, elected by the six Board members from outside the Board, usually from the county council. In this process, the state played only a passive role.[23]

In Sweden, because the private sector was too weak to take the initiative, it was the central bureaucracy, the National Social Welfare Board (established in 1912), which made efforts to bring together the medical profession and the sickness funds. In 1915 the Federation of Swedish Sickness Funds (*Sveriges Allmänna Sjukkasseförbund*) sent an open letter to the Social Welfare Board, asking that action be taken to stabilise relations between the sickness funds and the medical profession in order to improve medical benefits within the existing health insurance programme. The Board forwarded the letter to the SMA, recommending active interaction between the two sectors.[24] After three years of debate, the SMA acceded, offering a proposal which provided the basis for the first written regulations in 1918. The regulations consisted of two parts: (1) general agreements between the SMA and the Federation of Swedish Sickness Funds; and (2) draft tariff regulations for the local sickness funds and medical associations.[25]

Despite this general agreement to co-operate, however, active interaction did not occur until the late 1930s. This is evident in the proportion of medical benefits rendered by the sickness funds (see Figure 2.6). Between 1916–20 and 1926–30, less than 3 per cent of the sickness funds's expenditure went for medical benefits. Cash benefits consisted of 74.3 to 78.9 per cent of the total expenditure. The relatively low number of private practitioners and weak financial support from the state were probably the main cause of the quiescent inter-relationship between the medical profession and the sickness funds.

As we have seen, the reform of the 1930s was also initiated by the government rather than by the private sector, since neither the medical profession nor the sickness funds were yet strong enough to influence national policy. The number of sickness fund members in 1930 was

Figure 2.6: State Subsidies of Sickness Funds in Denmark and Sweden 1895–1950: Percentage of Total Income

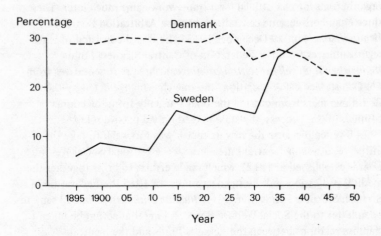

Source: *Statistisk Årbog* (Denmark) and *Registerade Sjukkassor Åren 1928–1930*, p. 16, *Historisk Statistik för Sverige* (1960), p. 143 (Sweden).

still low, with only 16.6 per cent of the total population active members, as compared to 46.5 per cent in Denmark. According to one report in 1930, about 65 per cent of the Swedish sickness funds were in deficit.[26] The government responded to these weaknesses by increasing the state subsidy, making medical benefits compulsory and, eventually, increasing the number of insured persons.

Hence, the tariff for medical benefits was also set by the government. In 1931, the new Sickness Funds Law (Law No. 280) was followed by the Tariff Law (Law No. 433),[27] which set the fees for non-surgical and surgical care and laboratory investigations, detailing 64 aspects. In 1938, also on government initiative, the fee schedule was revised and extended to 76 detailed aspects following the recommendations of the Board of Health (*Medicinalstyrelsen*).[28]

Due to the strength of the private sector in Denmark, the tariff question has always been in the hands of the medical profession and the sickness funds; in fact, the Danish sickness funds remained voluntary private organisations until as late as 1971, when the National Health Insurance Law was enacted.

In Sweden the smooth transition in 1947 from voluntary to compulsory health insurance was possible because the private sector was relatively weak and the public authorities strong. Since the 1931 law, the government had been actively involved in health insurance questions, both in terms of financial support and of active control of health insurance practice. This government activism was especially significant because the balance of political power engendered an increasing commitment to socialised medicine. The Swedish Social Democrats had maintained a stable government since 1932. Moreover, as director of the Board of Health between 1935 and 1952, the prominent Socialist physician Axel Höjer made great efforts for socialised medicine. In 1944, the Social Welfare Committee presented a report suggesting a bill for compulsory health insurance,[29] which led to the National Health Insurance Law of 1947 (Law No. 1, enacted 3 January 1947).

Between 1944 and 1946, the medical profession's reaction to this new policy direction was very limited. In fact, the profession as a whole did not seem to be aware of the trend until the late 1940s. In the SMA journal *Svenska Läkartidningen*, there were only six articles on this issue in 1945, and none at all in 1946. Dag Knutson, who became chairman of the SMA in 1946, was one of the few physicians alert to the challenge to the private sector. On 6 September 1946, at the twenty-fourth Congress of the SMA, he and Höjer held an open debate on whether doctors should continue to be members of a free profession or should become health care civil servants, Knutson insisting on the former position and Höjer the latter.[30] This debate drew the battle lines, and under Knutson's leadership the Swedish medical profession started to develop a consciousness of itself as a free profession. In 1947, the SMA was reorganised and strengthened. Thus, when Höjer suggested a reform of primary health care in 1948, a great many negative reactions appeared in the SMA's journal.[31]

Thenceforth, the SMA continued to become stronger, but never strong enough to defeat the public authorities. In some cases, it succeeded in postponement, but in the end it lost, and the state had almost full control of health insurance. Probably because of this measure of control, the scope of coverage grew rapidly from the mid-1930s, paving the way for a smooth transition from a voluntary system to a compulsory one.

Conclusions

The differences between Danish and Swedish health insurance policy development appear to outweigh the similarities. These similarities in policy profile can be briefly summarised. Action in both countries was, to some extent, inspired by German social insurance legislation during the 1880s. The first sickness funds laws were products of similar commissions appointed by the government for the purpose of studying workers' accident insurance – 1884 in Sweden and 1885 in Denmark – commissions apparently inspired by the German compulsory health insurance law of 1883 and the compulsory accident insurance law of 1884. In both countries, however, the accident insurance law proposals were rejected in parliament. Denmark and Sweden did enact health insurance measures almost simultaneously in 1891 and 1892 respectively. Although these health insurance proposals were accepted, neither of these Scandinavian countries followed the German compulsory model. In both cases, the choice was a voluntary health insurance programme based on a system of privately organised sickness funds. Thus, the health insurance laws were long called sickness fund laws in both countries.

Despite these parallels, both the content and developments following the first sickness funds laws differed significantly from one country to the other. One of the most significant differences between Danish and Swedish health insurance policy development was the rate of increase in insured persons. In Denmark the rate of increase was steady from the first sickness funds law of 1892. Swedish development, on the other hand, was quite moderate until the 1930s, increasing rapidly thereafter and culminating in the implementation of compulsory National Health Insurance in 1955.

The composition of various benefits was also quite different in the two countries. Since the first law in Denmark, both cash and medical benefits were obligatory for state subsidised sickness funds. Free medical treatment by GPs for fund members was included. Medical benefits in kind have always been an important part of sickness funds expenditure. In Sweden until the 1930s, the sickness funds almost exclusively provided cash benefits, there being no medical benefits in kind. Only after the late 1930s did the proportion of medical benefits increase drastically.

In Denmark, state subsidy was relatively large from the very beginning, lightening the economic burden for insured persons. In Sweden the relative importance of the state subsidy was small until the implementation of the Sickness Funds Law of 1931. Consequently the economic burden for the insured was relatively heavy.

All these factors suggest that Danish voluntary health insurance was, as Gibbon noted in 1912, quite successful from early in its history, whereas the Swedish voluntary system did not work well until the 1930s. There seem to be three major reasons why the Danish voluntary health insurance system was so successful:

1. high state subsidy, enabling many people to join the sickness funds;
2. large and well-organised private health care market facilitating an active relationship between the medical profession and the sickness funds;
3. widespread adherence to the principle of collective voluntarism, which made possible the early development of a well-organised medical profession and the sickness funds.

In Sweden these conditions were virtually non-existent. The lack of a strong private health care sector in Sweden particularly impeded the development of a voluntary health insurance system, necessitating active state initiative to make the existing voluntary system function. The Sickness Funds Law of 1931 was such an attempt.

The underlying philosophy of Danish health insurance policy, as in other Danish social insurance policies, was 'help to self-help', particularly in its early development. Both 'help' and 'self-help' were emphasised, ensuring a high level of state subsidy from the very beginning of the Danish voluntary system. At the same time, the law determined that only economically 'needy' persons were eligible for state subsidy as active members of the sickness funds. Those who were economically well-to-do, whose income was more than the average skilled worker's, were considered to be capable of 'self-help' (1892 Sickness Funds Law, Section 6). This principle remained virtually unchanged until 1961.

In Sweden, the emphasis on 'self-help' rather than 'help' prior to the 1931 Sickness Funds Law kept state subsidies small. Income regulation for membership in the sickness funds was first articulated with the 1931 law (Section 20). Prior to the 1930s, the 'self-help' philosophy created economic difficulty for the sickness funds; thus, as we have seen, in 1930 around 65 per cent of the Swedish sickness funds were in deficit.[32]

Notes

1. I. G. Gibbon, *Medical Benefits in Germany and Denmark* (P. S. King & Son, London, 1912), p. v.

2. H. C. Hansen, *Historien om Sygekasserne* (De samvirkende centralforeninger af sygekasser i Danmark, Copenhagen, 1974), pp. 195–7.

3. Steven Koblik (ed.), *Sweden's Development from Poverty to Affluence, 1750–1970* (University of Minnesota Press, Minneapolis, 1975), p. 335.

4. Barbara N. Armstrong, *The Health Insurance Doctor: His Role in Great Britain, Denmark and France* (Princeton University Press, Princeton, New Jersey, 1939), p. 159.

5. V. A. Fenger, *Den Almindelige Danske Lægeforening 1857–1957* (Nordisk Forlag, Copenhagen, 1957), pp. 1–2; Julius Petersen, 'Medical Associations', in *Denmark, its Medical Organization, Hygiene and Demography* (Jul. Gjællerup, Copenhagen, 1891), p. 33.

6. H. Daniel (ed.), *Danmarks Sygekassevæsen Gennem Aarhundreder*, 2 vols. (Forlaget Videnskab og Kultur, Copenhagen, 1937 & 1938), vol. 1, p. 13; Hansen, *Historien om Sygekasserne*, p. 9; Gösta Lindeberg, *Den Svenska Sjukkasserörelsens Historia* (Carl Bloms Boktryckeri A.B., Lund, 1949), p. 7.

7. V. Falbe-Hansen and W. Scharling (eds.), *Danmarks Statistik* (Forlagsbureauret, Copenhagen, 1881), p. 764.

8. Daniel, *Danmarks Sygekassevæsen Gennem Aarhundreder*, vol. 1, pp. 27–30.

9. Ibid., p. 53.

10. Gibbon, *Medical Benefits in Germany and Denmark*, p. 72.

11. Swedish Sickness Funds Law of 1891, sections 6 and 7.

12. Theofil Andersson, 'Läkare och sjukkassor', *Allmänna Svenska Läkartidningen*, vol. 11 (1913), p. 523.

13. Carl Dahlborg, *Provinsialläkareföreningen 1881–1905* (Schmidts Boktryckeri, Helsingborg, 1906); Gottfrid Törnell, *Svenska Provinsialläkare förenings Historia 1906–1930* (Svenska Tryckeriaktiebolaget, Stockholm, 1930).

14. K. F. Carøe, 'The Medical Profession', in *Denmark, its Medical Organization, Hygiene and Demography* (Jul. Gjællerup, Copenhagen, 1891), p. 30; V. Djærup, 'The Work of a Medical Officer of Health', in *Health Organization in Denmark* (League of Nations, 1924), pp. 410–11.

15. Dahlborg, *Provinsialläkareföreningen*, p. 42.

16. Fenger, *Almindelige Danske Lægeforening*, p. 219.

17. Ludvig Simon, 'Läkarkårens fackliga organisation', *Svenska Läkartidningen*, vol. 39 (1942), p. 2510.

18. W. Gårdlund, 'Tillfrågan om Sveriges läkarförbunds fackliga organisation', *Svenska Läkartidningen*, vol. 39 (1942), pp. 2203–13; W. Gårdlund, 'Något om fackorganisationerna inom läkarkåren och de privatpraktiserade läkarnas ställning', *Svenska Läkartidningen*, vol. 39 (1942), pp. 3099–107; Dag Knutson, 'Läkarkårens fackliga organisation', *Svenska Läkartidningen*, vol. 39 (1942), pp. 2786–97; Simon, 'Läkarkårens fackliga organisation', *Svenska Läkartidningen*, vol. 39 (1942), p. 2507.

19. M. Marcus, *Svensk Arbetarlagstiftning* (Hugo Gebers Förlag, Stockholm, 1907), pp. 100–1.

20. Daniel, *Danmarks Sygekassevæsen Gennem Aarhundreder*, vol. 2, pp. 1–10; Daniel, 'Statens tilsyn med sygekasserne m.fl.', in Daniel (ed.), *Fra Laugssygekasser til Folkeforsikring* (Sygekassenævnet, Copenhagen, 1942), pp. 195–202.

21. Gibbon, *Medical Benefits in Germany and Denmark*, p. 15.

22. F. Wittrup, *Danmarks Sociallovgivning*, vol. 2: *Sygekasseloven* (Indenrigsministeriets foranstaltning, Copenhagen, 1918), pp. 90–1.

23. Fenger, *Almindelige Danske Lægeforening*, pp. 7 and 133–4; Johannes Frandsen, *Sundhedsvæsenet 1927–1961* (Nyt Nordisk Forlag, Copenhagen, 1963), p. 23; P. J. Petersen, 'Sygekassernes Lægeordning-Voldgiftsraadet for Sygekasser og Læger', in Daniel (ed.), *Fra Laugssygekasser til Folkeforsikring* (Sygekassenævnet, Copenhagen, 1942), pp. 136–41.

24. *Svenska Läkartidningen*, vol. 13 (1915), pp. 936–9.

25. *Svenska Läkartidningen*, vol. 15 (1917), pp. 1612–18; vol. 16 (1918), pp. 1391–4 and 1738; *Läkaremöte* (1919), p. 6.

26. G. B. Lagerlöf, 'De statligt understödda sjukkassornas kontrollväsende', *Svenska Läkartidningen*, vol. 31 (1934), p. 346.

27. *Svenska Läkartidningen*, vol. 29 (1932), pp. 70–6.

28. *Svenska Läkartidningen*, vol. 35 (1938), pp. 1839–49.

29. Statens Offentliga Utredningar, *Utredning och förslag ang. lag om allmän sjukförsäkring*, SOU no. 15 (1944); Statens Offentliga Utredningar, *Kostnadsberäkningar ang. lag om allmän sjukförsäkring*, SOU no. 16 (1944).

30. *Svenska Läkartidningen*, vol. 43 (1946), pp. 2205–39.

31. Statens Offentliga Utredningar, *Den Öppna Läkarvården i Riket – utredning och förslag*, SOU no. 14 (1948).

32. Lagerlöf, 'Statligt understödda sjukkassornas kontrollväsende', p. 346.

THE DEBATE OVER 'SURPLUS OR SHORTAGE' IN SWEDISH MEDICINE IN THE 1930s

In the 1930s Swedish medicine was the centre of heated and value-laden debates over whether Sweden should train and/or import more physicians, and how this might be accomplished. While professional groups in many countries were embroiled in such debates as they attempted to protect their markets in a depression decade, the altercations in Sweden were perhaps more focused and public. Government-commissioned reports addressed the basic problem of professional employment – in medicine as well as the other professions – and were subjected to sharp rebuttal. The medical associations exerted strong pressure for the reduction of admissions to medical school courses, while Social Democratic and other groups argued that Sweden's almost uniquely low physician/population ratio should be raised to put it more in line with conditions in neighbouring countries. The discussion over whether physicians trained in other Scandinavian countries should be permitted to practise in Sweden was broadened later in the decade, when the government proposed to admit to practice some German and Austrian doctors. This debate provoked a dramatic session at the Karolinska Medical School, which culminated in a vote to oppose the entry of the refugee physicians.

Because it had held its physician production down more than the neighbouring countries had done, Sweden had in preceding decades experienced less fluctuation in physician employment opportunities. In Norway medical graduates would in one decade find that 'vacant positions and the blessings of the new medical reforms would fly toward us as "fried chickens do in the fairy tales" ', and their successors a decade later were told to expect, within a short time, 'a hungry doctor on every bay along the long Norwegian coast'. Consequently, as Torgersen found, there were ten or more applicants for most rural district doctor vacancies in the 'lean' years, and less than four applicants for the great majority of positions in the 'fat' years. Somewhat similar problems began to appear in Sweden in the late 1920s. In that decade the number of medical school places was expanded, in part in anticipation of increased demand due to health insurance reform, which however never materialised. This meant that young doctors had to wait much longer for established positions to become vacant, and by 1929 the average waiting period had increased to five years. During much of this time they had to accept unpaid assistant doctors' positions in the hospitals.

The Swedish discussion on whether and how to restrict physician numbers was stimulated by an article published in 1931 by Gunnar Dahlberg, an Uppsala medical professor. He argued that the problem of oversupply had been engendered by the preceding expansion of medical education and argued admissions curtailment through imposition of *numerus clausus*. An opposing interpretation was published in another journal by Sven Lingvar, a medical professor at Lund: 'In our nearest neighbour, Denmark, which has an education level and social structure similar to Sweden's, there are twice as many doctors per capita. Despite this the medical profession there maintains a good social and economic position, and one asks, inevitably, whether our country's need for doctors is really satisfied' (*Social Medicinska Tidskrift*, February 1932). An expansionist policy was also supported by Gunnar Helmstrom, of the Karolinska Institute, who believed that the imminent adoption of a health insurance scheme similar to Denmark's would help sustain many more physicians.

In part the discussion reflected the different interests of the three Swedish medical faculties. In 1933 Dahlberg spread the cautionary word directly, by sending reprints of one of his articles to prefects of the graduating classes in the various gymnasia, with the request that they be forwarded to students thinking of beginning medical study. He concluded: 'I say, therefore, that I do not want young students in large numbers to go to the expense of an education which does not provide them with livelihood possibilities.' His warnings seem to have had some effect, in so far as the number of applicants that year for the pre-clinical course at the Karolinska Institute was, according to Holmgren, less than half what it had been during preceding years.

The Medical Board, under Director-General N. E. Hellström, also backed the restrictionist solution. Hellström rejected the view that Sweden was worse off because it had less than a third of the physician density of Austria, and less than half that of the United States. He and others argued that Sweden needed fewer doctors because it used those it had more effectively. He declared that there was no evidence of a physician shortage. The medical association heartily affirmed this position, and strongly opposed exceptions to allow Scandinavian physicians in individual cases to be licensed to practice in Sweden.

Proposals to impose *numerus clausus* on medical and other professional schools had differing fates in Scandinavia in the 1930s; in

Norway the *Storting* defeated such a proposal in 1930, in Finland one was implemented. The Swedish response, of course, was to appoint a commission, but the two academic experts, Sven Wicksell of Lund and Tor Jerneman of Stockholm, were appointed by the recently installed Social Democratic government. Their report, published in 1935 — the same year that Axel Höjer replaced Hellström at the Health Board — accused the medical faculties of having reduced student admissions, 'supposedly because of space shortages, but in reality on the basis of a more or less striving for professional protection or monopoly'. Its conclusion from a review of the cross-national physician density figures was that, 'we in Sweden have, in comparison with other countries, all too few doctors, since it can scarcely be maintained that the need for medical care is less in Sweden than for example in Denmark, Norway, England or Germany'.

To support a goal of restoring the annual doctor production rate to 150, Wicksell/Jerneman predicted that health insurance, although hitherto 'humble', would 'henceforth come to give doctors in our country significantly more employment opportunities than has been the case up to now'. In its comments on the report, the Junior Physicians Association (SYLF) refused to count chickens before they were hatched. 'The development of a compulsory health insurance system, and doctors' relation to it, is at this time too uncertain for this factor to be now brought into the present discussion, or to be given the prominent place accorded it in the report.'

In the late 1930s further controversy was aroused by a government initiative to depart from the principle that medical licenses should only be issued to Swedes trained in Swedish medical faculties. At issue initially were petitions by individual doctors, Swedes trained abroad, or foreigners who had attained Swedish citizenship through marriage. Then in January 1939, Axel Höjer proposed to admit and give licenses to 20 German refugee doctors, many of them Jews who had lost the right to practise through Nazis decrees. The medical association through its secretary, J. P. Edwardson, raised 'strong misgivings' from the perspective of the 'general professional interest' which it represented. It pointed to the 'great surplus' of Swedish doctors, particularly the 300 to 400 young doctors who had only occasional incomes. The pro-German newspaper, *Aftonbladet*, carried an interview with a chief doctor who denied the Board's claim that Sweden needed the specialties practised by the proposed immigrants, and urged that young doctors be sent abroad for specialty training. The headline read, 'Travel Stipends for Doctors Better than Jew Import'.

The culmination of the prewar part of the struggle came in a February 1939 meeting of the Karolinska student body, presided over by Gunnar Björck, at which many speakers addressed themselves to Höjer's proposal. The opponents came partly from the political right and ultra-right, and partly from the SYLF leaders who stressed the priority of safeguarding economic interests. They carried the day against Social Democratic and other proponents, in a vote which went 263 to 180 against accepting any foreign doctors. The resolution called upon the Medical Association to bring about improvement in employment conditions for young doctors, and declared that, 'as long as the present difficult conditions for young doctors persist in our country, no action should be taken which could lead to a further worsening of the chances of young doctors to earn a livelihood'.

Compiled by Arnold J. Heidenheimer, on the basis of information from the following sources:

Seth D. Charney, 'Doctors: Surplus or Shortage' (Yale University Medical School, 1969), manuscript.
Walter Kotschnig, *Unemployment in the Learned Professions* (Oxford University Press, London, 1937).
Ulf Torgerson, 'The Market of Professional Manpower in Norway' (Institute of Social Research, Oslo, 1967), manuscript.

Part Two:

SWEDISH DECISION-MAKING STYLE AND THE
POLITICS OF HEALTH

3 HEALTH POLICY PROPOSALS AND WHAT HAPPENED TO THEM: SAMPLING THE TWENTIETH-CENTURY RECORD

Bo Bjurulf and Urban Swahn

Introduction

This chapter reports some of the results of a research project entitled *'Remiss* Consultations in the Political Decision-making Process'. It falls into two main parts. After a brief introduction to Swedish law-making procedures, the first part traces some general patterns of governmental medical policy-making during more than five decades (1922–76). Thereafter, we present the findings of analyses of the official decision-making processes leading to four momentous hospital bills, with a special emphasis on the role of the *remiss* practice.

The Swedish Law-making Procedure

The student of political decision-making processes in Sweden is extraordinarily well supplied with primary source materials. In most cases written documents are available from each stage of the legislative process. These documents present the standpoints of the different actors concerning the various issues (and specific aspects of them).

As the Swedish Government Chancery is a very small organisation compared to its counterparts in other countries, many of the basic documents on major issues are produced by outside sources. Specifically Swedish are the *ad hoc* commissions which are appointed by the responsible minister. The size of these commissions may vary, depending on the scope and complexity of their subjects, from one person to a dozen or more. The type of person appointed may vary as well. As a broad generalisation, the 'normal' commission (actually, about one in three) is still a one-man investigation on the part of a senior official. Larger commissions, however, usually include representatives of the major political parties and interested organisations.

After some years' work the commission presents its report to the minister. In about three cases out of four the recommendations are unanimous; the remaining one-fourth include some reservation(s) and/or dissenting opinion(s). Another specifically Swedish stage of the process then ensues. According to the 1809 Instrument of Government (in force until 1974) all government decisions should be prepared within a ministry, and this preparation should include, when necessary, the *consultation* of the central boards and agencies affected by the pending decision. By usage, the practice of remitting proposals for comment was gradually extended to other interested parties, such as local authorities, professional associations and other interest organisations. The 1974 Instrument of Government officially sanctioned this usage. Thus, not until the written desiderata of the various *remiss* bodies have been deliberated in the ministry, does the government decide the content of their bill proposition to the *Riksdag*. Bills usually contain extensive narrations of the basic documents and *remiss* desiderata.

In the *Riksdag*, individual MPs can make counter-proposals by introducing motions within 15 days of the submission of the bill. The final *Riksdag* resolution is preceded by a compulsory drafting in one of the (now 16) parliamentary standing committees (cf. Table 3.1).

Commission reports are published differently according to their topics. The *SOU* (Swedish Government Official Reports) series includes the most important commission reports (75 to 100 annually). *Ds*

Table 3.1: The Swedish Political Decision-making Process, Including a Commission Stage

Stage	Documentation
1 Commission is formed	The directives are issued. Also printed in the government's Annual Report (appendix to the *Riksdag* Records)
2 Commission works	Yearly statements in the government's Annual Report
3 Commission presents its report	Often published in the Swedish Government Official Reports (SOU) series
4 *Remiss* consultations	Desiderata narrated in the government's proposition
5 Government's bill is introduced	Appendix to the *Riksdag* Records
6 Private motions are introduced	Appendices to the *Riksdag* Records
7 Drafting in a Standing Committee	Appendix to the *Riksdag* Records
8 *Riksdag* debate and resolution	Minutes in the *Riksdag* Records
9 The government is officially informed of the *Riksdag*'s decision	A *Riksdag* Message is despatched (appendix to the *Riksdag* Records)
10 Law is issued by the government	Announced in the Swedish Code of Statutes (SFS)

(Ministry Reports, previously called 'Mimeographed Reports') is a second series of commission reports of somewhat lesser magnitude. Finally, minor drafts from the commissions are usually only circulated as duplicated memoranda. In our project, we distinguish only between *SOU* reports and 'other commission reports', which thus include *Ds* and 'memo' reports.

On minor issues, the decision-making process is often initiated outside the ministry, by an agency *request* or by an outside petition. Lesser shares of the decision processes are responses to international conventions or treaties or *Riksdag* messages demanding certain measures. In addition to the different types of basic documents, we have to consider the *'no basic document'* situation: the whole preparation process has been executed exclusively within the ministries.

In substantiating the stages of the processes, we work with 'hard data' only: written documents, express motives, manifest actions, etc. Our methodology relies heavily upon quantitative content analysis. It is important to stress the fact that we study only the *official* decision processes. Lobbying activities, mass media influences and anticipatory actions, while vital, fall outside the scope of our study. Here, the focus of analysis rests on *how the written desiderata of the* remiss *bodies are reflected in the minister's exposition of the motives for the policy measures chosen and, of course, in the deliberations and final resolution of the* Riksdag.

The Material Situation

The material situation is most easily described by reporting some crude measures of the official decision-making process.

For purposes of comparison, we consider the material in three distinct periods: 1922–45, 1945–57 and 1957–76. The points of division, which coincide with changes in regime, mark two important turning points in Swedish politics. In many respects, the 'grand coalition' of the war years detained an evolution emerging in the late 1930s. Secondly, the breaking of the Social Democratic–Agrarian Party coalition in 1957 was followed by changes in commission composition and in bill preparation patterns.[1]

During the years 1922 to 1976 a total of 13,532 government bills were presented to the *Riksdag* (budget propositions and a handful of other cases excluded). This makes an average of 246 bills per annum, but the variations are considerable (due to external conditions and a shifting balance of power between government and *Riksdag*), from a

maximum of 415 in 1939 to a minimum of 146 in 1972.[2] The
number of bills concerning different public sectors also varies.

More sophisticated analyses can be made when we consider the
proportions of the different cases (quantitatively and, if possible,
qualitatively).[3]

Observing how many bills rely on different types of background
material gives us an idea of the 'status' of the commission stage in the
policy process. On the whole, the dominant basic document is an
agency *request* (about 40 per cent of the bills until the 1950s,
thereafter decreasing to the present value of about 20 per cent), but
commission reports are steadily increasing their share as basic
document, especially during the postwar period (about 20 per cent
before 1940, about 30 per cent during the 1950s, and close to 45 per
cent – some years even more – during the 1970s). Other major basic
documents are external *petitions* (average: 11 per cent), and
international *conventions* and agreements (average 4 per cent); these
latter types of material show larger fluctuations, and their trends are
therefore more difficult to determine. *Riksdag* messages are used as
basic documents in only a handful of cases during each election period,
a bare 0.4 per cent of all bills. Finally, we find that the *'no basic
document'* situation has occurred in about every sixth case (average 17
per cent; individual years show sizeable variations, mostly dependent
on the government's parliamentary strength).[4]

Current Structure of the *Remiss Stage*

The different types of basic documents are handled differently as
regards their *remiss* consultation. In this section we will report some
results from a detailed study of the propositions introduced to the
Riksdag in 1974 – a year that for our purposes can be taken as
representative of the 1970s.[5] In 1974, *commission reports* were
remitted in 66 cases out of 67 (99 per cent), *requests* in 33 cases out of
46 (72 per cent), *petitions* in 15 cases out of 18 (83 per cent), and
conventions in 3 cases out of 12 (25 per cent).

The differences in *remiss* practice are even more evident if we take
into account the number of *remiss* bodies in each specific case.
Commission reports were remitted to an average 36 bodies, compared
to averages of 12 and 6 respectively, for requests and petitions.
Petitions are usually remitted to central boards and agencies only,
while requests are remitted to some private organisations as well as to
other boards and agencies. The sharp increase in the number of bodies
to which commission reports are remitted reflects the widened

spectrum of interests involved, while the proportions between public and private interests remain more or less unchanged.

The 'core' of state *remiss* bodies consists of the responsible central boards and agencies, county administrative boards (*länsstyrelser*), and the higher ordinary and specialised courts of law. In the private sector, apart from the relevant professional association(s), a number of large interest organisations can be said to represent a sort of 'generalist' knowledge in public matters. The most frequently consulted 'generalists' are the Swedish Trade Unions Confederation (LO), the Swedish Central Organisation of Salaried Employees (TCO), the Swedish Confederation of Professional Associations (SACO/SR), the Swedish Employers' Confederation (SAF), the Federation of Swedish Industries (SI), and the two national associations of local authorities: the County Council Federation (*Landstingsförbundet*) and the Swedish Association of Municipalities (*Svenska kommunförbundet*).

All these nationwide organisations have been consulted in at least one out of three *remiss*, as has the most frequently consulted professional association, the Swedish Bar Association. The very '*remiss* elite' is composed of LO, TCO, SACO/SR and the Swedish Association of Municipalities. These organisations have all been consulted in more than every second case (which, in other words, means *almost every time* any of each kind of organisation has been consulted!). In recent years the 'popular movements'[6] have increased their activity in the *remiss* stage, either as formally consulted bodies or as writers of desiderata on their own initiative. We might note that the preparation of government propositions in 1974 involved reading over 4,200 *remiss* desiderata!

The main part of this chapter will be devoted to the findings of a pilot study analysing the decision process in four selected issues of Swedish medical policy. Before turning to the details of that study, however, we should like to mention a more general analysis as an indication of the types of analyses the data bank permits. This latter study considers all government bills in the field of medical and health care since 1922, their basic documents, commission initiation and recruitment as well as *remiss* consultations.

Patterns in Swedish Governmental Medical Policy-making

Material Demarcation

Faced with 13,532 bills, our first problem was to define the range of *medical* policy-making. In order to include as much of medical 'politicking' as possible we decided to use a very broad preliminary definition. Our initial list of relevant areas included the following:

Internal Code	Policy Area	Number of Propositions
11	Medical Organisation	72
12	Mental Care	44
13	Dental Care	11
14	Care of the Aged and Disabled	10
15	Pharmacy and Veterinary Service	39
16	Public Health	47
17	Medical Building	121
18	Medical Funding	140
21	Health Insurance	48
82	Health Education	66
99	Other Medical – Health Topics	41
	Total	639
	(Of which areas 11–16	223)

We subsequently concentrated our attention on the first six areas. Borderline problems in allocating the bills to the respective categories were fewer than expected.

The Preparation of Medical Policy Bills

Figure 3.1 compares the distribution of medical bills among the different types of basic documents (thin columns) with the distribution of all bills (thick columns) during each of the three periods.

Looking to the relative volume of medical bills during the three periods (3.9, 6.9 and 4.4 per cent of total bills respectively), we find that medical policy has been a constant interest of every Swedish Government from 1922 on, but that a major effort was made during the period 1945 to 1957.

When we turn to consider the basic documents underlying medical legislation, we find a stable pattern over the years, with a slight over-representation of the 'heavy' *SOU* reports (roughly two medical bills per annum) and a corresponding under-representation of conventions and *Riksdag* messages. Interestingly, a special investigation of the post-1945 periods reveals that the number of bills, based on *SOU* reports, seems to be independent of the overall decline in number of bills and of changes in the government's parliamentary strength. During the most recent period agency requests are also over-represented. We also find that medical bills lack a basic document substantially less frequently than the average bill. The most striking deviation from the general

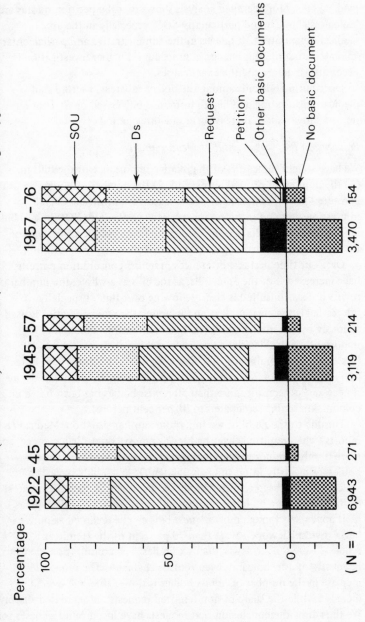

Figure 3.1: Distribution of Medical Bills (thin columns) and All Bills (broad columns) According to Type of Basic Document

pattern, however, is the 'disappearance' of petitions as bases for medical bills. More detailed analysis shows that the petition quotas are 'taken over' by *Ds* and particularly *SOU*, especially in the area of medical organisation.[7] Changes in the administrative and parliamentary 'climates' underlie this change in procedure. Further investigation is necessary to determine the exact causes.

Distributing our bills among the policy subareas, we find that medical organisation and health insurance bills based on *SOU* or *Ds* reports show a sharp increase over our three periods.

Preparation Patterns: Tentative Measurements

We have sought indicators of the relative importance of the bills in: (1) the number of printed pages; and (2) the number of bodies consulted in the *remiss* stage. Both measures confirm the overall impression that commission report-based (particularly *SOU*-based) bills are the 'heavy-weights' among medical policy legislation. Analysis of the latter variable further gave rise to the following observations.

Over our time periods differences in *remiss* consultation patterns have increased. For the *SOU* bills, as for bills as a whole, the number of *remiss* bodies consulted is clearly growing over time. Especially interesting is the clear indication (assuming the *remiss* practice is used seriously by the ministry) that *ad hoc* commissions dominate important medical legislative decision-making completely after 1957 (increasing the dominance they had before 1957). Since 1957, in fact, every bill of such a far-reaching character that the ministry has deemed it necessary to consult more than 50 *remiss* bodies has been based on a commission report (compared to 81 per cent before).

Turning to the *Ds* bills, we find quite another situation. Medical *Ds* reports (when remitted) have had fewer *remiss* bodies than average, and there is only a minor general increase in the number of consulted bodies. (Especially interesting are the ten *Ds*-based bills since 1957 which have not been remitted at all: an investigation reveals that most of these are in the building and funding areas, i.e. 'ex-petition' areas.)

It appears as though most *request* bills can be regarded as pure 'legislative spadework'. More than 70 per cent of the (remitted) requests were sent to fewer than six bodies. The consultation seems to be mostly of a technical or even routine character. The moderate increase in the number of *remiss* bodies is slower than the overall increase, while the share of non-remitted requests has increased sharply. We thus draw the conclusion that requests have lost ground as bases for important medical policy-making.

Ministry Revision of SOU *Reports*

Some published *SOU* reports are supplemented as basic documents by one or more *Ds* or 'memo' reports, especially in cases of revision. We have compared the share of medical *SOU* bills that also rely on one or more *Ds* reports with the corresponding figures for the total proposition population and find that ministry revision of *SOU* reports has risen considerably over the periods. The comparatively high revision activity on medical *SOU*s between 1945 and 1957 is interesting in view of a generally high level of medical policy activity and the tensions over the proposed Höjer reform.[8] In sum, however, the preparation methods as such do not differ between medical bills and other bills.

Medical Commissions: Initiatives and Composition

In the following section we shall comment on the initiatives behind and the composition of medical commissions of inquiry. (By 'commission' we now mean major commission, culminating in an *SOU* report.) We also confine our attention to subareas 11 to 16 (see p. 80), or what we consider the 'core' of medical policy.

It is generally difficult to trace the origin of the idea that a problem area should be investigated by a commission of inquiry.[9] Official statements by the minister in the instructions guiding the work of commissions indicate three main idea sources: the ministry itself, the *Riksdag* and other major commissions.

We have regarded those cases where no outside source of initiative is indicated as being initiated by the ministry itself. Meanwhile, we are quite aware that among these cases there may well be a number of inquiries at least partly initiated by outside sources like the large interest organisations. Keeping this reservation in mind, ministry initiatives constitute about 40 per cent of all cases (no specific trends can be ascertained). Direct initiatives in *Riksdag* messages were fairly common prior to 1957; the drop after 1957 is striking: from about 20 per cent to about 5 per cent of the cases. In addition, we have another group of *Riksdag* references: indirect references to motions and committee statements have been relatively stable at 25 per cent since 1945. However, Swedish political history tells us that many of these latter references should be regarded as 'bows' to the *Riksdag* rather than real initiatives. Other commissions have furnished numerous initiatives, and this trend is rising, from about 25 per cent before 1957 to about 35 per cent since. The sum of the figures above indicated that the residual initiatives from central boards and agencies, local authorities, professional associations and even the County Council Federation are very few (at least as manifestly stated).

Thus, it would seem as if most important medical propositions are initiated within three central political decision-making bodies: commission, ministry and *Riksdag*. We found no significant structural differences between our subareas.

It is very difficult to identify *one* comprehensive principle concerning recruitment to the major commissions. Our only general conclusions are that senior officials from the boards, MDs and professors are frequent overall. A second feature, however, is that MPs seem to be considerably less involved after 1957. MPs from all major parties participated in all types of medical commissions prior to 1957, whereas after 1957 'broad' parliamentary representation is found only on commissions concerned with dental care and care of the aged. A few Social-Democrats are represented on commissions on organisational issues and mental health care.

These tendencies seem to be more than purely coincidental. In another study, in which we examined recruitment patterns in the labour welfare area,[10] we found the same tendency: after 1957 the commissions were recruited from major boards, national organisations and professional associations.

Four Organisational Reforms

Hospital Decrees and Hospital Laws

The following discussion draws upon the findings of a pilot study which analysed several policy areas in respect of four or five momentous policy decisions each. These decisions were split up into sub-issues (20 to 100 each). The different alternatives presenting themselves with respect to each sub-issue at the commission, *remiss*, ministry, motion, standing committee and *Riksdag* resolution stages are treated as *roll-call motions*. The great advantage of the roll-call analysis approach is that it permits the study of coalition formation between commission members, *remiss* bodies, the responsible minister, MPs and political parties (or some of these) in respect of its *occurrence*, its *predictive value* for the subsequent development of the process and the *types of questions* in which a given coalition is (un)usual.

The principal part of the analysis concerns the *remiss* stage and the most frequent *remiss* bodies within the different policy sectors. The overall aim is to identify specific decision patterns which with reasonable certainty can be said to be caused by certain desideratum patterns during the process.

Keeping in mind the general medical decision-making structures outlined earlier, we now turn to a special investigation of four important medical bills:

Proposition 1928:101 (based on *SOU* 1927:3) establishing the county councils' obligation to arrange hospital care;

Proposition 1959:19 (based on *SOU* 1956:27) co-ordinating the successive partial revisions of the 1928 law and requiring the county councils to arrange ambulatory clinics in hospital (optional in the 1928 law);

Proposition 1961:181 (based on *SOU* 1958:15) requiring the county councils to set up out-of-hospital outpatient clinics or 'health centres';

Proposition 1972:104 (based on *SOU* 1971:68 and *Ds* S 1971:3)[11] providing guidelines for decentralising parts of the hospitals' specialist resources to health centres (and proposing new rules for the authorisation of MDs).

Our analytical interest is focused on the existence (during the later stages of the decision-making process) of any rejection, criticism or other proposed amendment concerning the different subproposals in the *SOU* reports. The four bills are treated as different entities when comparing the decision-making patterns. The bills may also be looked upon as a unit inasmuch as they constitute the reiterative process by which the societal output of health care services is regulated and co-ordinated. Doing so, we can discover and trace possible general trends in the reactions registered by different types of *remiss* bodies.

The five (including the *Ds*) commissions represent a good variety of different possible structures. The first commission consisted of four persons: a Judge Referee to the Supreme Administrative Court as chairman, and one representative each from the Board of Health, the medical faculties and the county councils. The second commission was headed by a former Social-Democratic MP, the other members being two other MPs (one Agrarian Party and one Conservative) and one representative each from the Board of Health, the Swedish Medical Association and the County Council Federation; a second Board of Health official was subsequently added to the commission in an expert capacity.

The third commission was the big 'ÖHS' Commission, formed to draft the reorganisation of Swedish public health and medical services.[12] At this time it consisted of 19 members, plus 5 'experts'. Chaired by a 'politically impartial' Director of the Board of Health, the commission included two other representatives of the Board, one medical professor (later an MP for the Conservative Party!), three county council representatives, five MPs (two Social-Democrats plus one each from the three non-socialist parties in the *Riksdag*), and seven members from the Swedish Medical Association and the different employees' organisations.

The fourth *SOU* report was the result of quite another type of Commission; the Board of Social Welfare[13] was charged to form a commission of inquiry. This 16-member commission, headed by Director Bror Rexed, was made up of six heads of division from the Board, three senior officials from other boards and two members each from the Swedish Medical Association, the County Council Federation and the Swedish Association of Municipalities.

The *Ds* report, finally, is a good example of a minor report from a minor commission. The sole member of this commission was a former Deputy Director of the Board of Health (and subsequently the Board of Health and Welfare), who had represented the Board in the *SOU* 1956:27 commission (serving as its secretary). A Head of Division from the Ministry of Social Affairs was subsequently attached to the *Ds* commission as an expert. The patterns of conflict within and between the different stages of the decision processes are illustrated in Table 3.2.

From Table 3.2 we can see that the commissions have by and large been agreed. Out of the 210 sub-problems considered we found only 5 reservations. The conflict level among *remiss* bodies was especially high for commissions 2 and 3, the two that included politicians. The ministry made most changes in the proposals emanating from commission 3, and least in commission 4. Turning to consider the *Riksdag* stage, the proposals of commission 2 (together with amendments made by the minister) were accepted to an especially high degree, whereas those of commission 1 were highly conflict-charged. When combining the different stages, it is interesting to compare the fates of the two 'bureaucratic' commissions, 1 and 4. In 1928, a ministry with weak parliamentary support accepted no less than 92 per cent of the commission's proposals, but met severe opposition in the *Riksdag*. In 1972, a minister with strong parliamentary support made more adjustments in the commission's proposals, most of which were successful at the *Riksdag* stage. The few sub-

Table 3.2: Intensity of Conflict at Different Decision-making Stages (*Percentage* Distribution at Each Stage)

	Commission No.			
	1	2	3	4
Within-commission conflict	0	5	6	0
Remiss body/bodies in conflict with				
commission proposal(s)	47	72	68	57
The minister:				
accepts commission proposal(s)	55	47	29	57
modifies commission proposal(s)	37	24	47	7
rejects commission proposal(s)	4	13	18	21
refrains from taking position	4	15	6	14
The *Riksdag*:				
accepts ministry proposal(s)	43	86	79	75
only private member's bill in conflict	49	9	15	4
Standing committee conflict	8	5	6	21
(Number of subproposals)	(51)	(97)	(34)	(28)

problems not accepted gave rise to more protracted conflict, however, in the form of opposition from Communist and Conservative MPs at the debate and standing committee stages. Commissions 2 and 3 (the 'parliamentarian' commissions) show evolutionary patterns that are very similar to each other.

Remiss *Body Access to the Ministry*

Being on the *'remiss* roll' is vital for anybody wishing to influence the ministry at the deliberation stage. When a minister puts an organisation, association, central or local board on the roll, it is generally because the body is assumed to have a substantial interest in or specific knowledge of the questions involved in the pending proposal(s). On the *remiss* rolls of our 4 *SOU* bills we find altogether 134 different bodies. Many of these have made sub-consultations. Indeed, we find explicit mention of 72 such bodies in the bills. Hence, over 200 bodies are known to have been involved in our 4 bills. In this study, we have measured a body's access to the ministry in terms of the extent to which it has been cited in the *remiss* narrations in the bills. Some 192 *remiss* bodies and 10 'collective instances' ('all the county councils', 'most *remiss* bodies', etc.) are cited in the 4 bills. In other words, only twelve of the bodies on the *remiss* rolls were not cited at all. (The reason for this seems to have been lack of interest; in none of these twelve cases had the body submitted comments of more than three pages.) Total *remiss* citations in our four bills amounted to 9,432 lines of text. These were distributed among our 202 bodies as shown in Table 3.3.

We find that 9 per cent (i.e., 19 bodies) are cited with 48 per cent of the lines. Moreover, 4 of these 19 bodies (the Board of Health, the County Council Federation, the Swedish Medical Association and the Association of Junior Physicians — SYLF) are cited with no less than 22 per cent of all lines. Our further analysis of individual *remiss* bodies will focus on these 19 bodies: the '*remiss* elite'. A notable fact is that all county administrative boards rank among the relatively 'deprived' bodies in this regard; while they represent a great share of *remiss* bodies, they are cited very sparsely.

A cross-tabulation of the types of *remiss* bodies filing views on different subjects reveals that interest groups, central boards and agencies, county councils, and the national associations of local authorities are heavily and fairly equally cited on all types of problems; together they cover 65 per cent of the cited lines. Medical faculties, county council subordinates (hospital directors and local boards of health), and county administrative boards (and their subordinates, mostly county medical officers), on the other hand, have much more profiled citation patterns.

Interest groups (the most prominent of which are the Swedish Medical Association, SYLF, and the Swedish Medical Society), by far the most extensively cited type of *remiss* body, are cited much above average on salaries and formal questions, while they are cited below average on public expenditures and central administration. Central boards and agencies are cited somewhat above average on economy, but rarely on formal questions. County councils are frequently cited on policy content, but sparsely cited on salaries and central administration issues. The national associations of local authorities are cited above average on economic matters only.

Other types of *remiss* bodies show more 'specialised' citation patterns. The medical faculties, not surprisingly, have exerted particular influence in the area of medical expert functions. The faculties also rank high on questions of central administration and, perhaps more surprisingly, formal questions. County council subordinates (hospital directors and local boards of health) are notably cited only on issues of central administration, whereas county administrative boards (and their subordinates, primarily county medical officers) are frequently cited on general policy content, but

Table 3.3: Extent of Citation of Various Types of *Remiss* Bodies

Type of *Remiss* Body	Number of Cited Lines					
	500+	499–100	99–50	49–10	9–1	Total
Higher public educational institutions	0	3	1	1	4	9
Ad hoc commissions	0	2	0	2	1	5
Central boards and agencies	1	3	4	8	7	23
All regional boards and agencies	0	0	1	43	15	59
County Councils, County Boroughs	0	3	6	17	4	30
County Council subordinates	0	0	3	8	6	17
Other County Council authorities	0	0	2	0	2	4
Nationwide interest organisations	2	2	5	16	8	33
National Associations of Local Authorities	1	1	2	1	0	5
Collective references ('all', 'some', 'many', 'most')	0	1	1	1	1	4
Other *remiss* bodies	0	0	0	6	7	13
N(%)	4(2)	15(7)	25(12)	103(51)	55(27)	202(100)

not on questions of central administration nor, surprisingly, on expert functions.

*Conflict Relations (Commission—*Remiss *Body—Ministry) and their Effects*

We now turn our attention to the relationship between the stands taken by *remiss* bodies and commission proposals in the four 'landmark' cases selected for analysis. Table 3.4 reports the reactions of 21 major *remiss* bodies to the 210 sub-problems identified (as cited in the bills). The reactions of the different *types* of *remiss* bodies are also summarised.

On the whole, the national associations, the county administrative boards and the commissions have been the most approving *remiss* bodies, whereas the medical faculties and the interest groups/ professional associations have been the most critical. It is also interesting in this regard to note a certain bias in ministry usage of collective references: 'most [county councils, *remiss* bodies, etc.]' means 'heavy support', while 'some . . .' means '(moderate) criticism'!

What effect, then, have these cited reactions had on the ministry? In attempting to answer this question, we shall first examine the cases in which *remiss* body and minister have taken definite positions (acceptance or rejection). That is, we study all *pairs of standpoints* in a four-field typology (see Table 3.5).

Table 3.5 shows the average pattern for each *type* of *remiss* body as well as selected members of the '*remiss* elite'. Here the medical faculties stand out as apparently the most influential 'veto group' in terms of having their rejections of commission proposals accepted by the minister. The professional associations, on the other hand, seem almost completely unsuccessful. The Swedish Medical Association has rejected 18 proposals, one of which was supported by the minister; the Swedish Medical Society scores 1 for 6; the Junior Physicians' Association 0 for 12! We should, however, note the generally low level of support of rejections (compare columns 2 and 4 in Table 3.5).

Finally, we should note that the County Council Federation has been cited as the most active endorser of commission proposals. Of 50 sub-problems, the Federation is recorded as favouring 47. The minister has rejected seven of the proposals supported by the Federation.

This analysis is, of course, a crude one, measuring only flat acceptance or rejection. Any student of written statements knows

Table 5.4. Remiss Body Reactions on 218 Sub-problems in Four Medical SOU Reports: Percentage Distribution (A.D. row
sum = 100%)

Remiss Body/*Remiss* Body Collective	Commission No.	*Remiss* Body Reaction Approval	Criticism	Rejection	Total N Citations in Bills
Medical Faculty of Uppsala	2, 3, 4	24	52	24	29
Medical Faculty of Lund	2, 3, 4	0	73	26	26
Medical Faculty of Gothenburg	2, 3, 4	20	48	34	21
Higher Public Educational Institutions (N = 9)		13	56	32	105
'OHS' Commission	2	64	28	8	25
Government *ad hoc* Commissions (N = 5)		50	41	10	44
Board of Health	1, 2, 3	42	45	11	79
Board of Social Welfare	2, 3	79	9	13	23
UKÄ	2, 3, 4	29	58	12	24
Central Boards and Agencies (N = 23)		48	40	13	187
Regional Boards and Agencies (N = 59)		54	29	16	275
County Council of Nyköping	2, 3	10	66	24	21
County Council of Örebro	2, 3, 4	23	54	23	26
County Council of Halmstad	2, 3, 4	56	31	19	16
County Councils, County Boroughs (N = 30)		38	43	18	249
County Council Subordinates (N = 17)		25	66	9	66
Swedish Medical Association	all	21	55	25	80
Association of Junior Physicians	1, 2	3	61	36	36
Swedish Medical Society	2, 4	5	63	33	22
Nationwide Interest Groups (N = 33)		22	50	27	339
Swedish Association of Towns	2, 3	44	44	11	27
Swedish Federation of Municipalities	4	78	14	7	14
County Council Federation	all	70	26	4	75
National Associations of Local Authorities (N = 5)		60	32	9	133
'Some county councils'	2, 3, 4	55	20	25	20
'Most county councils'	3, 4	77	24	0	17
'Some *remiss* bodies'	2, 3, 4	9	72	18	11
'Many *remiss* bodies'	2, 3, 4	38	52	10	21
'Most *remiss* bodies'	2, 3, 4	89	11	0	37

Table 3.5: *Remiss* Body/Ministry Patterns on 210 Sub-problems in Four *SOU* Reports. Percentage Distribution (N.B. *row sum* = 100%)

Remiss Body/*Remiss* Body Collective	Commission No.	*Remiss* Body/Ministry Pattern* 1	2	3	4	Total Number of Citations
Medical Faculty of Uppsala	2, 3, 4	46	23	8	23	13
Medical Faculty of Lund	2, 3, 4	0	67	0	33	6
Medical Faculty of Gothenburg	2, 3, 4	33	22	11	33	9
Higher Public Educational Institutions (N = 9)		27	32	5	37	41
'OHS' Commission	2	67	13	20	0	15
Government *ad hoc* Commissions (N = 5)		68	9	14	9	22
Board of Health	1, 2, 3	77	15	0	8	39
Board of Social Welfare	2, 3, 4	78	11	6	6	18
UKÄ	2, 3, 4	50	20	20	10	10
Central Boards and Agencies (N = 23)		75	16	3	7	102
Regional Boards and Agencies (N = 59)		75	21	2	2	187
County Council of Nyköping	2, 3	29	71	0	0	7
County Council of Örebro	2, 3, 4	33	67	0	0	9
County Council of Halmstad	2, 3, 4	57	29	0	14	7
County Councils, County Boroughs (N = 30)		56	28	9	8	115
County Council Subordinates (N = 17)		47	21	26	5	19
Swedish Medical Association	all	44	50	3	3	34
Association of Junior Physicians	1, 2	8	92	0	0	13
Swedish Medical Society	2, 4	0	71	14	14	7
Nationwide Interest Organisations (N = 33)		39	48	8	4	153
Swedish Association of Towns	2, 3	69	23	8	0	13
Swedish Federation of Municipalities	4	67	8	25	0	12
County Council Federation	all	80	4	14	2	50
National Associations of Local Authorities (N = 5)		73	13	14	1	80
Collective References (N = 4)		80	7	14	0	44

*Key:

		Remiss body Accepts	Rejects
Minister	Accepts	1	2
	Rejects	3	4

that this is hardly the complete picture. Therefore, in the following section we report and analyse the positions of different types of *remiss* bodies in relation to those of the ministry in greater detail.

Remiss *Body v. Ministry: A Detailed Analysis*

Here, our object of analysis is the group of sub-problems (N = 133) on which at least one *remiss* body has expressed criticism. This population involves a total of 202 *remiss* bodies, cited with a total of 1,413 opinions. *Remiss* body reactions have been classified in terms of acceptance, alternative or refusal and ministry reactions in terms of acceptance, modification or rejection.[14] Tables 3.6(a)–(g) show the distribution of these reactions among the total population and among different types of *remiss* bodies.

The total distribution of acceptance versus criticism is 40:60. Thus, there is no indication of bias in ministry narrations of the different *remiss* opinions. Slightly less than every second reported criticism is 'constructive', i.e., it offers an alternative solution to the sub-problem in question. On the whole, the ministry has accepted 40 per cent of the commission proposals, modified 45 per cent and rejected 15 per cent. Once again, these figures apply only to those sub-proposals encountering some form of conflict/criticism at the *remiss* stage.

Turning now to the different types of *remiss* bodies, the *medical faculties* have been cited with 82 reactions. The 'acceptance– alternative–refusal' distribution shows a very negative attitude pattern. Furthermore, the success of faculties as a 'veto group' is very clearly demonstrated: no less than 48 per cent of their refusals carry through the ministry! Constructive criticism on the part of the faculties is also comparatively successful. In addition, as Table 3.6(b) indicates, even in situations where a faculty has verbally accepted a commission subproposal, the ministry has made changes more often than might be expected. This reflects the fact that some faculty reactions have been 'acceptance in principle, but additional suggestions'. (Such opinions have been collapsed into the 'acceptance' column in the tables.) The influence of the medical faculties becomes even more apparent when we differentiate their critical reactions as to intensity. Doing so, we find that the ministry has rejected commission proposals more often than expected in the face of sharp faculty criticism and modified more often than expected when faced with only mild faculty criticism. One may conclude that the medical faculties have at least exerted a palpable 'counter-influence'. The

Table 3.6: Ministry Acceptance, Modification and Rejection of *Remiss*-Body Comment on Commission Proposals. Percentage Distributions (deviations, in percentage units, within brackets)

(a) All coded answers

Ministry:	acceptance	*Remiss* Body: alternative	refusal
acceptance	38	42	40
modification	51	44	41
rejection	11	15	19
(N =)	(563)	(409)	(441)
(% =)	(40)	(29)	(31)

(b) Medical Faculties

27 (−11)	32 (−10)	35 (− 5)
55 (+ 4)	42 (− 2)	18 (−23)
18 (+ 7)	26 (+11)	48 (+29)
(11)	(31)	(40)
(13)	(38)	(49)

(c) Medical associations

45 (+ 7)	46 (+ 4)	58 (+18)
35 (−16)	34 (−10)	24 (−17)
20 (+ 9)	20 (+ 5)	18 (− 1)
(49)	(95)	(109)
(19)	(38)	(43)

(d) County administrative boards and County medical officers

9 (−29)	20 (−22)	15 (−25)
88 (+37)	77 (+33)	78 (+37)
3 (− 8)	3 (−12)	7 (−12)
(128)	(60)	(54)
(53)	(25)	(22)

(e) County councils

26 (−12)	33 (− 9)	28 (−12)
59 (+ 8)	57 (+13)	47 (+ 6)
15 (+ 4)	10 (− 5)	24 (+ 5)
(54)	(49)	(78)
(30)	(27)	(43)

(f) Central boards and agencies

33 (− 5)	49 (+ 7)	38 (− 2)
62 (+11)	30 (−14)	44 (+ 3)
5 (− 6)	21 (+ 6)	19 (± 0)
(58)	(47)	(32)
(42)	(34)	(23)

(g) National associations of the local authorities

39 (+ 1)	25 (−17)	30 (−10)
37 (−14)	50 (+ 6)	55 (+14)
24 (+13)	25 (+10)	15 (− 4)
(46)	(20)	(20)
(53)	(23)	(23)

main areas in which this influence has been exerted are expert functions and formal issues.

Some 253 reactions on the part of the *medical associations* have been recorded. Their reaction pattern is very close to that of the medical faculties, although slightly less negative. The distribution in Table 3.6(c) is completely different, however. The table confirms our earlier indications of the 'non-influence' of the associations: criticism without an alternative is apparently non-influential, while constructive criticism (whether phrased in positive or negative terms) leads to ministry amendment more often than might be expected statistically. Differentiation according to the intensity of criticism shows an inverse relationship between sharp criticism and ministry rejection; mildly criticised commission proposals tend, on the other hand, to be rejected by the ministry more than might be expected.

The 242 cited reactions of *county administrative boards* and *county medical officers* are clearly more approving than the total average. Almost all these reactions, however, are found on proposals subsequently modified by the ministry (82 per cent) independent of the *remiss* body's reaction. Detailed investigation shows a positive covariation between criticism and ministry-originated modifications. In other words, while these bodies apparently have the 'wrong' solutions, they seem to pinpoint the 'soft spots' in commission proposals. As noted earlier, the citation pattern of county administrative boards and county medical officers was profiled with an emphasis on 'practical' matters like detailed organisation, expert-related questions, local administration and economy. Hence, we find a modifying influence of regional bodies on practical matters.

The *county councils* have had a total of 181 reactions cited. They show a somewhat more critical pattern than the total. More detailed investigation verifies the general impression given by the table; we find a positive covariation between specified criticism and *remiss*-based ministry modifications as well as between unspecified criticism and ministry-originated modifications. There is also positive covariation between unspecified criticism and flat ministry rejection.

Table 3.6(f) gives the impression that *central boards and agencies* have been moderately influential at this stage of the process. Detailed examination reveals a positive covariation between the various types of *remiss* criticism and the 'corresponding' ministry reaction, but negative covariation between the various types of *remiss* approval and ministry reactions.

Finally, the 86 reactions of the *national associations of local authorities* are as a whole more positive than the total. This attitude has produced one ambiguous finding: there are many more ministry rejections of proposals supported by the national associations than might be expected! Once again, especially constructive criticism has led to ministry amendment of commission proposals.

Concluding Reflections

Analysis of citations in the bills, and data as to the formal comments filed at various stages on each piece of legislation have permitted us to trace the activities of various interest groups and governmental bodies on selected issues in the field of medicine and health care between 1922 and 1976. Comparing the positions taken by these groups with the position of the ministry and the content of the subsequent Government Bill to the *Riksdag*, we have further been able to assess the instrumental effectiveness of the respective *remiss* bodies and groups of bodies.

Medical and health legislation occurred at a fairly constant rate over the years, with an increase (representing a major effort) between 1945 and 1957. The three main sources of major medical legislation have been *ad hoc* commissions of inquiry, the ministry and the *Riksdag*, with increasing use of the former in recent years.

Similarly, the number of bodies consulted by the average commission has also shown a steady increase. Looking to the composition of commissions, we find a general trend towards fewer MPs and greater representation of interest groups and the bureaucracy. Commissions have been strikingly unanimous, no more than 5 reservations being filed out of a total of 210 sub-issues.

In analysing policy-formulation processes our approach has been to treat the alternatives presenting themselves with respect to each sub-issue at the commission, *remiss*, ministry, motion, standing committee and *Riksdag* resolution stages as *roll-call motions*. This enables us to trace coalition formation between commission members, *remiss* bodies, the minister involved, MPs and political parties as well as how coalition formation relates to the subsequent development of the process and patterns in respect of the types of issues involved.

We have identified a '*remiss* elite' in 19 bodies which account for 48 per cent of the *remiss* citations in government propositions. Of these, interest groups, central boards and agencies, county councils and the national associations of local authorities are heavily and fairly equally cited on all types of problems, whereas other categories of bodies have much more 'profiled' citation patterns. The medical faculties show a markedly specialised pattern, but when cited, their (often critical) views have been highly influential. This forms a striking contrast to the professional organisations, whose views were seldom respected by the ministry.

Finally, a few words about the limitations of our approach. The analysis focuses on official decision processes only. Lobbying and expressions of public opinion, while vital, fall outside the scope of the project. Secondly, and perhaps most critical, we might note a source of error in assessments of *remiss*-body influence, for example, in what might be called the 'problem of silence', *viz*. our data do not take account of what is *not* on the record. Non-response (and/or non-citation), due to acquiescence or for whatever reason, should be introduced into the analysis.

There are numerous ways in which our analysis might be extended and refined to increase the precision of our descriptive variables. The need for knowledge of historical circumstances on the part of the user should be minimised. At present, the data bank offers a vast body of structured and structurable comparative data, providing an overview of Swedish legislative processes over the past half century. We believe it will prove valuable both as a reference resource and as a generator of research hypotheses.

Notes

1. See B. H. Bjurulf, 'Remissväsendet i den politiska beslutsprocessen'. *Statsvetenskaplig Tidskrift*, vol. 58, no. 2 (1976), pp. 144–58.
2. In 1939 the *Riksdag* was convened for two separate sessions. In conjunction with conversion to fiscal year sessions the 1975 session was shortened to a half-year. The 107 bills of that session should be added to the figure for the autumn session of the 1975/6 *Riksdag*, thus yielding a total of 194 bills.
3. These figures should not be taken as estimates of the total amount of work within the different ministries, as we have not taken into account all other administrative cases handled within the Chancery.
4. The yearly variations are considerable, from 10 per cent to 31 per cent. (The latter figure is for 1969, when the Social-Democratic Government returned with an absolute majority in both Chambers of the *Riksdag*.)
5. See C. U. Swahn, 'Departementen läste 5.000 yttranden', 'Intresse-organisationerna flitiga remissbesvarare' and 'TCO flitigaste remissvararen av organisationerna', *Administrations-TEMA*, vol. 4, no. 4 (1975), pp. 6f, 16f, 26f.
6. The 'popular movements', nationwide voluntary associations including consumer co-operation, temperance and adult education associations as well as evangelical churches, exert considerable influence, reflecting the relative uniformity and high degree of organisation of Swedish society.
7. The actual numbers of petition-based bills during the three periods are (for the most illustrative areas):

Code	1922–45	1945–57	1957–76
11	7	0	0
15	6	6	1
17	9	4	1
18	17	1	0

Thus, petition bills 'disappear' in two stages: areas 11 and 18 before 1945, and areas 15 and 17 before 1957.

8. For the details of this controversial proposal see Chapter 4 (pp. 101–3). Here it may be noted that many of the Höjer Commission's proposals were subsequently implemented.

9. See H. Meijer, *Kommittépolitik och kommittéarbete* (C. W. K. Gleerup, Lund, 1956), pp. 37 ff.

10. See Bjurulf, 'Remissväsendet', p. 149.

11. The two reports have been treated as a single report in the analysis.

12. For the details of the work of the Sterner Commission see Chapter 4 (pp. 105–6).

13. The former Board of Health was incorporated into the Board of Social Welfare to form the Board of Health and Welfare in 1968.

14. Our definitions are as follows:

remiss acceptance:	approval (with or without additional suggestions) or favourable criticism.
remiss alternative:	commission reservation approved or commission proposal rejected or unfavourably criticised and alternative solution proposed.
remiss refusal:	flat rejection or unfavourable criticism (without alternative solution).
ministry acceptance:	approval.
ministry modification:	commission proposal modified according to *remiss* body's suggestion or according to the minister's own view.
ministry rejection:	commission proposal rejected (no new solution proposed) or minister proposes new, quite different solution.

4 SWEDISH HEALTH LEGISLATION: MILESTONES IN REORGANISATION SINCE 1945

Uncas Serner

Government responsibility towards the sick is a basic principle that has always shaped Swedish health policy and politics. Postwar developments in the field of health care may largely be characterised as a development from basic security to equal access. This general principle of welfare has been and is being upheld by central government, mainly through legislation and funding. In other respects, central government has handed over the responsibilities of the welfare state to local government. Health care delivery has, for example, been shifted over to the county councils (*landsting*).

In various ways, however, central government continues to keep the sector under its control. Increasing county council responsibility, my next theme, therefore involves an interaction and power-play between central and local government. We shall consider this interaction in terms of both legislation and diversion of power.

In addition to the public sector, there is also a private sector — although of moderate size (15 per cent of all physicians and 50 per cent of all dentists). The attitude of the Swedish medical profession (as well as dentists and physiotherapists) towards policy proposals over the years will be considered in the latter part of this chapter.

Finally, policy can also be seen in the perspective of themes or issues, not directly related to specific actors. By way of conclusion, the issues of decentralised medical care and occupational health will be examined in such a perspective.

Background

The Swedish health care and medical delivery system has much in common with other national systems. Some more peculiarly Swedish characteristics should, however, be kept in mind.

Medical care ceased to be a service provided only on a commercial basis very early in Sweden. True, it was as elsewhere mostly a question of self-help in a self-subsistence society. Nevertheless, publicly-employed district doctors (*provinsialläkare*) have been offering medical care — although a scarce commodity — as part of a welfare system guaranteed by the community since about 1700. They were not only medical officers for preventive health, but primarily physicians for individual consultation and treatment, whose services were offered to some extent free of charge or at a fixed fee schedule.

The provision of hospitals and other Swedish health care institutions has always been predominantly a public duty, not a private undertaking, whether on a charitable or confessional basis or as a profit-making enterprise. Hospitals in particular were a state concern (on a regional basis under the provincial governors) and medical legislation, too, has concentrated on the organisation of the hospitals.

A fundamental restructuring of the representative system occurred in the 1860s, when the new parliamentary system succeeded the '*ständerriksdag*' or parliament of estates (nobility, clergy, bourgeoisie and landed gentry) and municipal sovereignty was given its constitutional base. The county councils were introduced as a secondary level of local government and given decisive legislative powers, among them, the power to levy taxes. After some deliberation as to what they should actually be entrusted with, they were in 1864 charged with responsibility for the provincial hospitals.

Much central control was retained within the central government bureaucracy, however. Hospital physicians (and others) were appointed by the King-in-Council, and a *Sundhetskollegium*, predecessor of the present National Board of Health and Welfare, maintained surveillance of hospital functions.

In time, some of the specialised branches of hospital care (control of tuberculosis and other epidemic diseases, etc.) were brought over to the counties. Legislation in 1928 gave county councils ultimate responsibility for providing hospital care where there was no other provider, which was generally the case.

Through the disbursing of government grants the county councils were subsequently – mainly in the late 1930s – charged with various non-hospital health care services, i.e. district nurses and midwives, maternity and pediatric health care, child dental care, etc. In the late 1930s less than one Swedish physician in three held a hospital post, with ambulatory care being offered mainly by private practitioners, in their own offices or on hospital premises. (Today, close to 90 per cent of ambulatory care is delivered by publicly-employed physicians.)

In 1938 Minister of Social Affairs Gustav Möller appointed a parliamentary commission on health legislation[1] and instructed it to look into the need for one comprehensive governing body for the county councils in the field of medical care delivery, in view of the number of health care responsibilities they had been entrusted with.

However, the result was a hospital law not very different from previous legislation.

In 1943 Axel Höjer, Director of the Board of Health, was instructed to form a new commission to consider ways and means to bring about a regulation of outpatient care at public hospitals.[2] The directives were no more specific than that. Unofficially, however, Minister Möller had discussed more extensive instructions with Höjer, requesting a comprehensive analysis of the entire health care delivery system, including doctors' fee-for-service remunerations.[3] For this or other reasons, Höjer interpreted the commission's terms of reference so as to focus on ambulatory medical care at hospital outpatient clinics and hospital doctors' offices, as well as outside the hospitals.[4]

The report of the Höjer commission treats a broad range of subjects. The convictions behind the various proposals are summarised succinctly, however, in the following:

> *All medical care services needed by the individual should be offered free of charge at the time of treatment.* It should be *the duty of the community to deliver this by means of an extended and (comprehensively) regulated organisation,* including and coordinating *public health, hospital care, preventive medicine on an individual basis and ambulatory medical care.* Especially *ambulatory medical care,* which has largely been left to medical doctors' private initiative . . . *should be extended and regulated by public provision.* This will pursue the general line of development of Swedish social medicine.[5] (Italics in the original.)

The report's proposals with respect to organisation, administration and financing were quite outspoken and very much in line with these commitments.

One of the principal legacies of the Höjer Commission is the presentation of a 'general organisational plan for ambulatory medical care', featuring a network of health centres, either at the hospitals or outside, to offer preventive as well as curative treatment. The concept is very similar to the *'vårdcentral'* favoured by all involved in Swedish health care today.

Turning to the report's actual proposals, immediate implementation[6] was proposed for:

1. county council responsibility for outpatient care at the hospitals, implying as well a contractual obligation on the part of hospital doctors to perform this service;

2. requiring the county councils to draw up a blue-print plan comprising all ambulatory medical care and to hasten its implementation;
3. increasing the number of district medical officers (*provinsialläkare*), still under state auspices, and related issues;
4. establishing a fixed schedule for doctors' fees.

In the longer term[7] the report proposed:

1. charging the Board of Health to draw up five-year plans for the assessment of medical and paramedical manpower;
2. drawing up formal provisions for accepting Scandinavian physicians in the Swedish service;
3. increasing the number of students at medical faculties (and creating new educational facilities);
4. decentralising administrative power from the National Board of Health to regional boards.

These proposals largely anticipate subsequent developments within the county council administration, but the creation of a regional politico-administrative body to administer health services has yet to occur.

Developments after 1950

The Höjer report was heavily criticised from many quarters, particularly the professional unions and especially the Swedish Medical Association. Consequently, it did not lead to immediate legislation or administrative reforms. There were many reasons and motives for this criticism. The report focused quite intensely on the sensitive issues of manpower supply, remuneration and specialty rules, which clearly impinged on the core interests of the medical profession. Another contributing factor may have been that the report itself was somewhat unsystematic in its reasoning and lay-out.

Certain of its principles, opinions and straightforward proposals, however, are still basically sound and of focal interest today:

1. The principle of access to all kinds of health services as an individual right, with all services provided free of charge by public institutions and a publicly employed corps of professionals.
2. County council responsibility for comprehensive planning and delivery of all health services, including ambulatory care in and outside the hospitals as well as preventive medicine.

Other perennial issues in the areas of administration and planning
are the emphasis on decentralisation, co-ordination of health and social
services, greater attention to the needs of the elderly and extended
home care.

From Basic Security to Equal Access

The gradual change in the field of health and medical care has occurred
at the same time as the policy of social welfare and equality has been a
major political issue. The general policy in the first decades of the
century was to provide basic security. Nobody should be left
altogether without medical care for lack of means.

Health insurance provided on a private basis, commercial or
co-operative, had been introduced in the first years of the century. It
gave uneven and inadequate coverage, which led to government
regulations in 1931 as a corollary to financial grants. Universal and
comprehensive health insurance was debated at intervals all through the
Second World War, and in 1946 such a bill was voted in Parliament.
Due to financial and other reasons, its promulgation was delayed until
1955, at which time coverage was extended to include drugs and
sickness compensation, as well.

The cost of medical treatment was not the main incentive for the
insurance, although this economic burden and that of drug costs was of
significance. With the traditional background of health care provided as
a public function, the charges for these services did not need to be
altogether overwhelming after all. The important item was sickness
compensation to cover loss of income. Although doctors' fees and drug
prices dominate the discussion below, the reader should keep this
emphasis on sickness and disability compensation in mind. These items
claim by far the greatest sums of money in the Swedish national health
insurance system.

Drug prices, notoriously high, had been regulated through
government intervention as early as 1936. When health insurance was
made part of the comprehensive social security insurance system in
1963, a ceiling of 15 crowns was set on charges for drugs acquired in
one transaction by a single prescription. Ultimately, the wholesale and
retail drug business was nationalised in 1971.[8]

Price controls were imposed in the actual medical delivery system as
well. The health insurance introduced in 1955 did not fix fees for
doctor's consultations. They were, however, regulated in the sense that
the insurance provided reimbursement for 75 per cent of fees below a

fixed level. The level served as a guideline, but physicians were not obliged to keep below it.

This reimbursement fee schedule for private practitioners soon made a strong impact on the fee-for-service earnings of hospital doctors, whose incomes were legally guaranteed in agreements, which since 1965 have been negotiated in collective bargaining. The rates for these fees were by and large fixed at the levels specified in the reimbursement fee schedule. (They were, however, gradually changed, and higher rates for specialist services, for example, introduced.)

Private beds and doctors' fees-for-service in hospital care had been abolished in 1959. In 1970, fees-for-service for ambulatory care provided by hospital doctors were abolished in the 'Seven Crowns Reform'. Technically, the reform actually comprised a provision in the hospital law that forbade employees to accept any payment from patients. In response to this provision, the SMA and the County Council Federation convened to renegotiate hospital doctors' incomes, which were converted into all-inclusive salaries for full-time work (see Chapter 6, pp. 152–4). Regulation of fees in the public sector – including DMOs – was followed in 1975 by a similar control on private practitioners, though fees differed somewhat. Dentists had been incorporated into a similar system in 1974. These regulations apply to all kinds of practice and specialties. Furthermore, the insurance system covers virtually all Swedish practitioners. Thus, a general pattern has been repeated in the health care field. Just as the basic old-age pension – to guarantee minimum security – was ultimately replaced by a supplementary pensions scheme (ATP) in 1960, minimum health insurance coverage was gradually increased to secure not only standards of living, but also equal access to diagnosis and treatment in private practice as well as public institutions.

This was one of the main reasons for the introduction of the 'Seven Crowns Reform'. The income policy effect among doctors was, after all, not the prime objective, although this, too, was one of the goals and hardly an unintentional by-product.

The principle of equal access to all health and medical care is a basic issue in the proposal (1979) of the 1975 Parliamentary Commission on Health and Medical Care Legislation.[9]

Increasing County Council Responsibility
Legislation
As noted above, the Höjer report did not result in new legislation or other immediate concrete effects. Instead, a new commission, headed

(after some months) by leading Social-Democratic ideologue Richard Sterner, was appointed in 1954[10] to look into much the same issues. A special subcommittee on mental health care (later set up as a commission of its own) was formed within the commission.

The directives given the Sterner, or 'ÖHS' commission were largely taken from the Höjer report. They included:

ambulatory care;
the relative growth of hospital care, inpatient as well as outpatient, as
    compared to ambulatory care outside the hospitals (Höjer had also
    stressed the need for expansion of hospital care);
preventive medicine and large-scale check-ups.

The first ÖHS report, published in 1958,[11] touches on nearly all current health delivery problems. The actual proposals, however, are more restricted in scope. Briefly, they involve:

switching responsibility for district medical officers from the state to
    the county councils;
increasing the number of DMOs;
increasing the supply of medical and paramedical manpower through
    educational expansion;
establishing a network of government employed and salaried regional
    medical public health officers (*länsläkare*);
general but unspecified encouragement of preventive and occupational
    medicine and health education.

ÖHS I also drew fire from the SMA but survived the *remiss* round. Most of its proposals subsequently materialised in government bills[12] or otherwise. Its most important results are the transfer of the DMO organisation to the county councils in 1963 and the creation of state-employed superintendent county medical officers (*länsläkare*) in 1962.

ÖHS left many major problems aside. Consequently, the commission was reconvened and requested to return to the remaining items. The directives to the 'renewed' commission particularly stressed hospital-based outpatient care, the balance between this delivery form and inpatient care and their relation to medical care in the home.

The ÖHS II report, issued in 1963,[13] presented a broad review of a number of medical delivery problems with ambulatory medical care the prime focus. Decentralised services, the report urged, should be given priority over hospital care and other specialised services. The report also pointed to the overall need to integrate hospital-based and decentralised care. In addition, ÖHS II emphasised long-term care and other facilities for the elderly as well as preventive medicine and industrial health.

Although furnished with an impressive display of statistics and a consistent and well laid out analysis, ÖHS II did not propose any concrete change or invention. Consequently, it did not generate any immediate government bill. It did, however, result in increased intake into the medical faculties.

ÖHS also helped to crystallise some ideas expressed in the health policy debate through the years. The proposal from the 1951 Parliamentary Commission on Hospital Legislation[14] that the county councils take over responsibility for hospital-based outpatient care was strongly endorsed by the ÖHS Commission and was enacted in 1960.

In 1958, the Commission on Regionalised Health Care Organisation, chaired by Arthur Engel, Director of the National Board of Health, published its report,[15] which laid the ground for a more rational expansion of specialised medicine so as to make such services available to all parts of the country. Sweden was divided into seven regions, each with a 'regional hospital'. The regional hospital was also to serve as a centre of medical training and clinical research; two of them were endowed with the nation's two new medical faculties as partners. The entire construction was left completely unregulated by legislation, however.

Ambulance services were made a county council responsibility in 1965. The ÖHS Commission on Mental Health Care led to an agreement between the County Council Federation and the government to transfer the mental hospitals to the county councils in 1967.

Thus, legislation enacted in the postwar period hastened the transfer of responsibility for the health and medical care delivery system to the county councils. The take-over of public medical care functions was practically completed by the end of the 1960s. In some cases no services were offered until after the take-over.

This development runs parallel to a thorough restructuring of government grants, in which some 20 grants for capital and operating costs for various health care activities were consolidated into one. Since the beginning of the 1970s, this has formed part of one global allocation to the county councils from the social security insurance funds, as negotiated yearly by the County Council Federation and the government.

Diversion of Power

The defeat of the Höjer proposals is usually assumed to have been brought about by the opposition of the medical profession, but their fate may also be seen in another perspective. Höjer was an intellectual and an idealist, but he was not a pragmatic politician. He had no close ties with county council politicians, nor did the others on his commission, who were all civil servants. It may well be that his ideas were simply before their time. As spelled out earlier, the greater part of his proposals are still valid (30 years — of very rapid cultural change — later). This in itself suggests that 'wrong timing' may well account for the negative outcome.

As we have seen, the general trend from the 1930s through to the 1960s has been a consolidation of county council administrative and political power in the health field. This is the period when the so-called 'county council party' (*'landstingspartiet'*)[16] held nearly absolute power in the *Riksdag*. The two CCF chairmen during this period, Erik Fast and Fridolf Thapper, both strong personalities with solid, central positions in the Social-Democratic Party as well as in Parliament, had a direct line to the (practically consistently Social-Democratic) government. In 1954, when Tage Erlander reopened the health policy debate and appointed the ÖHS Commission, reform efforts got a launching much more in tune with political realities.

Another example of adverse and propitious political 'timing' is the handling of regionalisation, i.e. co-operation on a level above the county council. In 1958 the county councils had accepted the principle of regional planning and co-operation as set forth by the Engel Commission, but rejected binding legislation on the matter. No outright obligation for the county councils to co-operate, set down in statutory law, was proposed when the government referred the matter to Parliament. Twenty years later, in 1979, a new commission on regional co-operation has looked over regionalisation again. This time regional co-ordination is being proposed with the endorsement of solid county council representation on the commission. Such legislation is quite certain to be included in the new health legislation to be enacted in the beginning of the 1980s.

County council momentum prevailed through the 1960s. In this decade, however, the state — principally the Ministry of Health and Social Welfare — emerges as a more commanding force. Rune Johansson had been in charge of health affairs as Minister of the Interior (subsequently carved up into the Ministries of County Affairs, Labour, Housing, etc.) through the latter half of the 1950s. Thanks to Johansson's close ties with the CCF, no real conflicts between the government and the Federation could be observed.

Health care was transferred to the Ministry of Health and Social Welfare in 1963. The same year saw the conclusion of CCF—government negotiations on the economic terms for the transfer of the mental hospitals to the county councils, which was the first occurrence of really tough bargaining between two almost antagonistic adversaries. This, of course, was related to the fact that time was running out for a period of expansion and almost unlimited funding.

The 1960s, however, was also the period when Sven Aspling took office as Minister of Social Affairs (1962). He held that office until 1976, an unusually long period, during which time he was able to establish close and effective collaboration with some key associates. Apart from a short stint with Ernst Michanek (1962–1963/4), he had only two under-secretaries during his 15 years in office – Lars-Åke Åström and Göte Fridh. Their tenure, too, was very long. What is more, Åström resigned, having 'schooled' Fridh in his thinking over a number of years, to become Director of the National Social Insurance Board – a key instrument in the shaping of health policy. The Ministry's chief legal officer, who also sat for a relatively long time, was subsequently appointed Director of the Board of Occupational Safety and Health. Clearly, this group of people had a palpable impact on the formation of health policy in Sweden from 1963 on. Actually, many of the changes brought about required both persuasion and coercion to obtain county council acceptance.

There was collaboration, to be sure. The county councils were represented on the Delegation on Health Care (*Sjukvårdsdelegationen*), set up as an advisory body to the ministry in 1965, as were a number of other ministries, agencies and organisations. Although formally only an advisory body, the delegation has undoubtedly been a power nexus. Deliberations there, however, have come increasingly to replace the traditional balanced co-operation between government and the CCF.

Aspling and his deputies set to work on the 'Seven Crowns Reform' on their own initiative. The CCF was kept informed, but Fridh and Åström were the ones who conceived the structure of the reform. When everything seemed ready, in January 1969, the whole plan had to be kept secret until a conference of all county council chairmen and their administrative directors could be convened. Grave doubts had been registered as to the advisability of the reform, concerning among other things the effect that abolition of fees-for-service might have on production in terms of the number of consultations and doctor–patient continuity (both current topics today). After some debate, a majority of the conference gave its approval. Some CCF people remained dubious, however, as shown in later off-the-record comments.

Even greater dissidence was manifest when private dentistry was brought under a virtually compulsory insurance system. Bitter suspicions prevailed among most dentists in the face of their 'socialisation', but quite a number of CCF representatives also had serious doubts as to the effects insurance financing of private dentistry might have. Was there not a risk that county council-employed dentists would turn private? This is indeed what happened, and it provoked additional regulations, which virtually inhibit the establishment of new practices by means of special rules for dentists' affiliation to the insurance organisation.

Another case of central government power prevailing over the county councils was the 1969 bill (Proposition 1969:35) on postgraduate medical education. It clearly stated that government (and, though not stated, the central agencies, Board of Health and Welfare and National Social Insurance Board) intended to use regulation in this field as an instrument in directing health policy. It implied an elaboration of the legal right of the Board of Health to franchise new doctors' posts, and connecting the planning and franchising of junior doctors' posts in postgraduate training to the individual county councils' plans, thus gauging the number of trainees in each specialty by the total number of qualified specialists in each specialty. Specialists' posts, too, were distributed through a similar procedure. Although not altogether successful, the system as such is a sophisticated invention, well deserving both the praise given it by planners — not least foreign experts envious of its formidable total control — and the resentment of the medical profession, who primarily sense the potential for curtailing professionals' freedom to choose their place of work.

The decade 1965—75 witnessed the formation of a well-conceived government policy. This involved legislation regarding the medical delivery system and control of government grants and health insurance financing. One more aspect should be mentioned: all capital investments for building were now to be centrally authorised. The ability of the state to give 'stop' or 'go' signals to the construction of hospitals and other medical care facilities has proven very practical with a strong and direct impact.

At present, however, it seems as though the situation has stabilised somewhat. The 1975 Commission on Health and Medical Care Legislation proposes new health legislation entrusting county councils with 'total responsibility' for planning the delivery of all services. 'Total responsibility' will give them more discretion over their own affairs. A case in point is a revised system for medical manpower distribution, which is to be left entirely to the county councils — in co-operation with the National Board of Health and Welfare and other central organs, but altogether unregulated legally. (Medical care legislation currently requires franchising by the Board in accordance with a distribution plan authorised yearly by the Health Planning Committee of the Ministry.) The intention is to get the county councils to assume responsibility and not simply rely on central administrative authorities. The new policy was all but unanimously supported by the 1979 CCF congress, an unprecedented demonstration of political determination that may possibly mark a new phase of mutual solidarity among the county councils.

On the other hand, a greater share of funds disbursed through government channels (due to strained local and national finances) will enable the central government to attach 'strings' to the funds, to initiate new directions, and to maintain national balance, etc.

Attitude of the Medical Profession

When the Höjer report was published, it contained dissenting opinions from two of Höjer's three collaborators on the commission, namely the two physicians on that body. The difference in opinion was hardly coincidental. The medical profession was vehement in its opposition to the Höjer proposals, so much so that this is generally assumed to be the reason for their failure to materialise in legislation.

Twentieth-century health insurance history up to 1955 offers many examples of a 'dragging of the feet', forestalling counter-proposals, 'smearing' and opposition verging on defiance on the part of the profession. The profession had been forced to accept the 1931 insurance legislation against its will, but at a time when many doctors were jobless and depression reigned. Be that as it may, medical corps opposition had helped to keep comprehensive insurance proposals from being effected ever since 1920.

The ÖHS I report of 1954 was signed by seven doctors, five of whom filed (the only) dissenting opinions. The remaining two were Arthur Engel, Director of the Board of Health, and Gunnar Inghe, prominent Social-Democrat and notable proponent of social medicine. Inghe and two of the dissenting doctors remained on the ÖHS II commission, but none of them dissented from the majority this time (1963). As related earlier, ÖHS I was much criticised, but produced changes in the delivery system and in legislation, primarily the transfer of the DMO organisation to the county councils (which was precisely what the dissenters opposed). ÖHS II, on the other hand, did not present any specific proposals, which probably explains the lack of medical profession opposition. Still, this acquiescence is somewhat surprising, considering that the need for an increased number of physicians is very explicitly expressed in the report (as it had been in the Höjer report).

In the beginning of the 1960s, however, and over subsequent years, the profession – above all its spokesmen after Dag Knutson – has very gradually come round to the government viewpoint. Since the beginning of the 1960s the SMA leadership has grown increasingly pragmatic and has been seeking to open a dialogue with the government and other central bodies.

The launching of the SCR in 1970 was preceded by unofficial contacts with the SMA leadership, entailing their informal approval. The 1975 extension of insurance coverage to private practice took quite some bargaining as to figures and estimates of assumed and demanded incomes; the basic principle, however, was undisputed. Indeed, affiliation to the insurance plan was much desired, towards the end of the bargaining process at least.

Since the beginning of the 1970s medical manpower distribution has been based on comprehensive plans (cf. p. 109) drawn up by a joint working party, including the SMA, the Board of Health and Welfare and the CCF. In 1975 the SMA – together with two other unions (nurses and auxiliary staff) – got a seat on the Delegation on Health Care of the Ministry of Health and Welfare (cf. p. 108). Seen in retrospect, the relationship seems to have grown all the more fraternal over the years.

We may, however, be witnessing a relapse into a more antagonistic attitude instead of the more pragmatic co-operation of the 1960s and 1970s. The SMA has recently expressed second thoughts about its co-operation with respect to manpower distribution since the 1979 CCF Congress demanded (with the tacit consent of the Ministry and Board) harsher measures to force doctors out to more peripheral posts. In early 1979, in response to deliberations on the part of the 1975 Commission on Health and Medical Care Legislation, the SMA, together with the national associations of dentists and physiotherapists launched a nationwide campaign for the 'protection of free enterprise'.

The commission has proposed that county councils assume 'total responsibility' for all health and medical care delivery, including private practice, within its area. This does not imply a 'nationalisation' of private practice; no changes in trusteeship are proposed. The county councils, however, are to be charged with the total planning of all delivery, which presupposes agreements with all health and medical care entrepreneurs.

This blueprint – not yet published by the commission – provoked the fighting opposition of the professions, who in February 1979 launched a vehement, nationally co-ordinated campaign protesting at the 'socialisation of free private practice'. Their protests were given publicity, but largely of a negative sort which may prove counter-productive to their aims. County council and Board of Health spokesmen have criticised the professional organisations for stirring up a debate about a proposal that had not yet appeared and for incorrectly alleging that it would 'socialise' private practice. (The organisations have been represented on the commission and were thus fully informed of its deliberations.)

The three professions have countered that the commission also discussed means of reallocating insurance fund contributions to private practitioners via the county council as part of its 'total planning' responsibility and that such a measure would in effect put practitioners at the mercy of county council politicians. The professions undoubtedly have an argument there. The commission, however, was not instructed to draft any insurance fund legislation whatsoever. Eventual changes on that front, if any, are rather an open question.

In sum, the protest campaign of 1979 is unlikely to have much effect on the political feasibility of increasing county council power over insurance moneys. In view of the persistent strain on state and county finances, the burden of health and medical care costs will doubtless be reapportioned successively in comprehensive agreements. These will deal with the whole economic balance in the country, including the distribution of national and county taxes. Medical entrepreneurship plays a small role in a drama that deals with the economy as a whole.

Private practice may well be able to avoid an outright 'socialisation'. The professions' campaign, however, has raised a question heretofore all but unknown in Sweden. Is it reasonable that private practitioners, whose expenses are nearly completely covered by national health insurance funds, should not be required to give anything in return?

It is, in itself, rather remarkable that this has not been an issue in Swedish health politics until the 1970s. (The private insurance organisations that operated in the first decades of the century did deal with it, though.) Swedish doctors can open their practices wherever they like and have an unconditional right to enlist with the local branch of the insurance organisation. Only if they ask for an elevated fee schedule — as was granted to existing group practices when the SCR was introduced — need they comply with county council rulings as to location and Board of Health approval (a regulation very limited in scope in that it applies to no more than 60 doctors throughout the country). As noted earlier, such conditions were made compulsory for dentists practically from the start. (Cf. p. 109. This provision is temporary and is scheduled to expire in 1984, when there will supposedly no longer be a shortage of dentists.)

If it proves easy to stave off 'socialism' in the sense that private practitioners will continue to be allowed, it will no doubt prove more difficult to stay as completely free of regulation as has been the case to date. Health is gradually becoming a volatile and exploitable political issue. The Liberal Party scored points when in 1976 it introduced the 'family doctor' (*husläkare*) concept. (The idea, subsequently killed in the 1979 session of the *Riksdag*, has been resurrected, slightly remodelled, in a 1980 proposal of a Conservative minister of health.) Private practitioners, too, are envisioned, albeit with some reluctance on the part of planners, to co-operate in the family medicine scheme. In this context they are to co-operate with a county council health centre, the cornerstone of the system. 'Family doctor' systems in Denmark and the United Kingdom are pointed to as models for the proposed scheme. British and Danish general practitioners work under a complete and comprehensive planning and franchising system; they are also on call nightly, which Swedish private practitioners virtually never are. Much of Swedish doctors' freedom seems doomed as general practice gradually takes over as the delivery form.

Although this debate is yet to come, it seems unavoidable and will no doubt be a focal point of Swedish health politics in the 1980s. Should a surplus of doctors develop, as many believe will happen, such an eventuality will most certainly influence the outcome.

Decentralised Medical Care and Occupational Health as Issues

One of Höjer's main points was *decentralised ambulatory care* administered as a public service. ÖHS brought about county council adoption of the district medical officers from the state. ÖHS I and II both turned attention to the disproportionately large share of resources claimed by hospitals and warned of their growth. This critical view has prevailed ever since. The need for realignment of priorities, with decentralised care on top, has been stressed in almost complete unanimity. The emphasis on primary care has been endorsed and promoted at a number of CCF congresses, and the 'Seven Crowns Reform' was very much an attempt to direct the demand from hospital to decentralised care. The issue permeates the planning documents of the National Board of Health and Welfare as well as those of the individual county councils and SPRI (the Swedish Planning and

Rationalisation Institute of the Health and Social Services), the quasi-governmental planning agency of the ministry and the CCF. It recurs as a prime issue in the government's annual budget estimates for the Ministry of Social Affairs.

Still, all statistical and other evidence shows that the hospital sector, and not least its outpatient departments, continues to grow and claim ever greater shares of resources. Well may one wonder: How can this be?

Diversion of power on the way from central to local government seems to be accountable only in part. More attention should perhaps be directed to the level(s) between local (county council) government itself and the various service units, hospitals and others.

It seems as though the already well-equipped hospital attracts even more resources, that when competing with other service units it gets higher priority. A number of reasons for this have been offered in the current debate. One such reason, of a perhaps more specifically Swedish character, could very well be the fact that the Swedish 'county hospital' — of which there is one in each county — is located where the administrative and political powers also converge, in the provincial 'capital', (normally) the largest city in the county, the seat of the provincial governor, the bishop of the diocese, etc. Although local politicians have their origins in all parts of the area, this is where they meet and make their careers.

The failure of official health policy to promote primary care has drawn attention from various quarters. The matter was brought before the 1978 CCF Congress in a motion by Ruth Kärnek, leading Social-Democratic health politician, that has yet to produce any result. It is also the object of investigation by a group within the National Accounting and Audit Bureau.

To support the periphery within each county new and different measures are required. In line with the decentralisation-oriented policy of the 1970s proposed legislation will make it possible for the county councils to introduce politically elective boards (on a level below the county council medical services board) for separate parts of the delivery system. In the debate leading up to this proposal much hope has been vested in special 'primary care boards', which are foreseen to be able to fight more successfully for their own sphere of activity. Such a development could possibly have effects on the distribution of power between county council and the municipalities.

The *occupational or industrial health* sector was broached in a joint venture by labour and management (the Swedish Trade Union

Confederation and the Swedish Employers' Confederation) in 1942.
When the sector was regulated in 1949, the legislation did not change
this basic approach, but instead pivoted the system on local agreements
between labour and management at the various industrial sites. When
the 1978 Work Environment Act consolidated the occupational health
organisation with the workers' protection and safety organisation, it
was with the unanimous consent of the labour market organisations.

The unanimity was not total, however. The CCF had spent time and
effort preparing to assume responsibility for industrial health units to
serve conglomerates of small enterprises located together. The service
was preferably to be combined with ordinary health centres. The National
Board of Health and Welfare also advocated a policy aimed in the same
direction; all individual health and medical care should be delivered
mainly in the individual's immediate environment. Primary care should
comprise industrial health as well as family medical care. The principle
of comprehensive primary care is a cornerstone in the whole of
Swedish health care philosophy.

The open conflict was tentatively resolved in 1975, when the CCF
Congress backed off from a direct confrontation, supporting a
declaration by CCF board member and prominent Social-Democrat
Sven Wilander to the effect that the CCF should not press for county
council management against trade union opposition. The issue remains
unresolved, although armistice prevails. The Board of Health has made
no declaration of non-intention to date.

One motive for not turning this sector over to the county councils
has been the desire to guarantee that resources will be allocated to
preventive health measures, and not to curative medicine in the
hospitals — which has been a tendency in county council
administration. Another reason, ironically, is that 'occupational health
services' are something one does not willingly give up. Having ready
access (usually free of charge) to a doctor on the premises has clearly
been a valued fringe benefit.

Occupational health is growing and is becoming a major issue, as
well. If the worst comes to the worst — seen from an opponent's
point of view — an occupational health organisation embodying a
complete delivery system may emerge. This would deal a serious blow
to the principle of 'equal rights for all'. Segments of the population —
singled out on the grounds of profession, collective bargaining power,
etc. — would have access to far superior health and medical services. In
a country like Sweden, where 'welfare' is by tradition the right of
everyone, the arguments against such a scheme are self-evident, but

limited economic resources in the public sector, coupled with the so-called 'granny boom', could render this problem a real dilemma. Whether such an occupational health scheme will become a reality is really an open question. The strength of the labour market organisations makes it more than a theoretical possibility. On the other hand, Swedish egalitarian traditions should militate against it.

Notes

1. 1938 års hälso- och sjukvårdssakkunniga.
2. The mission was given to the Board of Health, which appointed the Director and three other civil servants to the commission.
3. A. Höjer, *Den öppna läkarvården i riket* (SOU, Stockholm, 1948), p. 14.
4. Ibid., p. 14.
5. Ibid., p. 241.
6. Ibid., pp. 293 ff.
7. Ibid., pp. 307 ff.
8. The basis for this move was SOU 1969:46, *Läkemedelsförsörjning i samverkan*, which had been preceded by two unsuccessful commission reports (in 1951 and 1959).
9. *Hälso- och sjukvårdsutredningen* (SOU, Stockholm, 1979:78).
10. Kommittén för översyn av hälso – och sjukvården i riket.
11. *Hälsovård och öppen sjukvård i landstingsområdena* (SOU, Stockholm, 1958), p. 15.
12. Prop. 1961/181, 1962/22.
13. *Sjukhus och öppen vård* (SOU, Stockholm, 1963), p. 21.
14. Report with proposals for new hospital legislation drafted by an expert committee, popularly referred to as the 'hospital legislation committee' (SOU, Stockholm, 1956), p. 27.
15. *Regionsjukvården* (SOU, Stockholm, 1958), p. 26.
16. This widely used term (cf. R. Ejvegård, *Landstingsförbundet. Organisation, beslutsfattande, förhållande till staten* (Landstingsförbundet, Stockholm, 1973), pp. 335 ff., (i.a.) refers to the circumstance that many Members of Parliament also sat on the county councils of their home districts. When matters pertaining to county councils were treated in Parliament, these MPs often formed an informal alliance that wielded formidable power in the pre-1970 bicameral Parliament.

Part Three:

HEALTH POLICY REFORMS AND THE MEDICAL PROFESSION

5 CONFLICT AND COMPROMISES BETWEEN PROFESSIONAL AND BUREAUCRATIC HEALTH INTERESTS 1947–72

Arnold J. Heidenheimer

Introduction

The reasons why Swedish health system development during the third quarter of the twentieth century has drawn such a disproportionate amount of world attention can best be understood in relation to two longer-term trends. One of these trends expresses a growth rate. During this period the Swedes accelerated their spending on health and on the training of doctors, so as to approach in the health sector the position of the 'most rapidly growing Western system', which they had previously achieved for their economy as a whole in the century since 1860.[1] The second trend reflects a pattern of decline. It becomes evident if one contrasts recent 'deprofessionalisation' patterns with the privileges which academically-trained professionals have enjoyed in Western societies since their modern incubation in the Italian city-states of the thirteenth century.[2] For it has been during the past quarter century that many aspects of professional autonomy have become more circumscribed in Sweden than elsewhere in the West. It is the relationship between these two trends which constitutes the framework for my attempt to interpret Swedish health policy developments in the period from 1947 to 1972.

The values which were articulated during the recent Swedish struggles suggest analogies to the cosmologies of the great religiously-inspired poets of earlier ages, such as Dante and Milton. From the perspective of the traditional ideologists of professionalism, the transformation is often portrayed as a 'descent' from a lost paradise of professional autonomy to the nether depths of bureaucratic enchainment.[3] Conservative medical journals abroad came routinely to report real and fabricated humiliations visited upon their Swedish colleagues at various junctures.[4] From the opposing ideological position, that of the rationalising planners, the Swedish development has been portrayed, conversely, as an 'ascent' towards an integrated system, which has compelled physicians to purge themselves of base and impish desires to manipulate treatment and payment methods towards egotistical ends.

119

For the analyst who, lacking the poet's license, must use the modest credential of the social scientist, it seems useful to redesign the Dantean model. Let us, instead, conceive of the Swedish health 'system' as being composed of three discs intersecting on a common hinge, each of which supports a distinct set of structures. Let us label these:

1. the political-administrative disc;
2. the professional education and status disc;
3. the health care delivery disc.

We will further assume that certain actors, the 'pluralists', seek to maintain the angles of incidence which separate the three discs from each other. Other actors, whom we can label 'corporatists', have the contrary aim of manipulating the central systemic hinges so as to reduce the angles of divergence as much as possible, and even to collapse the three discs onto a single plane.

Institutions and populations are distributed on the three discs, some being located more towards the centre and some more towards the periphery, and some at the middle-rings. All participants are concerned with the distribution of resources – financial, scientific and political – within each of the planes, but some are more concerned than others with linkages between the three discs. Research scientists in the medical schools seek to divert resources to central institutions of the education and status disc, and are less concerned with what goes on elsewhere. Medical school clinicians defend turfs on both the education and the health delivery discs. Finally, actors like the National Board of Health and the medical associations pursue goals on all three discs. They are also directly concerned with the divergences between the discs, and how they affect the 'degrees of freedom' enjoyed by the actors on them.

On the political-administrative disc are located the central authorities, like the Ministry and the Board of Health, the county authorities which raise and allocate resources to be channelled to the health care delivery disc, and the hospital directors and head district doctors, who are charged with seeing that resources are devoted to the meeting of certain goals.

On the professional education and status disc, university medical schools dominate the centre, and extend their influence outward through medical specialist societies. Some of the professionals at the periphery, like general practice physicians, are not represented at the centre. Status positions are highly correlated with length of training, and specialty accreditation, which reinforces the strong centripetal dynamics on this plane.

On the health care delivery disc, facilities and personnel are distributed spatially, with large regional hospitals at the centre, county hospitals at the middle rings, and health centres and district medical officers at the periphery. Private practitioners are ambiguously placed, being concentrated mainly in the cities but insulated from hospitals. Centripetal pulls here are generated mainly by specialised technology and high professional status, while centrifugal forces are based on popular demands for readily accessible health care.

Convergence Options in the 1940s

As against the view that the seven-fold increase in doctor production and the 20-fold increase in expenditures in the 25-year period between 1947 and 1972 were the product of a purely economic imperative, I would advance the interpretation that priorities were powerfully affected by political options which were set in the late 1940s. As in other countries which could afford to do so in those postwar years, Sweden debated plans for a large-scale reform of its health system, which engendered strong conflicts between a left party-bureaucratic coalition on the one side, and the medical profession and its allies on the other.

In this context it is important to recognise that Swedish physicians were distinguished from their equivalents in other West European systems in three important ways:

1. There were far *fewer of them*; only about half as many per capita as in the U.S., and only about one third as many as in central European countries like Germany and Austria.
2. They retained ideological positions which induced the *projection of prewar confrontations* into the postwar setting.
3. By defeating the reform proposals of Axel Höjer, they won the first round of the postwar struggle, unlike their British colleagues who had to accept a National Health Service.

The issue of the low number of physicians was raised soon after the Social Democrats first came to power. In March 1933, Karl Evang, then head of the Norwegian Socialist doctors' association, told a Karolinska Institute audience that it was especially absurd for the Swedes to talk about the dangers of 'overproducing' doctors. Two years later a governmental commission attributed medical school admission barriers to 'more or less conscious professional protection, or monopolistic striving on the part of medical societies and medical faculties'.[5] In 1945 another report pointed out that Sweden was turning out only 150 new doctors per year, far fewer proportionately than Denmark and Norway. Then, in 1946 Höjer's Health Board (*Medicinalstyrelsen*) recommended a sharp increase in medical school admissions, from 185 to 400 per year, so as to meet an anticipated need for 7,200 doctors by 1960.

In the depression decade of the 1930s, physicians and other professionals in many European countries had raised the spectre of an 'academic proletariat' to reinforce their protectionist demands. But there were several reasons why these later proved more of an albatross for the Swedish medical profession. Not only was it numerically more exclusive, but it was also rather disproportionately susceptible to some anti-democratic elitist ideologies. Such tendencies were manifested somewhat openly in the debates of the 1930s, but even after the war Höjer felt entitled to label the SMA executive director a 'pro-Nazi'.[6] The very consistency of the Swedish Medical Association (SMA) opposition to the immigration of non-Swedish doctors invited the linkage between prewar and postwar attitudes, for the slogans used in the late 1940s to combat the import of doctors were markedly similar to those used a decade previously. Since many Swedes entertained some guilt feelings about how their neutrality goals had minimised their assistance to war victims, the SMA's obdurate position shamed even many of its former adherents. Two decades later, an American medical student recorded that 'these are the years which Swedish doctors today avoid discussing with foreigners or even with one another'.[7]

Höjer's relations with Dag Knutson, who was to emerge as his main SMA adversary, dated from 1937, when the two men met in a pullman coach as Höjer was on his way to Stockholm to assume control of the Health Board:

In the corridor we became engaged in a lively discussion which lasted long into the night. At his request I elaborated on my views. . . . We needed more doctors and nurses. Doctors should be given a privileged position among white-collar workers in society, but should be placed in salaried employment rather than having to take payment for individual services. Knutson listened appalled. . . . Later, he and his colleagues on the SMA board laid down the line: 'We must refuse to cooperate with the *Medicinalchefen*. He is dangerous and must be removed from his post as soon as possible'.[8]

Nine years later, in 1946, Höjer called on the doctors to admit their error in opposing medical expansion. Acknowledging that 'the Swedish medical corps had shown its tenacity and unity in defence of old positions', he called on it to recognise that 'the time has arrived for the physicians to participate more actively in the attempt to make the Swedish health care organization more modern'.[9] Instead the Medical Association elevated Knutson to the chairmanship.

Axel Höjer's 1948 health delivery reform proposals represented a novel and unusual strategy in an attempt to by-pass the vested interests at the centres of the professional education and status discs. Höjer had not been a member of the medical school establishment, and he was appointed in 1937 only after five clinicians previously offered the job had declined.[10] His plan to initiate reform at the level of primary health care was based on a proposal to expand the number and scope of district doctors, and to focus delivery on health centres as well as hospital outpatient departments. This constituted a direct challenge to the profession's desire to hold on to the fee-for-service principle.[11] But it also affronted organised medical and administrative groups who occupied the central professional and health care echelons. Even in Britain, where the contemporaneous National Health Service reform was more successful, the proposal to develop municipal health centres for primary care was the one component of the NHS programme to prove stillborn in 1948.[12]

The breadth and intensity of the opposition to the Höjer reform were aroused by the proposed remuneration changes. But varied professional and bureaucratic interests also felt threatened by his attempt to surmount the demarcation lines between preventive, ambulatory and acute care. These considerations triggered opposition from Höjer's three fellow commissioners, as well as from the numerous bodies who submitted negative *remiss* responses. Not only did all three Swedish medical faculties join the opposition alliance which was organised by the SMA, but numerous representatives of the county council and administrative authorities also joined the coalition.

Had some version of the Höjer reform been enacted, in conjunction with a health insurance programme, the immediate effect would surely have been to stimulate medical sector expenditures and expansion in the number of medical students. It is possible, however, that the rate of both physician and total expenditure growth over the next several decades might have been lower than it came to be.

This conjecture is related to the probability that the adoption of the Höjer proposals, at a time when options were still open, would have drawn subsequent Swedish developments closer to those in Denmark and Norway, whose health expenditures as a percentage of GNP grew to 6.6 per cent and 7.3 per cent by 1973, compared to Sweden's 8.3 per cent.[13] Höjer's professional experience and background, primarily as a district doctor serving poorer patients in Stockholm and Malmö, had affected his attempt to give priority to improvements at what academic and other professional leaders regarded as the periphery of the health delivery disc. Had his plan been adopted at the time, it might well have led to greater emphasis on health centres rather than outpatient clinics of large hospitals, and to more support of primary care physicians rather than clinical specialists.

If such an option for the development of the Swedish health system had been pursued, it could have produced another strategy for reducing the 'angles of divergence' between the discs in our tri-disc model. A multi-stage reform effort which commenced at the delivery sites away from the centre could have mitigated some tendencies; such as the increase in the number of recognised medical specialties, and the resulting multiplication of hospital wards, and thus engendered a different set of convergence dynamics. Those dynamics might have been more analogous to those actually applied in the Swedish education system, where reform initiated with the lower-level schools, and then extended in successive steps to the 'higher' level secondary and university institutions. If health centres and primary care personnel had been given sequential priority in Swedish reforms, this might have engendered 'weights' at the peripheries which would have induced greater convergence between, for instance, the service-delivery and the professional education status discs.

But as this option was foreclosed, the central political decision-makers on the political disc were impelled to pursue another strategy, which placed emphasis on 'lubricating' the system's hinge mechanisms through an accentuated flow of both financial and personnel resources. For the Social Democrats, the ideological rationale for pursuing this strategy had been moulded by the preceding series of confrontations.

The Role of the Younger Doctors

The decade which followed the demise of the Höjer reform was relatively void of conflict. Dr Arthur Engel, an internist and chief medical officer of a county central hospital, took over the Health Board directorship in 1952 as a consensus candidate. He had the explicit endorsement of the leaders who had led the attack on Höjer, but also

the support of Höjer himself. He seemed to please Prime Minister
Erlander by telling him that he envisaged his role as that of an
'unpolitical adviser'.[14] In this phase of depoliticisation, a Liberal like
Engel could work in harmony with the conservative SMA chairman
Dag Knutson, the Agrarian Party Minister of the Interior Gunnar
Hedlund, and the Social-Democratic chairmen of the County Council
Federation (CCF), Erik Fast and Fridolf Thapper.

It was during the 1950s that the groundwork was laid for the great
expansion of hospital capacity, which was rationalised and legitimated
through the regionalisation programme during the latter phases of
Engel's tenure at the Board. The hospital boom has been attributed in
large part to 'the great influence of the medical profession, primarily
that part based in the academic institutions and teaching hospitals . . .
in determining priorities within the health sector'.[15] The ambitions of
the academics were readily endorsed by the county politicians, and
legitimated by planners at the Board who developed new definitions of
health 'needs' to support the expansion plans. The hospitals also
became a favoured instrument of the more Social-Democratic-oriented
ÖHS Commission, which advanced plans to transfer additional
primary care responsibilities away from the district doctors and
towards the outpatient hospital clinics. The total number of
ambulatory consultations grew by some 150 per cent while Engel was
director, and the proportion of those given at hospitals increased to
half. This created many new positions for doctors who were completing
their medical training during the 1950s, when medical school
admissions were gradually raised to the target of 400 per year which
Höjer had recommended in 1946.

The new generation which now took over the Association of
Junior Hospital Physicians (SYLF), thus pursued interests which were
quite different from the leadership which had developed the organisation
in the 1930s. Then J. P. Edwardsson had mobilised the young doctors
in good part against the tendency of the chief doctors to monopolise the
extra income provided by outpatient care, as well as against the
competition from immigrant doctors. That cohort then made
Edwardsson secretary, and Dag Knutson chairman of the parent Medical
Association. For more than a decade, Knutson built on strong personal
control of the SMA staff, and especially the support of private
practitioners and senior hospital doctors, to lead the Association with
a strong hand. Relying on a private fortune, he was able to devote great
energy and time to the task, and no one ever challenged his repeated
re-election.

The expansion of hospital positions made the younger physicians less dependent on their seniors' goodwill in career preferment. By the same token they had a high stake in establishing better negotiating conditions with the county and national health authorities. With the passage of the 1959 Hospital Law, the SYLF leaders displeased Knutson by entering into negotiations with the government to ensure improved remuneration for the junior doctors. In the subsequent struggles, the groups backing Knutson, such as the chief doctors and the private practitioners, were challenged by the young hospital doctors. Up to that time the relative success of the SMA in exercising its monopoly lay in its ability to conduct salary negotiations with the counties one at a time, playing the counties off against each other. SYLF's pressure to enter into more consistent negotiations with the political centre threatened to erode that strategy, especially after the counties strengthened the County Federation as a bargaining instrument.

In the late 1950s, however, the new leadership group which had emerged within SYLF began to assert greater independence. They were also able to mobilise their members both within the SMA's general assembly, and gradually within the Executive Committee. Throughout

Table 5.1: Swedish Medical Association Executive Committee Representation of Constituent Groups, 1950–60

Year	Chief Doctors' and Senior Hospital Doctors Associations	District and Municipal Doctors Associations	Association of Doctors in Private Practice	Junior Doctors' Association (SYLF)
1950	7	3	2	1
1951	7	3	2	1
1952	7	3	2	1
1953	6	3	3	1
1954	6	3	3	1
1955	6	3	2	2
1956	6	3	2	2
1957	5	3	2	3
1958	6	2	3	2
1959	5	2	3	3
1960	4	2	3	4
1969	8	1	2	3
1975	5	1	1	6

Source: SMA Documentation.

the decade their executive committee representation gradually increased, largely at the expense of the more senior hospital doctors associations, from one out of thirteen in 1950 to four in 1960 (see Table 5.1).

Towards the end of the 1950s, the younger leaders began to feel that the continued poor relations between Knutson and the Social-Democratic government constituted a grave handicap. SYLF leaders like Bo Hjern, Åke Lindgren, and Nils Terner were able to win allies among the other physician groups for their view that the removal of Knutson was a prerequisite for the normalisation of consultative relationships with the ministries and other national agencies. Under this pressure, Knutson resigned office and initiated a new career as a successful sheep-farmer in Värmland.[16]

The Erosion of Professional Self-government

A new era of more aggressive national health policy initiative commenced in 1959, and continued into the 1960s to bring about radical jurisdictional shifts for many power centres in the health system. These changes were attributable most directly to the return of an all-Social-Democratic cabinet, with the replacement of Gunnar Hedlund by Rune Johansson in the Interior Ministry. Johansson's assignment was important for health policy because this very powerful county politician was in an unusually good position to align the interests of the Cabinet and the CCF, on whose executive he continued to sit while minister.[17] With Carl Persson as State Secretary, the Interior Ministry began to crank up the legislative machinery to handle many of the proposals which had been produced by the ÖHS Commission (under Richard Sterner's chairmanship), but which had not been actively promoted as long as Hedlund was minister. In a reversal of Höjer's strategy, this commission seemed to concentrate reform initiatives at more central processes on the professional and health delivery planes. Its most important initiative helped stage the 1959 Hospital Law,[18] but it was also active in the discussion of the specialist licensing law, which was placed on the legislative agenda in 1960.

Through its Proposition 141, the Interior Ministry proposed to replace 1915 legislation regulating medical licensing, by making licensing the exclusive basis for the right to practice, and by initiating the legal basis for license revocation. Its politically most sensitive component made the physician's ability to label himself as a specialist conditional on the fulfilment of qualifications determined by a governmental agency, such as the Health Board.[19] This innovation infringed on the prerogatives of the SMA, which, in the absence of any mention of specialties in the 1915 law, had institutionalised the granting of specialty accreditation. Its committee on graduate medical education had been issuing specialist credentials under rules adopted by the Association. The most recent version, dating from December 1951, listed 25 different specialties, and required candidates to offer proof of five years of specialised training following the first medical degree. Most of this was practical hospital training, since the medical faculties did not offer a developed programme of graduate training.

Among those who had initially opposed the statutory regulation of specialist competence was Director Engel. It appears that Engel discounted the ministry's ability quickly to present a completed draft law, and to an SMA observer it seemed as though 'the Ministry especially enjoyed putting Engel's horoscope to shame by getting a draft law ready to spite his pessimism'.[20] Perhaps encouraged by these apparent divisions, the SMA in April 1960 expressed 'vehement criticism' of the draft proposition, and a meeting with ministry officials in which Dag Knutson led the SMA side had to be 'adjourned without the group being able to reach agreement on a single major point'.[21] The ministry basically held that the SMA's regulations were legally inadequate because they were applicable only to SMA members, and because in possible future court cases 'the courts could not be expected to base their decisions on norms established by a private organ like the SMA'.[22] The SMA argued that there was no basis for direct state regulation since there were no formal educational courses or institutions at the graduate level. It asked that the Health Board confine itself to registering the credentials which the SMA committee awarded.

In the subsequent development, the ministry insisted on going beyond the recommendations of a study commission which largely had praised the adequacy of the SMA scheme, and opposed the transfer of specialty recognition to a state organ.[23] One of the loopholes which it was able to exploit was the SMA's practice of allowing chief doctors 'to be granted the right to advertise themselves as specialists, even though they may not completely fulfil the requirements for competence in the specialty in question'.[24] About one-third of the deputy chief doctors — mainly surgeons, radiologists and psychiatrists — did not hold specialty credentials. Since the 1955 health insurance law provided for different remuneration rates for specialists, there was a question as to which doctors were eligible for payment at which rates.

Credentialing authority might have been placed under the office of

the University Chancellor, then still elected by the professoriate. One
proposal called for the creation of a 'Council on Medical Specialties',
financed by the SMA, and composed of representatives of the SMA, the
Board of Health and the Chancellor of the Universities. But the SMA's
bid to keep this council under its sponsorship was rejected by
Johansson in the subsequent parliamentary discussion.

> Specialist issues must be handled by an organ which is an authority
> in the proper sense of the word, and the proposition provides that
> these matters might be entrusted to the Board of Health, if the
> Crown so decides. This is the same organ that licenses doctors . . . it
> seems natural, then, that the Board also have jurisdiction in questions
> of specialist competence, which after all is an extension of the basic
> competence to practice medicine . . . I am not at all opposed to the
> thought of instituting a committee for specialist questions within
> the National Board of Health, composed on roughly the same
> principles as the SMA Specialist Council . . . There is nevertheless
> one point on which there is no room for discussion . . . the demands
> for public insight and government control are non-negotiable.[25]

For the opposition, the case for allowing the SMA to retain overall
control of specialty licensing was put by the Liberal, Gunnar Edström.

> Society has confidently placed the matter of regulation in the hands
> of the respective professional organization, sometimes under the
> supervision of the authorities, sometimes not . . . To transfer the
> entire procedure from the province of the Medical Association to an
> organ of state seems poorly motivated . . . Allowing the professional
> organization to continue as the regulatory agent will allow it to
> better follow the intensive pace of development . . . In the face of
> rapid development the state bureaucracy will, by virtue of its very
> structure, always be one step behind medical associations
> themselves.[26]

Parliament endorsed the government's bill.

Compared to those of 1948, the comments made by the organisations
showed a diminution of the strength of the coalition which had
defeated the Höjer proposal twelve years earlier. Favouring the
transfer to the Health Board were most of the official agencies, apart
from *Medicinalstyrelsen* itself. These included the Board of Social
Welfare, a number of county boards, both the CCF and the Municipal

Federation, as well as the majority of the ÖHS commission. The medical faculties were divided, with the Karolinska and Lund faculties tending to support continued SMA control, while the Gothenburg faculty supported lodging powers with a public authority.[27]

The new arrangements for specialist accreditation institutionalised patterns through which decisions were made jointly by professionals and bureaucrats, and laid the groundwork for subsequent efforts to plan the allocation of medical manpower. The joint committee of Board officials and SMA representatives made no sharp changes in accreditation practices, but the Board's Office for Further Medical Education won increasing influence in manpower allocation policies. This led both to changes in graduate education and, from 1969, to intensified efforts to set up specialist training quotas which were linked to physician positions in the larger hospitals. Taken together, these changes had the pronounced effect of bringing about further convergence between the professional education and status disc and the other two discs in the Swedish system.

Rationalising the Bureaucratic Monopoly

During the 1960s, those employed in the Swedish public health system saw their bureaucratic and political superiors frequently changed as the result of reorganisation. The main beneficiaries of these changes were the counties, whose control over health delivery became monopolistic as the Health Board relinquished to them operating responsibilities for the district doctors (1961) and the mental hospitals (1967). At the cabinet level the Health Board was transferred from the Interior to the Social Affairs Ministry (1963), and later merged with the Board of Social Welfare (1968). Politicians and bureaucrats seemed to have an equally strong stake in supporting these changes. The bureaucrats perceived the elimination of overlapping jurisdictions as a prerequisite for more effective steering and planning capacity.[28] The politicians saw the creation of a more streamlined network of political responsibilities as a prerequisite for eroding the Medical Association's ability to outmanoeuvre officials by negotiating nimbly on a case-by-case basis, often anticipating and exploiting loopholes in the gradually emerging health-planning apparatus.

The Board might perhaps have retained administrative control over the district doctors, and used them to develop a set of health centres as an alternative to hospital outpatient departments for supplying primary care. But the district doctors were regarded as lacking the infrastructure to improve the range and quality of their services. They were something of an embarrassment to the Interior Ministry, whose officials felt that the county administrators could transfer some of the expertise gained in running hospitals to the improvement of the district doctor system. Opposition to the move was limited to some district doctors, and to perpetual nay-sayer Gunnar Björck, a traditionalist Karolinska professor.

One reason for integrating the two services was to arrest a tendency towards clientele stratification according to fee levels. In 1958 the district doctors charged at the suggested fee levels of the insurance programme (patient reimbursement rate: 74 per cent), while the hospital doctors and private practitioners charged at higher rates (reimbursement rates of 67 per cent and 61 per cent, respectively).[29] Another motivation at the ministry was to shift the county politicians' preoccupation away from hospital construction. As Carl Persson put it: 'Johansson and I hoped that transfer of the district doctors to their jurisdiction would cause the county councils to pursue more balanced policies, but they retained their traditional commitments to hospitals.'[30]

Borgenhammer found that the county board chairmen were more generous towards hospital expansion developments than even the physicians, and that this attitude was particularly strong among chairmen aged over 60. More recent evidence has certainly not disproved his suggestion that 'there might be a connection between the sense of influence of political decision-makers in this area and the fact that Sweden has, by international standards, a comparatively high bed/population ratio'.[31]

The strong vested position of the counties is highlighted by comparison with the municipalities, where vested interests were shaken up by a two-wave amalgamation, which reduced the number of communes by 90 per cent in two decades. Another model for reorganisation of county jurisdiction might have been suggested by the three large cities. There health administrators had to compete more rigorously for resources because the health sector accounted for some 25 to 30 per cent of expenditures, compared to 80 per cent for the counties. Perhaps Johansson would have found it harder to use his influence with the County Council party[32] to reshape county and municipal responsibilities. Instead, integration was achieved on paper by transferring the Health Board to the Ministry of Social Affairs in 1963. But at the county level, where the financial power resided, new hospital construction was given priority. Thus the strengthening of the monopoly of the middle-ring authorities on the political disc had the result of increasing the dominance of the central institutions on the health care delivery disc.

There was also relatively little opposition to merging the Board of Health into the Board of Social Welfare (*Socialstyrelsen*). King Gustaf Adolf VI expressed some concern to Arthur Engel about the apparent disappearance of the traditional *Medicinalstyrelsen*,[33] but few of his subjects in the health sector seemed willing to undertake a mobilisation campaign. Even the *Riksdag*'s arbitrary action in striking the word 'Hälso' from the proposed compound Board title seemed to provoke little protest. Perhaps the physicians had, by this time, learned to take symbolic put-downs in their stride. But, labels notwithstanding, after Dr Bror Rexed took over the combined Board directorship in 1968, some 24 out of 28 division heads in the Board came to be physicians.

These changes at the centre of the political-administrative disc had diverse consequences on the health delivery disc. Some senior physicians perceived that 'social administrators and Social Democrats were taking over' control of the health system, especially in the Social Affairs Ministry and at the level of the county health directors. However, the hospital directorships created by the 1959 act seemed to have been filled more by relatively apolitical economists. The studies by Borgenhammer make evident that the leading hospital physicians got along extremely well with the elected local county chairmen, of whom most of the more senior ones were Social Democrats. Compared with levels of party 'colonisation' of administrative organs in other countries, the politicisation of the Swedish health system seemed to remain modest even in the 1960s.

Rexed's appointment to the *Socialstyrelsen* chairmanship was eased by the fact that the senior medical educators had learned to discount their distaste for his party politics because of his success in winning approval for the great expansion of medical education and research, and related hospital facilities. If the number of full professorships in Swedish medical schools multiplied much more rapidly than those in other university departments and schools, it was in good part because of Rexed's skill as a bureaucratic negotiator. Rexed's strategy for reconciling the different demands in the social welfare complex was to expand budget rather than to knock heads. The Board's powers to disapprove county construction and personnel plans were minimally used in the 1960s. The Ministry of Social Affairs demonstrated its success at integrating functions, he maintained in 1969, by growing to absorb a quarter of the government budget, or 'three times as much as the Defence Ministry'.[34] Observers found Rexed's formula for assuring the success of integration efforts rather expensive.

Figure 5.1: The Projected Growth of the Medical Profession, 1930–2010

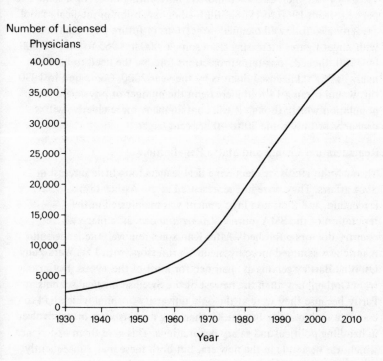

Source: *Läkerbrist-överskottet* (Landstingsförbundet, 1978).

In June 1969, after Rexed had been in office for four years, he and the Finance Minister Gunnar Sträng both addressed the County Federation congress, meeting in Örebro. Sträng acknowledged that it was good to have a 'fiery soul' like Rexed present the case for medical needs, but accused him of employing 'Gaullistic' thinking. 'De Gaulle presents things so that first comes France as a great nation, then comes the need for nuclear bombs, and only then comes the economy, positioned somewhat like the Army Supply Corps behind the battle field.'[35] Newspaper editorials, commenting on the encounter, pointed out that whereas, in a typical county, it had taken 20 years for health expenditures to double between 1920 and 1940, the doubling was now recurring every four years.

Total health care expenditures, which had grown 231 per cent from 1950 to 1960, increased even more rapidly during the 1960s, some 346 per cent from 1960 to 1968. Still further expansion of medical school capacity also followed biennial projections of future physician need, with target figures increasing from some 6,000 in 1965 to over 16,000 by 1980. Indeed, long-term projections foresaw the need to have as many as 35,000 licensed doctors by the year 2000. Compared to 1930, this would mean a 14-fold increase in the number of physicians for a population which, though it will contain many more elderly, will probably be only some 30 to 40 per cent larger.

Remuneration Change and Status Redefinition

Through the 1950s, academic medical leaders took little interest in SMA affairs. They were not represented in the Association's leadership, and their non-involvement was manifested in the reputation of the SMA journal, *Läkartidningen*, as 'a place where country doctors published'. After Knutson's removal, the leadership mantle *was* assumed more by medical professors, with Lars Werkö and Osborne Bartley serving as chairmen for most of the 1960s. Both came from Gothenburg, then the newest of the Swedish medical schools. Partly because they were at the only university hospital which had to compete within a city budget, Gothenburg doctors were more involved in handling political and salary negotiations. This gave them experience which was desirable in the new era. But both these men subsequently left their academic careers, and one may conclude that there was some structural incompatibility in combining the position of SMA chairman with that of a 'normal' Swedish medical professorship. Having managed to unseat the redoubtable Dag Knutson, some young SYLF leaders were also unwilling to grant his successors the deference which they had been accustomed to expect within a medical school setting.

The organisational changes wrought in the 1960s affected the relationship between two relatively unique organisations – the counties with their own tax bases, and the SMA with its tightly-organised political blocs based on career stages. The counties' affluence grew immensely as they outdistanced other government levels by doubling their tax rates, and in the mid-1960s they significantly strengthened the County Council Federation as a negotiating instrument at a time when national legislation legalised strikes by public employees. At the same time, SYLF grew disproportionately in membership and – as it

became accustomed to plentiful resources – also in ebullience. It was
the SYLF leaders who became most outspoken in giving the SMA's
trade union functions clear precedence over its 'professional' status.
This implied lesser concern with protecting professional 'autonomy' or
the status distinctions between medicine and other occupational
groups, and greater concern with successful economic bargaining
results.

Greater centralisation of negotiations over salaries and working
conditions made differences between various groups of hospital
doctors more transparent than they were when the countries had
negotiated on a more individual basis. This revealed that both junior
and senior physicians in some specialties were earning much more
than those in others. Yet, since the internal organisation of SMA was
not based on specialties, it was difficult to cope internally with these
differences of interest. In fact, since salary negotiations usually
involved across-the-board percentage increases, the more successful
the overall SMA negotiations, the wider the differentials in incomes
between doctor groups became. Differences were also accentuated
between those physicians – primarily junior hospital physicians, whose
salaried incomes were fully visible to the tax authorities – and those,
especially the private practitioners, whose fee-for-service incomes were
believed to be less totally subject to tax officials' scrutiny. Later it
developed that the tax officials were able to utilise insurance records
more effectively than had been expected, partly because the National
Tax Board concentrated its scrutiny efforts on physicians for two
successive years in the late 1960s. As a consequence, many hundreds of
physicians, primarily private practitioners, were fined for unreported
income located in small-town banks throughout Sweden.

Peer Control – via Sister Professions?

The outcome of the negotiations over 'salary only' remuneration in
1970 (see Chapter 6) left many physicians dissatisfied. A little later, the
consequences of low increases given to the higher-level public
employees in the aftermath of the 1971 'SACO-conflict' raised intense
dissatisfaction among some doctors. This triggered the development of
a 'grass roots' revolt against the ongoing incorporation tendency which
came close to forcing the Medical Association to cancel its membership
to SACO, the peak professional association which it had established and
nurtured for several decades. This thrust came predominantly from
younger specialists at the university and larger county hospitals – that
is, from junior physicians towards the centre of the professional disc.

They had been subjected to several relative deprivations, which repeatedly reduced their anticipated incomes in relation to various reference groups. Many were first deprived of their supplementary fee incomes; then some specialties had their income bases 'relativised' downward in the consolidated salary schedules; and finally many saw their claims to a smallish 'professional salary improvement pie', sacrificed in favour of the claims of other SACO groups, such as librarians and other lower-grade professional employees of the counties. Their grievances were articulated in a letter from 54 doctors in the summer of 1972.

> Prior to the Seven Crowns Reform our remuneration was acceptable. Since that reform our negotiations adversary, the government, has in the last analysis in practice dictated the conditions of settlement. This means that real remuneration will decline by at least one-fifth during the present contract period.
> During the 1971 wage negotiations the other SACO member organizations were willing to accept a final settlement giving advantages to low-income groups within SACO at the expense of high-income groups. They did not feel it necessary to take the wishes of the Medical Association into consideration.[36]

Their grievances were further excited by what might happen if a weakened SACO should enter into merger negotiations with TCO, the white-collar federation, a possibility under discussion in 1972. The result might have been that the same negotiators would have to represent the claims of both doctors and nurses. They felt that this 'would not improve our situation. One may think what one will about the egalitarian principle voiced in the political debate of the day, – in union activity it has no place.'

Previously other groups of physicians, working more in smaller hospitals and in the district doctor service, had attacked the negotiation outcome because it was not egalitarian enough. The focus of their complaint was that the negotiators had not altered the fact that physicians remained the only occupational group which was exempted from the legal work-time limit of 40 hours a week.[37] The demand was seized upon by a dynamic SYLF chairman to develop backing for a motion to have the SMA executive council give notice of quitting SACO.

This was a direct attack on the leadership of Osborne Bartley, who had for four years combined the roles of SMA and SACO chairman.

Bartley had been a strong ally of Bertil Östergren's, and after the latter resigned in the aftermath of the failure of the 'SACO conflict', Bartley found it necessary to emphasise his SACO responsibilities in order to contain that organisation's membership and other losses. For a while it looked as though the rebels might win. Several of the other SMA groups seemed to be willing to support a cohesive SYLF delegation. But in the end, the leadership arguments against precipitate action prevailed, and the motion was defeated by nine to three.[38]

This conflict reinforced Bartley's impression that it was necessary to choose between the two chairmanships, and he left the SMA post at the end of 1972 to give full attention to SACO. In an interesting parting interview with *Läkartidningen*, Bartley strongly defended his strategy on the Seven Crowns law, claiming that it was 'implemented in a manner basically beneficial to doctors', and that the number who had experienced income increases exceeded those who had to accept decreases. The scars he suffered in the difficult role of demand-aggregator in the negotiations following both conflicts may help explain his sharp criticism of the 'factional voting' prevailing in the SMA Executive Board. He argued that 'there had been a bit too much' mandated voting, suggesting that 'each member of the Board should let himself be influenced by factual considerations and vote according to his conviction – not on the basis of a mandate'.[39]

His successor as SMA chairman, Dr Stig-Bertil Nillson, also suggested in the same issue that local affiliates of SYLF, the hospital doctors, and other subgroups should negotiate initially through the *local* SMA associations, 'so that the leadership of the Association will be able to consult a single organ as regards bargaining questions, etc.'[40] The SMA leaders, amid the pressures of mediating corporate interests in a situation in which the public employers had sharply increased their monopoly powers, were thus groping 'back' to more 'Liberal' principles of representation within their own organisation. In earlier phases of the conflicts, the professional organisations had tended more towards what might be called a 'syndicalist' strategy. This was manifested in emphasis on the development of strike funds, and a tendency of the SACO leadership in the late 1960s to 'defend its members' interests less through reliance on alliances on the political tier, and more through the solitary exercise of its economic power on the labor market tier'.[41] Even after the SACO strike had shown that the government could risk interruptions of professional services, the protesting doctors argued that an independent Medical Association could pursue a tougher conflict strategy because of 'the consumers' high degree of urgent need, and valuation of the services we offer'.[42] In both conflicts, doctors' dismay at the lack of significant support from any of the bourgeois party leaderships reinforced their 'anti-political' tendencies. They scoffed at those colleagues who thought that a government change would improve the situation. 'It is quite unlikely that a bourgeois government would provide Social-Democratic propaganda with ammunition by altering the tax rates so as to grant favours to a group of so-called high-income academics. Hence, doctors' only alternative to economic catastrophe is markedly increased collective bargaining activity.'[43]

Conclusion

During the quarter century surveyed here, the Swedish health system altered greatly, even though it did not undergo any one single cataclysmic change. Conventional terminology serves poorly to capture the essence of the transformation. If there was a 'revolution', which institutions or practices were jettisoned? The further shift into a system of 'socialised medicine' is hard to pinpoint, for while the public 'monopoly' was extended and the sway of market forces further reduced, it is difficult to identify critical thresholds. Should, then, the outcomes of these conflicts in this period be portrayed as marking the end of the era of 'pluralist' bargaining in Swedish health politics, and as the beginning of acceptance by the medical profession of the need to conform to a 'social corporate' form of interest accommodation? Did organised interests decline in their ability to be fundamental elements in the institutionalised pluralism of the Swedish industrial welfare state, in that they constitute 'countervailing powers' to political and administrative decision-makers?[44] Probably, yes. But did they also accept corporate recognition for the right to 'deputize for the state in whole sectors of public life, and to have duties delegated to them that properly belong to the civil service'?[45]

Those acquainted with the Swedish policy-making process, as presented in Chapter 3 of this volume, know that it is very difficult to distinguish functions which are 'properly' those of bureaucrats, from those which are 'properly' those of associations. The Medical Association was representing a profession whose members were increasingly employed in the public sector. The main issue in the Seven Crowns Reform was how strongly the SMA could or should mobilise its members to oppose a remuneration system which further shaded the distinctions between physicians and the regular civil servants.

The changes described above have obviously reduced the 'degrees of freedom' which the medical profession and its association could take advantage of in conflict situations. But in so far as a societal corporatist trend has been evident, it has impinged on the autonomy of professional associations generally. What especially affected the position of the physicians were the consequences of the politically-based policy of expanding health care and medical manpower which was pursued so persistently after 1950. Greatly increasing the 'population density' on the professional education and status disc had the effect of generating additional pressure to reduce the angle of incidence to the health delivery plane.

As the health system grew, physicians drew an increasing proportion of their income from public salaries and insurance reimbursements. That by itself did not engender a collapse of professional autonomy claims. In Germany and elsewhere, doctors have long combined reliance on public income with sustained control over key portions of the professional status and health delivery discs. In Sweden, even the leaders of the traditional position, such as Dag Knutson and Gunnar Björck, had held public hospital positions. What was most difficult in Sweden was the way in which the change in remunerations basis was related to changes in professional values and symbols.

The bar against fee-for-service practice was seen by some older private practitioners as a mortal abridgement of professional privileges, which were so deeply rooted in European societies, in part because they antedated the rise and legitimation of national bureaucracies. While maintaining the distinction from ordinary civil servants was a viable ideological goal as long as the profession was small and 'aristocratic', it became less attractive as the annual production of new doctors approached 1,000. When they were so few in number, Swedish doctors were responsible for the work of more hospital personnel, and the care of more patients, than physicians in other European countries.[46] But by 1970 the number of hospital admissions per doctor had been reduced by one-third compared to 1950, and the number of patient-days per doctor by more than one half since the 1930s. The increase in practising doctors projected for the 1970s, 8,000, was more than three times larger than the *total* number of physicians in 1930 (when the population was only one-quarter less).

What occurred can be captured conceptually in terms of the model discussed at the beginning of the chapter. On all three discs there have been strong tensions between central and peripheral pulls on resources. Most important was the gradual convergence between the three discs.

The distinctiveness which traditionally set apart health administration, professional education and status, and health care institutions, has lessened. The angles of incidence between the discs have been considerably reduced.

Reduced, but not completely eliminated. The three discs have not been collapsed into one, and there is still no single decision-making hierarchy which can ensure absolute compliance. In the case of medical specialty manpower, we have traced how the bureaucrats won power to reduce the freedom of choice of young doctors in terms of centrally defined needs for different specialists. But a decade after the channelling mechanism was put into effect, the 'priority' specialties were still short of trainees, while close to 1,000 young physicians in high status, but low priority specialties, were floating on the lookout for a permanent position.[47] Their degrees of freedom of choice had been narrowed, but not eliminated.

More than 20 years earlier, Höjer had prophesied that 'if the system develops in the projected way, there should by 1960 or 1970, only be a very few physicians employed at the hospitals who would not be willing or obliged to enter the civil service compensation systems'.[48] The ways in which the system developed after Höjer's time, with the greater emphasis on hospitals and the yet sharper increase in physicians production, tended on balance to increase the proportion who were 'willing'. Some of the younger specialists who were highly paid under the preceding system, such as surgeons and laboratory specialists, were among those who felt 'obliged', and who resisted the change. But the larger number of new recruits to the profession had indeed become 'willing'.

Notes

1. For the period 1871–1970, the Swedish economic growth rate, at about 2.1 per cent annually on a per capita basis, was second only to that of Japan. Assar Lindbeck, *Swedish Economic Policy* (University of California Press, Berkeley, 1974), p. 1.

2. Carlo M. Cipolla, 'The Professions: The Long View', *Journal of European Economic History*, vol. 2 (Spring 1973), pp. 37–52.

3. 'Fran "liberal profession" till tjänsteman', *Läkartidningen*, vol. 75 (1978), pp. 1994–6.

4. Characteristic were the editors of the popular journal *Prism*, published for a while by the American Medical Association. In one 1974 issue, they commissioned an artist to draw an illustration, which was printed as a double-page drawing accompanying a critical article on the Swedish health system. It

showed an unhappy-looking doctor waiting to punch a time-clock, a practice which, I am told, Swedish doctors have not engaged in.

5. SOU 1935:52, Wicksell-Jerneman Report, p. 39.

6. J. Axel Höjer, *En läkares väg* (Stockholm, Bonniers, 1976), p. 193.

7. Seth D. Charney, 'Doctors: Surplus or Shortage', unpublished paper presented at Yale University Medical School, 1969, p. 48.

8. Höjer, *En läkares väg*, p. 192.

9. Ibid., p. 194.

10. Odin W. Anderson, *Health Care: Can there by Equity?* (John Wiley & Sons, New York, 1972), p. 78.

11. Statens Offentliga Utredningar, 'Den Oppna Läkarvården i Riket, SOU 1948:14.

12. Harry Eckstein, *The English Health Service* (Harvard University Press, Cambridge, Mass., 1958), pp. 202, 248–52.

13. *Yearbook of Nordic Statistics* (1975).

14. Interview, Arthur Engel, March 1973.

15. Vicente Navarro, *National and Regional Health Care Planning in Sweden*, DHEW Publication no. (NIH) 74-240 (Government Printing Office, Washington D.C., 1974), p. 76.

16. Interviews with Prof. Gösta Tunevall, Dr Bo Hjern, Dr Nils Terner, Dr Ake Lindgren, 1973–4.

17. Rolf Ejvegård, *Landstingsförbundet* (Stockholm, Grafisk, 1973), p. 361.

18. Statens Offentliga Utredningar, 'Halsovard och Öppna Sjukvard', no. 15 (1958).

19. Proposition 141, 1960.

20. Sveriges Läkarförbund, Husmark Memorandum A 49/60, 1960.

21. Sveriges Läkarförbund, Eriksson Memorandum 121/60, 1960.

22. Proposition 141, p. 82.

23. Ibid., p. 81.

24. Ibid., p. 78.

25. Riksdagsdebatterna, Upplaga D. Nr. 49 Första kammaren, 1960, 25 May 1960, p. 34.

26. Ibid., p. 23.

27. Proposition 141, pp. 83–5.

28. Vicente Navarro, *National and Regional Health Care Planning in Sweden*, pp. 110 ff.

29. 'Oversyn av sjukförsäkringens aterbäringstaxa', Social-department, SO 1967:4.

30. Interview with Carl Persson, 1974.

31. Edgar Borgenhammar, 'Hospital Budgeting Processes and Attitudes Toward Costs: Report on a Research Study', *The Swedish Health Services System* (American College of Hospital Administrators, Chicago, 1971), pp. 110–11; Edgar Borgenhammar, *Makten over Sjukhuset* (SNOS, Stockholm, 1968).

32. Ejvegård, *Landstingsförbundet*, Ch. 10. (See Ch. 4, n. 16.)

33. Navarro, *National and Regional Health Care Planning in Sweden*, Ch. 3; A. Engel, *The Swedish Regionalized Hospital System* (National Board of Health, Stockholm, 1967).

34. Bror Rexed, 'Public Policy and Medicine', in *The Swedish Health Services System*, p. 202.

35. *Landstingsnytt: Medelanden fran Örebro Läns Landsting*, vol. 16, no. 4 (1969), p. 8.

36. *Läkartidningen*, vol. 69 (1972), p. 3948.

37. *Läkartidningen*, vol. 68 (1971), p. 3650.

38. Interview, Osborne Bartley, 1974.

39. *Läkartidningen*, vol. 70 (1973), p. 39.
40. Ibid., p. 42.
41. Arnold J. Heidenheimer, 'Professional Unions, Public Sector Growth and the Swedish Equality Policy', *Comparative Politics*, vol. 8 (October 1976), p. 62.
42. *Läkartidningen*, vol. 69 (1972), p. 3948.
43. Ibid., p. 3949.
44. M. Donald Hancock, *Sweden: The Politics of Post-Industrial Change* (Dryden Press, Hinsdale, Illinois, 1972), pp. 68, 147.
45. Philippe Schmitter, 'Still the Century of Corporatism?', *Review of Politics*, vol. 36, no. 1 (January 1972), p. 86.
46. *Läkartidningen*, vol. 55 (1958), p. 2880.
47. *Läkerbrist – överskottet* (Landstingsförbundet, Stockholm, 1978).
48. Höjer, *Den Öppna Läkarvarden*, p. 316.

6 TOWARDS A SALARIED MEDICAL PROFESSION: HOW 'SWEDISH' WAS THE SEVEN CROWNS REFORM?

Mack Carder and Bendix Klingeberg

The Seven Crowns Reform (SCR), perhaps the most significant and highly publicised of the post-1950 Swedish health care measures, represents a landmark in the restructuring of the remuneration system which underpins medical professionalisation in Sweden. The SCR is of special interest also because the procedures which produced it appear uncharacteristic of the Swedish policy process. In this chapter, we will attempt to determine to what degree and for what reasons the Seven Crowns Reform was an exception to the 'normal' pattern of decision-making in Swedish health politics.[1]

The Seven Crowns Reform was a two-stage revision, the first of which primarily involved statutory changes in national laws governing medical care and general insurance.[2] It was at this primary stage that the 'normal' pattern of decision-making seems to have been clearly violated. As previous chapters have borne out, major changes in the Swedish health sector have usually been preceded by years of careful research, often carried out by *ad hoc* research units called Royal Commissions (see Chapter 3, pp. 75–9). The Seven Crowns Reform was, on the contrary, designed and implemented with considerable haste and secrecy. No Royal Commission was appointed, and open deliberations took place only among representatives of the Ministry of Social Affairs and the principal employers of public physicians. What seems most startling is that representatives of the Swedish Medical Association (SMA) were not openly included or extensively informed publicly about the deliberations leading to the statutory reforms. The procedural deviations in this first stage of revision may have had a significant impact on the latter stage as well, since the statutory changes necessitated and set the tone and content of the collective bargaining negotiations between the representatives of publicly-employed physicians and their employers which comprised the second stage of the reform.

The content of the Seven Crowns Reform as it emerged from its atypical gestation process was wide-ranging; it stipulated a uniform flat-rate fee for outpatient care, removed physicians from financial

transactions, abolished fee-for-service compensation for outpatient care
and physicians' reception of private patients at public facilities, sought
to equalise incomes within the medical profession, increased inpatient
fees by 100 per cent, and increased insurance coverage for some
patients. The number of working hours for physicians was reduced and
some physicians actually suffered real income losses as a consequence
of the SCR. And these major changes in remuneration methods and
levels were achieved without the serious conflicts with medical
professional groups which had accompanied similar attempts in Sweden
and elsewhere.[3]

The ease with which the statutory reforms were decided and
implemented and the late and mild resistance of the medical profession
have been attributed to the hasty and secretive tactics and clever
political manipulations of a reform alliance composed of the Swedish
Ministry of Social Affairs, the Swedish County Council Federation
(CCF), and the hospital authorities of the major municipalities.

This analysis, which puts prime emphasis on the process by which
the revision was achieved, raises a series of provocative questions about
the motivations and intentions of the policy-makers who resorted to
such an abbreviated procedure. Above all, the avoidance of open
consultation with physicians might be interpreted as an attempt by the
reformers to limit the possibility of the development of a strong and
unified medical coalition similar to the one which had defeated the
Höjer reform some 22 years before (see Chapter 5, pp. 121–4).

Further, highly visible measures like the Seven Crowns Reform can
translate into additional political support for the governing political
party. In this light, it would be helpful to explore whether the reform
constituted a political move to bolster lagging voting support, or
whether it simply represented the latest fruition of the Social Democrats'
post-1959 push in health policy. This political consideration is further
augmented by the fact that the timing of the reform coincided with
certain constitutional changes in the electoral cycle and the
parliamentary system initiated in 1971.[4] Such a coincidence warrants
consideration in itself.

The potential benefits of the hasty and secretive proceedings
surrounding the reform for the Social-Democratic government and the
employers are self-evident. However, the tendency to view the reform
as the imposition by government of 'salary-only' compensation on a
free medical profession seems to have kept some analysts from asking
an additional important question: whether the SMA leadership could
have benefited from their exclusion from the Swedish consultation

process. The SMA's lack of success in the *remiss* procedure on health care policy might indicate that the association could have benefitted from a redefinition of its relationship with health policy-makers. Could the behaviour of the association have been a gesture of *rapprochement* to the Ministry of Social Affairs or the public employers? And what of the internal problems within the SMA? It is conceivable that these difficulties prompted the leadership to co-operate with, or restrain opposition to, the reform measures and that the prevailing system of physician remuneration was as problematic for the SMA leadership as it was for the national and local health authorities.

The attempt, in this chapter, to reach fuller understanding of these possibilities is essential for accurate understanding of the Seven Crowns Reform itself, yet their significance extends far beyond its particular historical and geographical confines. The answers to these questions hold the key to the very definition of the 'professions' in Sweden and perhaps other post-industrial societies. And the content of that definition may greatly influence the future direction of public policy, the nature of the polity and the strength and adaptability of society.

The Reform Alliance, Electoral Politics and Deviations from 'Normal' Decision-making

After a phase of rapid expansion, structural and administrative reorganisation and a redistribution of responsibilities, the health delivery system had in many ways been consolidated by the beginning of the 1960s. At that time, however, a number of systematic and structural deficiencies surfaced that were initially and most directly felt by the counties. This is due, in part, to the fact that they are the political and administrative units closest to the patients, physicians and voters, thus to all potential interests.

The County Councils

Because of their historic responsibility for public hospitals and their autonomous taxation power, the counties were the logical basis for the health care delivery system that was to develop in Sweden following the Second World War. Assuming more and more of the functions and responsibilities once performed by the primary communes or the state, by 1967 they had become responsible for administering, funding or delivering almost the entire spectrum of health care services. Since 1945 the counties had taken over chronic patient and long-term care (1945), the care for the mentally retarded (1954), the funding of maternal care

(1959), the system of district medical officers (1961), ambulance service (1965), and psychiatric care (1967).[5] The county councils had also embarked on a drive to expand their system of hospitals and had considerably increased their capacities for vocational training, especially of nurses and other ancillary medical personnel.[6] Relying primarily on their own taxation power, but partially on financial grants from the state, the counties had expanded into authorities that were 'close to unique in the degree to which they are "uniservice health jurisdictions" '.[7] The chairman of the CCF could with some justification be called the 'unconstitutional minister of hospitals'.[8] Pushed by inter-county competition and the demands of physicians for more and better-equipped hospitals[9] and encouraged by national health and labour policies,[10] the county councils and their hospitals became the backbone of the health care delivery system.

While the expansion of the hospital sector provided Sweden with some of the finest facilities, it also created many problems. Expected to fulfil most health care functions, the hospital sector developed into a 'resource magnet'[11] — monopolising investments, personnel, technology and patients at the expense of other health care delivery subsystems. Hospital inpatient care is the most expensive type of health care. For these reasons, alternatives to inpatient care became important to the county councils. In tandem with an emphasis on alternative delivery modes outside the hospital, the predominant inpatient orientation of the hospitals began to change. After 1959, hospitals were required to maintain outpatient departments for the treatment of ambulatory patients. The number of outpatient visits at the hospitals had grown from 7.4 million in 1952 to 18.4 million in 1963, which meant that the hospital ambulatories handled over 40 per cent of Sweden's medical consultations in 1963.[12] Though the use of ambulatories increased significantly during this period, the shift from inpatient care to ambulatory care was slowed by the fact that the former was financially advantageous for patients. This situation obtained because of disparities in the payment and insurance reimbursement systems, which will be elaborated in the second major section of this chapter.

The counties also faced tremendous problems of staffing and general manpower planning, especially in outpatient care. Many hospital positions were among the most prestigious and financially rewarding positions in the health care system, and consequently drew physicians away from such positions as district medical officer or health clinic physician. Young doctors were generally not interested in serving outside the hospital, since hospitals provided the opportunity for professional advancement, research, teaching and access to the latest technology that health clinics and district doctor units did not. If alternatives to hospital care were to be viable, competent personnel were a necessity. Also, the non-hospital facilities were generally designed to utilise the services of from one to four doctors, which meant that general practitioners were needed for this type of work. The trend in training physicians in Sweden, as elsewhere, had been towards specialisation at the expense of general practice.

The National Health Authorities

Planning and administration at the national level are carried out by a two-tiered civil service comprised of the ministries and agencies or national boards. In the health sector, policy-making, co-ordination and planning are primarily the responsibility of the Ministry of Social Affairs. The lower level Board of Health and Social Welfare is charged primarily with policy implementation and administration.[13]

The Seven Crowns Reform was prepared within the Ministry of Social Affairs, apparently without the direct participation of Bror Rexed and the Board of Health and Social Welfare. To the ministry, the Seven Crowns Reform represented a further step in the rationalisation of Swedish health care pursued by the Social-Democratic government since 1959.

In 1963, the report of the ÖHS Committee, the Royal Commission on Hospitals and Outpatient Care, strongly emphasised the need for increased outpatient facilities and alternative modes of health care delivery for medical as well as economic reasons. The report also analysed some of the systematic and structural barriers to effective outpatient care.[14] Among these was the extant system of physician remuneration. The ÖHS Committee report noted that:

> One way to improve the chances of other sectors within the health care system to compete for physicians would be to deny the physicians the additional incomes from outpatient work, in other words to integrate outpatient work into those service duties that are compensated for by salaries.[15]

The national health authorities shared the county councils' interest in the use of outpatient care, and recognised the personnel problems which hampered progress towards that goal. For the perception had steadily grown that the income possibilities for various specialties and the form of physician compensation had strongly affected the production and distribution of medical manpower and contributed to the overproduction of certain medical specialties at the expense of others that were badly needed. Thus, the goals of the county councils and the national authorities overlapped to some extent and it was only a matter of timing and opportunity when these partially complementary interests would be transformed into action.

Complementary goals do not always make for the closest relationships, however. While health care planners at the national level demanded further investment and expansion of the delivery system, especially in psychiatric care, long-term care and the development of outpatient facilities, the counties saw their financial capacities eroded while expenditures increased. Government showed little interest in reducing the cost burden of the counties significantly. Fridolf Thapper, long-time Social-Democratic chairman of the Federation of County Councils, summed up the situation as follows:

> In all negotiations with the State, they bring up the strained national financial situation . . . but we have to realize that even the county councils have limited possibilities to create financial resources.[16]

The controversy is vividly illustrated by a confrontation between the Minister of Finance, Gunnar Sträng, and Bror Rexed of the Board of Health and Social Welfare, on the occasion of the inauguration of a hospital in the summer of 1969.[17] Sträng maintained that investments in the health care sector could not be expanded, given the projected 4 per cent maximum increase in GNP. Rexed answered sharply that he didn't care if the health delivery system grew to take a 13 per cent share of the GNP. He demanded an annual investment increase of 10 per cent, and admonished Sträng to provide these resources rather than meddle in health care policies.[18]

Politics: Deviations from 'Normal' Decision-making

Coming just before the parliamentary elections of September 1968, the CCF's move to increase inpatient fees can be characterised as an attempt to affect Social-Democratic health policy. The county councils had been trying to force a full reconsideration of the health care finance system for several years with little success. The decision to double the fees charged for inpatient care was sure to attract attention to the health policy area and perhaps was partially responsible for putting the Seven Crowns Reform on the political agenda.

In 1968, the Social Democrats (SAP) were unsure of their electoral strength, primarily as a consequence of their rather poor showing in the 1966 communal elections. Their share of the vote had slipped to 42.2 per cent, the lowest since 1934. In response to the slim vote margins, the SAP had developed a new policy thrust, of which the so-called 'equality policy' was a major component. The 'equality policy' laid the foundation for income equalisation and on-the-job equality between the sexes. Further, it emphasised the protection of underprivileged groups in Swedish society such as the infirm, the poor and the elderly. The adoption of this general policy orientation permitted the Social Democrats to present the electorate with a series of real and perceived achievements, which were described by Prime Minister Erlander at the party congress of June 1968 as follows:

> Labour market and localisation policies have been extended with expenditures of 520 million Crowns. A security system for older unemployed persons have been introduced . . . general pension plans have been increased by 150 million Crowns . . . new housing construction has increased to 400,000 units . . . This entire reform program has been implemented with virtually no increase in taxes.[19]

In September 1968, the Social Democrats won the national elections by an unexpectedly large margin. On 6 November 1968, the first meetings between the CCF, the Ministry of Social Affairs and the Ministry of Finance were called to discuss the county councils' demands and other health policy matters. The Ministry of Social Affairs presented a preliminary paper outlining some of the issues, and after four November meetings, a working committee was formed to evaluate and analyse the various proposals. This resulted in a 'package' proposal presented on 6 December 1968, which was refined in subsequent meetings on 17 December, 1 January 1969, and 9 January. The Seven Crowns Reform was prepared during these last three meetings, with the contents presented as a binding agreement to the respective parties.[20] The parties to the reform fought hard to avoid amendments in Parliament, and despite the *remiss* procedure designed to allow input from other interested parties, the reform was passed and implemented virtually unchanged.

Why was the Seven Crowns Reform formulated hastily within the Ministry, rather than more cautiously by a Royal Commission? The reasons are many. First, the reform provided the party with an excellent opportunity to solidify electoral support by demonstrating a commitment to the equality policy. Recent developments in the health care sector clashed with the ideology of equality, especially the disproportionately high incomes of most physicians. Equalisation, and in some cases reduction, of physician incomes provided symbolic reassurances that the party was serious about equality. The reform also increased health benefits, reduced out-of-pocket expenditures for outpatients, provided additional facilities for construction, and increased the number of free hospital days for pensioners. Secondly, following the substantial victory, the Social Democrats could continue with increased confidence the ambitious health sector reforms begun in the late 1950s. The Seven Crowns Reform was not an isolated measure, but one further development in the ongoing rationalisation of the Swedish health care system. This is evidenced by the fact that the SCR included unimplemented recommendations from the Engel Report, the Report of the Royal Commissions on Hospitals and Outpatient Care, the Hultström Report, the Report of the Royal Commission on Insurance, and the various demands of the Federation of County Councils. The haste and apparent lack of research can be partially explained by the fact that the package was composed of proposals that had been accumulated, researched and subjected to interest group scrutiny over the years. In reality, then, although the package was rushed through without the Royal Commission procedure, most of the individual proposals had previously received thorough consideration.

The Social Democrats' desire to determine the future shape of the health sector was further influenced by the constitutional revision of 1971. This measure transformed the Swedish bicameral Parliament into a unicameral body and set the date of the next elections two years hence. With elections only two years away and unsure of their electoral prospects, the party chose to act while it had the chance. Also, creating a unicameral body and making county elections coincide with national ones diminished the influence of the county councils in Parliament. The county councils had enjoyed considerable parliamentary power through what had come to be known as the *County Council Party*. The need to act before the changeover imposed a kind of deadline for reform.

The establishment of a Royal Commission, or extensive public information and debate on the ministry's deliberations, could theoretically have given interest groups and organisations more time with which to mount opposition to the reform package. This was perhaps most true of the medical profession. A Royal Commission or more open deliberations within the ministry might have catalysed stronger and more timely opposition among rank-and-file physicians.

From this perspective, the avoidance of the Royal Commission route and the exclusiveness of the deliberations perhaps facilitated a pragmatic compromise among the reform coalition that could later be 'sold' to the Swedish medical profession and the remainder of Swedish society.

It seems unlikely, however, that this reform alliance would have chosen flagrantly to violate medical preferences on proposals for changing remuneration methods. As monopolistic providers of essential services, physicians generally exercise considerable power in decisions determining the methods of their payment in all Western industrial nations. According to Marmor and Thomas:

> Western industrial states will never risk a medical strike . . . The failure to satisfy widely understood medical preferences is presumed . . . to be a sufficient condition for a medical strike . . . Hence, whatever the political and medical structure of the western industrial country, medical preferences determine the methods of payment in public health care programs.[21]

Attention to the implications of this argument raises the possibility that though governmental tactics may have played a role in the reform process, a fuller explanation must include an examination of the preferences and reactions of the medical profession in general and the SMA leadership in particular. In fact, one interesting possibility that remains to be explored is that the absence of the SMA leadership from public deliberations was not involuntary and that the leadership did not want to be openly included in the deliberations. This possibility will be explored in depth after a discussion of the SCR from the public authorities' perspectives.

The Reform Proposals: The Public Authorities' Perspectives

The national government's role in the health care system has been primarily one of co-ordination and planning, especially since the adoption of the recommendations of the Royal Commission on Regionalisation (Engel Report) in 1961.[22] Through voluntary planning, co-ordination and regionalisation, divergent groups with varying degrees of interest and power are expected to reach consensus.[23] Recent years have seen a growing demand for better co-ordination and joint utilisation of health care resources among the various sectors of the system. The consolidation of health care responsibilities with the counties during the 1960s exemplifies this strategy of integration, and the Seven Crowns Reform itself was, among other things, aimed at co-ordinating the work of doctors within the system.[24]

The parties to the negotiations leading to the Seven Crowns Reform shared a limited consensus on several points. However, the priorities and interests of the reformers diverged somewhat. These divergent priorities were determined to some extent by the administrative, financing and delivery responsibilities of the actors, and led to the development of different criteria for formulating and evaluating reform proposals.

Proposals Relating to Outpatient Care

Clearly, a shift from costly hospital inpatient care to less costly ambulatory care was one tactic upon which the reformers could agree. The county councils faced a rather curious dilemma which made the shift difficult, however.

Under the old system, the outpatient was required to pay the entire fee for his visit directly to the doctor. The fees doctors could charge were regulated by a compensation schedule (*ersättningstaxa*) which was determined in negotiations between the Swedish Medical Association and the insurance authorities. The rate of reimbursement to the patient was regulated by an insurance reimbursement schedule (*återbäringstaxa*) which was based on the principle that the out-of-pocket expenditures of patients should not exceed 25 per cent of the total fee.[25] In practice, however, patients often expended more than the prescribed 25 per cent because the compensation and reimbursement schedules did not correspond, and because physicians often demanded fees in excess of those prescribed by the compensation schedule. The problems with this '*taxa*' system made the desired shift in utilisation patterns very difficult by making outpatient care financially disadvantageous to patients.

This problem had already been recognised by the 1963 Royal Commission on Hospitals and Outpatient Care and was made the focus of the Hultström Report, a report commissioned internally by the Social Affairs Ministry in 1965.[26] The introduction of a flat rate payment system, one solution to this well-known problem, was favoured by all the public authorities involved in the reform negotiations. Negotiations focused on the amount of the fee, with the Social Affairs Ministry proposing a patient contribution of 5 crowns with an additional contribution of 25 crowns from the insurance fund. The CCF demanded higher amounts, and the final compromise set the rate at 7 crowns from the patient and 31 crowns from the insurance fund.

The flat rate system would theoretically reduce the demand for the more costly inpatient care and promote the use of hospital outpatient departments and other ambulatory care facilities by removing the economic incentives favouring utilisation of inpatient care. Further, the system was a political bonus for the governing party since it represented a net decrease in out-of-pocket expenditures for many outpatients. The adoption of the new flat rate system was, then, a highly visible and popular political reform. It was totally consistent with the new equality emphasis of the SAP and could be presented as the implementation of reforms that had been promised before the 1968 national elections, especially since it would serve to equalise physicians' incomes and facilitate the control of increases in physicians' incomes in the future.

Manipulation of fee schedules can alter the manner in which medical manpower responds to the twin phenomena of technological development and medical specialisation. Specifically, the patterns of recruitment among high- and low-paying specialties, and between specialists and generalists can be more efficiently regulated by the public authorities if variations in fees are eliminated. The flat rate system could thus facilitate more effective and efficient recruitment and utilisation of medical manpower.

With the adoption of the seven crown flat fee for ambulatory visits, a major component of the statutory stage of the SCR, fee-for-service compensation became less attractive to physicians than it had been previously. Though this rate represented an increase over previous fee schedules for some treatments, the projected overall effect was a reduction in extra income derived from outpatient work. Thus, by reducing the economic benefit derived from fee-for-service outpatient visits, the statutory stage of the reform may have greatly facilitated the introduction of *totallön* in the subsequent bargaining stage. Though the county councils had long supported the practice of fee-for-service compensation, they came to recognise that the stage had been set for its demise. The county authorities had previously used the promise of extra fee-for-service compensation to attract and hold highly qualified physicians, but the utility of this ploy was greatly diminished by the seven crown flat fee. Thus, the interests of the county councils, and the national planners who had long recognised that total salary (*totallön*) was the most rational payment method,[27] had finally come into agreement on this point. By the time of the collective bargaining negotiations between the employers and the physicians' representatives, total salary compensation was the most effective method of physician remuneration for the counties, and perhaps for physicians also. *Totallön* was an idea whose time had come. The correspondence of interests between the national and local health authorities, the political attractiveness of the reform, and the weakened opposition of the medical profession had combined to make the hitherto problematic total salary system a viable and necessary alternative to supplemental fee-for-service compensation.

The delivery system was further altered to exclude physicians from all financial transactions. All payments were to go directly to the hospital. The county council and municipal authorities favoured such a direct payment system because it put the financial administration of outpatient care under their control, thereby increasing their organisational power *vis-à-vis* physicians and the state.

The ministry and the insurance authorities favoured the direct flat rate system because it greatly simplified the insurance system and rendered it more efficient. Clearly, the new system would reduce the paperwork required for outpatient care by eliminating the need to reimburse patients individually; institutions could be reimbursed in lump sums at regular intervals.

The ministry proposed to include all physicians in the new payment system, arguing that the county councils should subsidise the private practitioners in return for their promise to adapt private fees to the flat rate of seven crowns. The ministry was concerned that all medical manpower should be put to use as efficiently as possible and that health care costs for all services, whether performed by public or private health care providers, should be kept at the lowest possible level.

The county councils rejected this idea totally. The counties had long regarded private practice as 'an irrational element' in the health care system, responsible for many of the staffing and cost problems they experienced.[28] As long as private practice offered an attractive alternative to physicians, the county councils could not gain the leverage needed to staff the less desirable positions in the system. The county councils were therefore unwilling to subsidise the private practitioners, but instead suggested that all private practitioners should enter public service.[29] The medical association claimed that the availability of public care at seven crowns would seriously endanger the private practitioner, and it is likely that the county councils were attempting to do away with private medical practice by their exclusion from the new payment system. The county councils were adamant on

this point, and government officials agreed to exclude the private
practitioners, though a study group was formed to look into the
problem of compensating them.

Proposals Related to Inpatient Care

Inpatient fees had been the focus of attention at the CCF Congresses of
1957 and 1963, and in 1964, the Federation had suggested to the
Crown that inpatient fees be increased from five crowns to ten crowns
per patient day to improve cost coverage and to decrease the attractiveness of inpatient care. The county councils financed inpatient care
almost entirely from their own resources. By arrangement with the
insurance authorities, the hospitals received five crowns per patient day
from the insurance fund and financed the remainder on their own.
These payments from the insurance fund had covered about 9 per cent
of the expenditures of the counties in 1961, but by 1965 they covered
only about 6 per cent.[30]

Though the national authorities recognised the problems with the
insurance system, they were not sympathetic to the demands to double
inpatient fees. Indeed, the December 1967 report of the Royal
Commission on Insurance suggested the abolition of all inpatient fees
and the introduction of free health care. They reasoned that the
collection of fees, however small, would in the long run become a
barrier to full public utilisation of health care facilities.[31]

The Federation's reply to these proposals demonstrated both the
distance between their position and that of the Insurance Commission
and the relationship between inpatient and outpatient care:

> The Executive Committee finds the attempt to solve, as the
> Commission has done, the economic problems of the patients in
> inpatient care without unconditional and simultaneous examination
> of costs in outpatient care totally unrealistic . . . Fee policies
> constitute . . . an important instrument in health care politics and
> should be used to transform outpatient care to an economically
> equivalent alternative to inpatient care . . . As long as the utilization
> of outpatient care is combined with often considerable costs for the
> patients, the Executive Committee is not prepared to discuss the
> principle of free inpatient care.[32]

To the counties, inpatient and outpatient care were inextricably linked.
Though the proposals to install a direct seven crown payment system
for ambulatory care would reduce the gap in attractiveness between

ambulatory care and inpatient care, the CCF remained steadfast in its demand for a 100 per cent increase in inpatient fees. By the time the negotiations began, the national authorities' position seemed more flexible, though they still favoured free health care. In any case, inpatient fees were doubled, further reducing the attractiveness of inpatient care.

The inpatient fee question presented a problem for the Social Democrats, since an increase in fees would not be consistent with the equality policy. The group of voters that would be most alienated were the pensioners, a powerful and important group in Swedish politics. With the narrow political and electoral margins characteristic of Sweden, the pensioners could play a decisive political role. The inpatient fee increase directly affected their interests because it constituted a very radical solution to the *överskott* problem, i.e., the possibility of pensioners accumulating sums of insurance money while under treatment in inpatient or long-term care facilities. The increase was a radical change because it did not take into account the ability of the pensioners to pay the double fees. Of the CCF's demands for increases in inpatient fees, the Royal Commission on Insurance warned that:

> It has not been taken into consideration, that a hospital fee of 10 crowns per day is more than a pensioner who depends exclusively on his pension would be able to pay.[33]

Even for the pensioners who had additional income or benefits, it would still create considerable financial strain and individual hardship. Clearly, this was not a policy that meshed with welfare state concepts or the Social Democrats' emphasis on increased social equality. With parliamentary elections only two years away, the SAP could not afford to alienate this very important group.

The problem of the pensioners' capacity to pay for inpatient care was solved by prolonging the period of free care for pensioners from 180 days to 365 days. Thus, the Seven Crowns Reform was said to offer increased benefits to pensioners.

The efficient delivery of health care services required the CCF to seek increased inpatient fees. This tactic reduced the financing burden of the counties, served to make outpatient care more attractive to the patient than costly inpatient care, and was instrumental in bringing the reformers to the negotiating table. Perhaps the persistent demands for increased inpatient fees forced the consideration of more basic issues by applying considerable political pressure to the governing party.[34]

General Proposals

The CCF demanded a two-year extension of state loans for the construction and expansion of long-term care facilities. The government was prepared to extend the programme for only six months, but the volume available was increased to 100 million crowns.

The extension of the loan programme was a political bonus for the SAP because it allowed them to claim responsibility for the building of long-term care facilities. Capital investments of this sort are among the most visible of all political activities, and the provision of long-term care facilities served further to solidify the pensioners' support for the governing party. Thus, the construction loan question resulted in a pragmatic compromise that allowed the counties to obtain state monies for construction of facilities while the governing party was able to solidify its electoral support.

The various components of the Seven Crowns Reform resulted in an increase in health care expenditures. For outpatient care, national insurance expenditures were calculated to increase by 121 million crowns and out-of-pocket expenditures of outpatients were expected to decrease by 4 million crowns annually.[35]

If the inpatient fee increase was not to be passed on to the patients directly, expenditures from the health insurance fund would have to be increased. New monies for the insurance fund could come from an increased subsidy from the national government, increased employer contributions or from increased employee contributions. If these expenditures were to be financed partially by an increase in the employees' contributions, the authorities warned that:

> greatest care must be taken if the health insurance contribution was not to become unacceptably high, as the premium contribution is in principle not depending on the person's level of income.[36]

Clearly, the increase of employee contributions was not consistent with the equality policy of the SAP. A further increase in this regressive insurance contribution would serve to stabilise rather than equalise the distribution of benefits, and hence to perpetuate any inequality in the system. On the other hand, government was not prepared to increase its contribution. The solution was to increase the employers' contributions to the insurance fund. The government's 40 per cent grant to the

insurance fund was not increased. The only new money that was to
flow into the system came from an increase of the employers'
contributions to the health insurance fund from 2.6 per cent to 2.9 per
cent. This decision was apparently made within the Finance
Ministry.[37]

The SMA in Search of a New Image

Under the leadership of Dag Knutson, who became Chairman in 1946,
the Swedish Medical Association accentuated its role as a 'free
professional association'. Free professions strive to extend their control
over such relevant characteristics of their occupational milieu as:

> . . . the manner of recruitment, the evaluation of merit, the control
> of occupational behavior, the formation of occupational attitudes,
> the occupational culture or external ethos, and the rate of growth or
> decline.[38]

The legitimacy of such claims are in turn based on the professional
authority of individual physicians which derives from two sources:

> First, as a result of the long period of training undergone by the
> practitioner, he is expected to have acquired a body of expert
> knowledge and to have internalized a code of ethics which governs
> his professional conduct. Second, this self-control is supported by
> the external surveillance of his conduct by peers . . . Professions in a
> given field constitute a colleague group of equals. Every member of
> the group, but nobody else, is assumed to be qualified to make
> professional judgements.[39]

As an advocate of professional autonomy for publicly employed
physicians as well as the smaller group of private practitioners, the SMA
under Knutson often found itself in opposition to the health care
reform aspirations of the governing Social Democrats. Though Knutson's
confrontation politics were initially successful in stalling some reform
efforts, they contributed significantly to the deterioration of relations
between the SMA and government. These strained relations were soon
translated into telling policy defeats on issues dear to Swedish
physicians. Of monumental importance were the increases in the
numbers of medical students admitted to Swedish medical schools
during the 1950s. Also, the specialty accreditation controversy of the

early 1960s touched directly on the central facets of professional control referred to above (see Chapter 5).

The SMA was charged with representation of its members' interests in at least two important stages of the health decision-making process: formulation or review of policy, and collective bargaining with public employers. Clearly, the SMA under Knutson had become ineffectual in the first of these stages. Further, the profession could expect a continuation of aggressive health policy given the exclusively Social-Democratic composition of the cabinets of the 1960s. Partly because of these considerations, but partly because he had failed to remain abreast of changes in SMA membership attitudes, Knutson resigned in 1962.

Knutson's resignation opened the door to the creation of a new and more productive image for the association as well as a more congenial relationship with government health authorities. The direction in which the medical association leadership was moving represented an abandonment of the 'free professional model' and an emphasis on the collective bargaining role of the SMA. According to the SYLF (Swedish Association of Junior Physicians) chairman Hjern, the new sentiment was to view the practice of medicine as one qualified profession among many. Blurring the distinctions between 'work' and 'profession', the new SMA image was that of a modern 'white-collar trade union'. The Seven Crowns Reform provided the medical leadership with an excellent opportunity to institutionalise this change, but this new sentiment was by no means universally shared by SMA members. Consequently, association leaders could not openly participate in the reform process, though they could benefit greatly from the content of the reform.

Government–SMA Contacts

On 17 December 1968, eleven days after the Ministry's initial reform package was introduced, leading representatives of the SMA were publicly informed by Minister Aspling of plans to install a new flat rate payment system for ambulatory care. The flat rate was to be tentatively set at about five crowns and physicians' fees were not to exceed this amount.[40]

The SMA representatives replied that faced with such low-cost outpatient care the income possibilities of the private practitioners would be adversely affected, and that, as a consequence, these physicians would have to refer the more complicated cases to the public facilities. This effect, plus increased utilisation due to low cost, would increase queues and time pressures for the already overworked physicians in understaffed hospital outpatient departments.

A second meeting took place on 22 January 1969, at a time when the SCR had practically been decided, but the information released was hardly more extensive.[41] It was not until the memorandum of the ministry outlining the reform proposals was passed on to the SMA in early February 1969, that physicians were informed of plans to remove them from all financial transactions and allow hospitals to collect fees from patients directly. This new rule did not preclude fee-for-service payment, and in March 1969, the SMA asked its members to consider the various forms of physician's compensation available.[42]

Though the public record indicated that they were only cursorily informed, the leading representatives of the SMA seemed to be aware of the proposal's consequences.[43] In an article in *Läkartidningen*, the SMA leadership explained that the association had practically no chance to influence the decision of the public employers. Citing the formal legal regulation that left these kinds of employment conditions up to the employers, it pointed out that 'the medical association can consequently not negotiate the question whether or not the physicians should receive their compensation through payments from the patients'.[44] This disavowal of influence can be considered as an indication that the SMA intended to avoid open conflict with the employers over the direct payment proposal. It was not yet totally clear, however, that compensation would come in the form of full salary.

Conflict Within the SMA

By the 1960s, the SMA was an organisation riddled with internal conflict. Perhaps the most important source of that conflict was the unjust and unequal income profile that had developed among physicians, especially among hospital physicians. All Swedish hospital doctors received a basic salary for inpatient hospital services, but some were allowed to accrue additional fee-for-service income for treatment of outpatients in the hospital ambulatories. Doctors in paediatrics, psychiatry, neurology and neurosurgery, and some other specialties often earned considerably less than their colleagues in other fields. Income problems related to technological development were also important sources of conflict. This income distribution problem cut across the horizontal specialty lines as well. The chief and assistant chief physicians, by rank and seniority, generally monopolised outpatient work and the extra income it provided. Hence, the junior doctors were often left with only their salary income.

Many senior hospital physicians objected to the old system because their routine outpatient work provided economic rewards but also consumed too much of their time. This created a conflict between professional status and personal satisfaction on the one hand and income on the other. Routine duties in outpatient departments provided extra income but diminished the time and effort spent in qualified specialty work from which physicians gained intra-professional status and personal satisfaction.

The expansion of the delivery system and the increased diversification and specialisation of the medical profession had increased conflict potential and widened differences within the medical association. By the late 1960s the professional unity that had contributed to the defeat of the Höjer reform two decades earlier had become seriously eroded. The problematic issue of *totallön* preoccupied the SMA in 1968, producing considerable strain within the association. The internal conflict over compensation questions was quite vocal, active and often took the form of formal competitive debate, with teams travelling the country to debate the pros and cons of each compensation alternative.

In 1968 the CCF had approached the SMA with a proposal for full salary and working hour regulation for specialists at Stockholm's Annex Hospitals and at the Vetlanda Hospital in southern Sweden. By mid-1968, the Executive Committee of the SMA had decided that *totallön* was an alternative worthy of consideration and had agreed to partake in these pilot 'salary-only' programmes. This was not an easy decision. The question had been hotly disputed within the SMA, and was finally decided by a delegate meeting in June 1968. The debate became so heated that a vote of no-confidence was demanded, but the SMA Executive Committee was vindicated by a slim three-vote margin (45–42) in an election where about 25 per cent of the assembly abstained. Hans Österberg, chairman of the private practitioner group (SPLF) later called the decision to negotiate 'a most important collapse of the battle-front'.[45]

His accusation led to a bitter exchange in *Läkartidningen* with SYLF chairman Bo Hjern, who pointed out that the so-called Vetlanda agreement was a one-year experiment with the new wage and employment conditions designed to gain information and experience with the system, to facilitate a rational decision on the matter, and to avoid repetition of previous conflicts.[46] To this Österberg replied:

If one is aware of the fact that there are public employers who are

convinced that all employed physicians should be salaried within a
few years, there is very little cause to call the agreement an
experiment, something one could later get away from . . . It is more
honest to say that this has come to stay and will include all
employed physicians.[47]

Though the issue was highly controversial, the outcome of the
conflict was acknowledgement and confirmation of the Executive
Committee's policies. Clearly, a kind of 'taboo' had been broken, in so
far as the SMA would consider full salary and working hour regulation
a negotiable alternative.

The Social Affairs Ministry's official memorandum on the Seven
Crowns Reform came just before SYLF's annual meeting in March
1969, and the issue totally dominated the meeting. The SMA
circulated the Ministry's memorandum among its approximately 70
subgroups and, on the basis of their replies, wrote the SMA's *remiss*
answer to the ministry.

The *remiss* statement did not reject the proposals out of hand, and
professed general agreement with the reform's goals of facilitating
access to health care and to reducing costs for patients. The Medical
Association, however, believed that the SCR proposals would achieve
exactly the opposite of these intentions. Instead, they warned it
would result in increased costs for the chronically ill and patients in
long-term care as well as for those who needed repeated minor
therapeutic services which had been cheaper under the old system.
The SMA pointed out that the expected steering effects from
inpatient to outpatient care were uncertain and had not been
researched. Further, the association believed it likely that queues
would grow and physicians would have much less time per patient. The
adverse affects on private practitioners who were faced with such low-
cost public health care delivery were strongly emphasised. The SMA
demanded a postponement of the plans, more extensive research and
careful preparations, and offered its services for these tasks. It
concluded:

These proposals cannot, in their present form, be the basis of the
intended reform. The proposals should be improved considerably
and be backed with documentations and data on the important
issues.[48]

When the *remiss* procedure to the memorandum was completed, it
became clear that the SMA was virtually alone in its negative stance.

The general response was overwhelmingly positive, though the employers' organisations (SAF and SHIO) suggested that the reform should be financed by an increase in the employees' contribution to the insurance fund. Other *remiss* statements expressed the wish that the reform should go further, and inclusion of the private practitioners was favoured strongly by the union confederations TCO and LO, the insurance authorities, the Board of Social Welfare and the communes. The pensioner's organisation, backed by LO and TCO, suggested totally free inpatient care.

These proposals were once again strongly rejected by the county councils and the other members of the reform alliance. It was clear that the negotiated compromise would not be upset by unwrapping the entire package in order to fulfil these demands.

Apparently, the SMA *remiss* answer was a formality, representing compliance with some of the more militant rank-and-file expectations of proper behaviour rather than a real effort to slow the reform. Regardless, the overwhelmingly positive response of the other *remiss* writing bodies removed responsibility for the reform from the shoulders of the medical leadership. Seen in this light, the SMA call for delay seems but a symbolic gesture.

In May 1969, the SMA Executive Committee prepared and distributed among its sub-organisations a confidential paper which dealt with the medical profession's situation and options under the Seven Crowns Reform and outlined alternatives and positions for negotiation with the public employers.[49]

It appears that this and other SMA strategies were informed by a bit of reconaissance work done by some of the medical leaders. Bo Hjern, then chairman of SYLF, hosted dinner meetings with the reformers to gain information vital to the interests of the profession. In this manner, Hjern and others were informed about reform plans and thus were aided in praparations for their all-out effort at the collective bargaining stage of the Seven Crowns Reform. The meetings also represented a symbolic gesture of limited solidarity between the medical leadership and public health authorities uncharacteristic of the Knutson period. Though much information was gained, it appears that the medical leadership chose not to inform the rank-and-file of the profession of the government's plans, but rather allowed the reformers to control the timing and content of announcements regarding the plans for the reform.

They did try, however, to prepare the profession for the remuneration change to come and it seems that the leadership was well aware that *totallön* was on the reform agenda. Though a number of possible compensation structures were described and discussed, the paper distributed by the SMA Executive Committee left no doubt that the negotiations would centre on the question of full salary and working time regulation. The paper even indicated, though not expressly, that *totallön* was the most advantageous solution for the profession, and that the Executive Committee favoured its introduction.

One of the advantages the paper emphasised was the opportunity to equalise incomes within the profession, while fee-for-service payment would perpetuate income differences. The level of incomes, traditionally thought to be higher under fee-for-service compensation, would not depend so much on the compensation system as on the price the public employers were willing to pay for the introduction of the salary-only compensation plans. The paper pointed out that with increasing numbers of physicians and available positions in the delivery system, fee-for-service would, in the future, not guarantee the same income levels as in the past. This could only be achieved through high salary levels and regulated working hours.

The Executive Committee also warned that it could not guarantee all physicians' incomes at as high a level as before. In order to raise some of the lower ones, some of the top incomes would have to be cut. It was, however, pointed out that physicians could temporarily receive individual compensation for income losses (*personlig avlösning*) as a special concession from the public employers, but only in return for SMA acceptance of the *totallön* proposal.

As a whole, the paper clearly indicated a change in attitude among the SMA leaders, who by now regarded themselves more as representatives of a type of white-collar union than a 'free' professional interest group. *Totallön* was regarded as the optimal solution in regard to income levels, future security and working conditions. Even though the problems of the private practitioners were evaluated at some length, their interests no longer dominated the SMA.

Shortly before the June SMA conference where this internal paper was to be discussed, SYLF produced an answer to these confidential considerations which was to show clearly how close SYLF's position and that of the SMA leadership really had become.[50] SYLF backed the *totallön* system openly, warning that such willingness could only be bought at the expense of working time regulation and the best possible employment and income conditions. Their written response, in fact, centred on tactical guidelines for the expected negotiations, guidelines which seem to have been followed rather closely by the SMA in the tough and bitter negotiations that ensued.

With the proposals for the Seven Crowns Reform on the docket of
the *Riksdag* in September, negotiations between the SMA and the public
employers finally began and the public employers presented their
proposal for a full salary remuneration system. This was described by
the SMA as a 'surprise move' and a special delegate conference was
called to decide what the association's reaction should be.[51] An article
in the association's journal pointed out that the 'salary-only' decision
of the employers must be considered a very serious expression of their
intent.[52] Though it was not accepted as the final word, little hope was
expressed of changing the employers' decision.

At a special meeting to decide on these obviously expected proposals,
SMA leaders gained unanimous support for their negotiation goals and
strategy. In general, these were guidelines worked out on the basis of
SYLF's response to the confidential paper of the Executive Committee.
A confrontation on 'matters of principle' did not take place.

Through October and November the *Riksdag* debates and the
negotiations between the SMA and the public employers were carried
on concurrently. They were accompanied by a late and final crescendo
of warnings and criticisms from physicians all over Sweden in almost
every daily paper. The SMA leadership came under heavy fire once
more when a senior clinician, in an article in *Läkartidningen*,
demanded a general referendum on compensation issues, claiming that
the leadership had lost contact with the members of the Association
and had misjudged and misinterpreted, if not disregarded, the real
opinion within the Association.[53] The Executive Committee reacted
with a sharp and firm statement, rejecting the 'utopian idea' of a
referendum, especially in this case, since the issues were too complex
and complicated to be decided in that manner. In regard to the more
general problem of decision-making within the Association, the
Executive Committee claimed that participatory structures and
opportunities were sufficient for those who really took an active
interest in SMA policies:

> Those who do not take advantage of participation processes have by
> their own free will given up their opportunities to influence policies
> and decisions of the Association.[54]

Conclusion

We have attempted to elucidate the complex nexus of issues, tactics and
circumstances that led to the Seven Crowns Reform. The negotiations
were set in a context of increased demand for health services at a time
of skyrocketing service costs. These pressures impacted most directly on

the county councils, and consequently the CCF moved to begin negotiations by instructing hospitals to raise inpatient fees by 100 per cent. This tactic was designed to increase cost coverage of hospital expenses, reduce the attractiveness of inpatient care, and more importantly to facilitate remedial action related to other deficiencies in the health care system. Because of the interrelated nature of health systems, alterations in one area may have significant consequences for other areas of the system. This was especially true of the composite insurance/direct service delivery system characteristic of Sweden in the 1960s, and it was precisely this interrelatedness which the CCF sought to exploit. By demanding increased inpatient fees, the County Council Federation may have induced the government to undertake more widespread and comprehensive reform.

Though the CCF was undoubtedly responsible in part for the timing and content of the reform, we must not overemphasise its role. The decision to raise inpatient fees may have forced the reform package on the political agenda, but it did not dictate the terms and conditions of the subsequent negotiations. The problems and proposals were issues of long standing whose time had come. No amount of clever political manipulation or backroom manoeuvring by the CCF could have brought about the reform in a hostile economic, social or political context. Cost economics demanded systematic reform while the socio-political situation was dominated by the sentiment of equality. Many of the reform proposals of the late 1960s and early 1970s were influenced by the reports of the SAP's Working Group on Equality and publications of the Low Income Commission, which pointed out that little progress had been made towards income equalisation between blue-collar and white-collar workers with university training and other workers.[55]

The Social Democrats were under pressure to develop political support for the parliamentary elections of 1968 and articulated the 'equality policy' towards that goal. Against this backdrop, the demands of the county councils would have proved embarrassing to the SAP had they not been accompanied by other measures. Taken alone, increased inpatient fees constituted exactly the type of regressive scheme against which the Low Income Commission had warned. Coupled with increased benefits for pensioners, the new outpatient payment system, the equalisation and regulation of physicians' incomes, and the provision that new monies would come from the employers' contributions to the insurance fund, the Federation's demand was turned into a political bonus for the governing party.

Undoubtedly, the atypical decision-making process which brought about the Seven Crowns Reform diminished the ability of opponents among the medical profession to solidify their opposition. A unified medical profession could possibly have blocked or seriously diluted the statutory reform which preceded and opened the door for *totallön*. We find it unlikely that the local and national health authorities would have risked a medical strike by imposing a new remuneration system on an unsuspecting medical profession by governmental fiat.

Granting the validity of these last comments places great importance on the preferences and responses of the medical profession in general and the medical leadership in particular as factors leading to the reform. First, as alluded to above, the composition and attitudes of the medical profession had undergone considerable change in the decades following the unsuccessful Höjer reform. These shifts were precipitated by a rapid increase in the number of medical schools (from three in 1947 to six in 1970) and the concomitant increase in the size of entering medical classes. The increased output of medical schools was absorbed primarily by the hospital sector, where most junior doctors were compensated on a full salary basis.

Further, the demise of fee-for-service and the introduction of a *totallön* system were supported by other groups among physicians and hospital workers for a variety of reasons. Perhaps of greatest importance were the great differences in incomes between different specialties. Figure 6.1 portrays these serious income differentials for one group of physicians in the medical hierarchy of the public hospitals, the chief physicians. Clearly, clinical chemists, pathologists, X-ray specialists, and ear, nose and throat specialists were compensated at a much higher rate than colleagues in other specialties. Most of these differences obtained because of fee-for-service outpatient work rather than from salary differentials. This unfortunate income distribution created serious morale problems in the hospitals and reduced the unity of interests and sentiments among publicly-employed physicians. Another dimension of the morale problem existed because the highly skilled and experienced chief doctors had to devote much of their time to relatively minor outpatient work and the administrative duties associated with it rather than the more specialised inpatient care for which their training qualified them. The payment system in operation before the reform worked against the preferences of many of the chief physicians who received the greatest economic benefit from it.

Also, the Swedish health system has been characterised by relatively low physician/patient ratios. In combination with the hospital-intensive nature of the system, this low ratio made for rather long working hours.

Figure 6.1: Composition of Average Annual Income of Chief Physicians by Specialties, Before and After the SCR

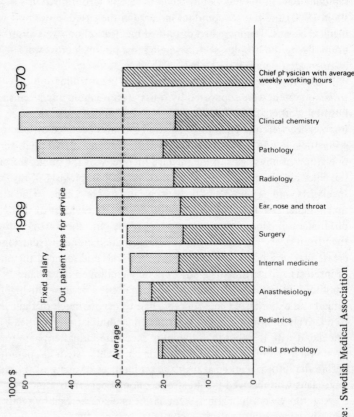

Source: Swedish Medical Association

Swedish doctors worked considerably longer hours than most other public employees and were not always compensated accordingly. Considering the high marginal tax rates on extra income, longer working hours often had little pay-off in real income. These conditions combined to make salary-only compensation and regulated working hours an attractive alternative to the supplemental fee-for-service plan.

It is painfully evident that the medical leadership faced very serious obstacles to the performance of their policy-making and collective bargaining roles in the late 1960s. What was needed was some strategy by which the conflicting goals of establishing congenial relations with public health authorities and diminishing internal conflict could be simultaneously served. Yet even in the face of strong and widespread support for remuneration reform, they could not openly participate in the reform deliberations. It appears that the leadership had been waiting for, even soliciting, outside help to settle their internal differences in a manner that would facilitate closer relations with the national and local authorities. The Seven Crowns Reform, with its deviant decision-making process, provided exactly the vehicle to accomplish these two important leadership goals.

By meeting with officials of the Social Affairs Ministry and the public employers, the SMA leaders, either tacitly or overtly, demonstrated that they could co-operate with ambitious reform aspirations. By not making the information gained in these meetings available to the rank-and-file of the profession, they allowed the reform to progress unhindered. Surely, this strategy was designed to facilitate future participation in health policy-making.

Besides promoting a rapprochement with government, the avoidance of open consultation had the additional benefit of placing primary responsibility for the statutory stage of the Seven Crowns Reform squarely on the public health officials. In this manner, the medical leadership could reap the benefits of the substance of the reform while accepting little responsibility for its formulation. As events occurred, the SMA could present the statutory changes as the dictates of an overly zealous reform coalition, demand further study in their *remiss* answer, and be assured that the content of the reform would facilitate future professional unity with little fear of endangering their own positions in the organisation.

From the perspective of the SMA leadership, the Seven Crowns Reform provided an opportunity to solidify and institutionalise the new role that had been developing since the resignation of Knutson. The behaviour of the leadership was intended to obtain the best possible employment conditions for public physicians in the context of a rapidly changing health sector. With the equalisation of incomes among the various specialties, the issues which had divided the profession were diminished. And professional unity on compensation issues is an important resource in collective bargaining negotiations.

We have described a reorganisation of relationships and institutions which produced no clear losers and with potential benefits to all. What remains to be seen is the impact of these revisions on the health care consumer. Only then will the final verdict on the Seven Crowns Reform be in.

Notes

1. For descriptions of the 'normal' Swedish policy process, see e.g., Thomas J. Anton, 'Policy-Making and Political Culture in Sweden', *Scandinavian Political Studies*, vol. 4 (1969); Lennart Hörnlund, 'Historical, Cultural and Social Characteristics', in *The Swedish Health Services System, Lectures from the A.C.H.A.'s Twenty-Second Fellows Seminar, Stockholm, 1969* (American College of Hospital Administrators, Chicago, 1971), p. 1.

2. The reform has two main parts, the revision of National Law No. 381 (General Insurance) and No. 242 (Medical Care).

3. For the USA see, e.g., David Hyde and the editorial board of the Yale Law Journal, 'The A.M.A.: Power, Purpose and Politics in Organized Medicine', *The Yale Law Journal*, vol. 63, no. 7 (1954); also Robert Alford, *Health Care Politics* (University of Chicago Press, Chicago, 1975). For England see, e.g., Rosemary Stevens, *Medical Practice in Modern England* (Yale University Press, New Haven, 1966).

4. Vicente Navarro, *National and Regional Health Care Planning in Sweden*, DHEW publication No. (NIH) 74-240 (Government Printing Office, Washington, D.C., 1975), pp. 10–15.

5. Rolf Ejvegård, *Landstingsförbundet-Organisation, Beslutsfattande, Forhallande till Staten* (Landstingsförbundet-publication, Stockholm, 1973), p. 79.

6. Ibid., p. 88.

7. Arnold J. Heidenheimer, Hugh Heclo and Carolyn Teich Adams, *Comparative Public Policy: The Politics of Social Choice in Europe and America* (St Martin's, New York, 1975).

8. Sven Svenson, *I Maktens Labyrinter* (Grafisk, Stockholm, 1968), p. 83.

9. 'Sjukhus och Öppen Vård', SOU, 1963:21, p. 162.

10. For more detailed analysis and description of the co-ordination of labour policies and health care policies, see Stig Winzer, *Landstingen och Staten*, Kommunalforskningsgruppen, Avahandlingsserien 26, Umea 1971, and also Assar Lindbeck, *Swedish Economic Policy* (University of California Press, Berkeley, 1974).

11. Heidenheimer's formulation, *Comparative Public Policy*, p. 23. He also makes some interesting comparisons between the USA, the UK and Sweden on hospital development. See also on this Odin W. Anderson, *Health Care: Can There Be Equity? The United States, Sweden and England* (John Wiley & Sons, New York, 1972), p. 122.

12. Gunnar Wennström, 'Training of Health Care Workers in the Swedish Medical Care System', *Annals of the New York Academy of Science*, vol. 166 (1969), p. 986.

13. Navarro, *National and Regional Health Care Planning in Sweden*, pp. 18–30.

14. SOU 1963:21, 'Sjukhus och Öppen Vård', p. 17 and *passim*.

15. Ibid., p. 165.

16. *Landstingsnytt*, 54 (1967):11, p. 10.

17. *Landstingsnytt*, 4 (1969):16, pp. 4–10; reprints of the speeches.

18. Ibid. See also *Svenska Dagbladet*, 11 June 1969, pp. 2 and 9 (Leader: 'Sträng or Rexed?'); *Dagens Nyheter*, 10 June 1969, p. 12 (Leader: 'Sträng-Rexed totally opposed on future health care!').

19. Donald Hancock, Gideon Sjoberg (eds.), *Politics in the Post-Welfare State – Response to the New Individualism* (Columbia University Press, New York, 1972), p. 140.

20. Ejvegård, *Landstingsförbundet-Organisation*, pp. 379–83.

21. Theodore R. Marmor and David Thomas, 'Doctors, Politics and Pay Disputes: "Pressure Group Politics" Revisited', *British Journal of Political Science*, vol. 2, no. 4 (October 1972), p. 437.

22. Arthur Engel, 'Regionsjukvården', SOU, 1958:26.

23. Navarro, *National and Regional Health Care Planning in Sweden*, p. 5.

24. *Swedish Medical Care in the 1980's – Ways and Means* (Federation of Swedish County Councils, Stockholm, 1973), p. 15.

25. 'Den Öppna Läkarvården i Riket', SOU 1948:14, p. 225.

26. 'Översyn av sjukförsäkringens återbäringstaxa', SOU 1967:4.

27. SOU 1963:21, 'Sjukhus och Öppen Vård'.

28. Örebro County Council *remiss* answer to the Hultström-report, signed by Nilsson and Allard; A 60 1 A: c 1, 16 October 1967.

29. CCF's *remiss* answer to RFV report, Dnr 1942:69, 20 January 1970, p. 11.

30. 'Förmåner och Avgifter i sluten sjukvård mm', SOU 1967:63, p. 52.

31. Ibid., *passim*.

32. CCF's *remiss* answer to SOU 1967:63, Dnr 27/68, 1 July 1968, p. 3.

33. SOU 1967:63, p. 89.

34. Former Social Desk director Sverre Royen and CCF director Bengt Olsson in interviews with Ben Klingeberg, September 1976.

35. Figures are from the CCF-memorial 188/68 and Ejvegård, *Landstings-förbundet-Organisation*, pp. 377–9.

36. SOU 1967:63, p. 87.

37. According to the Social Desk director at the CCF, Sverre Royen.

38. Theodore Caplow, *The Sociology of Work* (University of Minnesota Press, Minneapolis, 1954), p. 101.

39. Peter M. Blau and W. Richard Scott, *Formal Organizations* (Chandler Publishing Company, San Francisco, 1962), pp. 62–3.

40. Internal SMA memorandum to the Executive Committee, 1 January 1969, U 5/69.

41. Internal SMA memorandum to the Executive Committee, 22 January 1969.

42. *Läkartidningen*, Leader, 66 (1969):10, p. 978.

43. Former SMA chairman Professor Bartley, interview in *Läkartidningen*, 70 (1973):1, p. 35.

44. *Läkartidningen*, 66 (1969):10, p. 978.

45. *Läkartidningen*, 65 (1968):36, p. 3444.

46. *Läkartidningen*, 63 (1968):37; 38; 39.

47. *Läkartidningen*, 65 (1968):39, p. 3764.

48. SMA *remiss* answer to the SCR memorandum of the Ministry of Social Affairs, stencil, U 91/69, 20 April 1969, p. 17.

49. 'Fackliga konsekvenser av förslag om enhetstaxa', stencil, F 55/69.

50. 'SYLF's fackliga program inför 1969/70 års förhandlingar', stencil, Dnr 21/21, 2 June 1969.

51. *Läkartidningen*, Leader, 66 (1969):41, p. 4166.

52. Ibid., p. 4167.

53. *Läkartidningen*, 66 (1969):47, p. 4826. Senior Clinician E. Sundmark, ' 'Har vara förhandlarna fått ratt grepp på opinionsläget?' ('Have Our Negotiators Gotten the Right Feel for the General Opinion?').

54. 'Folkomröstning-Nej!', *Läkartidningen*, 66 (1969):48, p. 4870.

55. Alva Myrdal, *Towards Equality: The Alva Myrdal Report to the Swedish Social Democratic Party* (Prisma, Stockholm, 1971), pp. 24, 34.

COMMENTARY ON PART THREE

Bo Hjern

I have worked within the Swedish Medical Association for many years
— first as a delegate and during the past five years as a staff employee.
The Swedish Medical Association celebrated its 75th anniversary in
1978. When we look back in this connection on what has happened
during the past 75 years we are forced to note that very little has been
written about the history of the association. It is quite a remarkable
fact that, while we ourselves have hardly bothered to take an interest in
the role of the association regarding the development of medical care,
people from across the Atlantic have taken the trouble to put together
facts about the association and its way of acting during different
periods of time.

Arnold Heidenheimer has made a very interesting analysis of the
development since the Second World War. The first question is then: is
it correct? Yes, I believe that on the whole it is a true account of what
has happened, at least after 1957, which is a period I myself can verify.
In 1948, when Höjer presented his reform regarding ambulant care, I
had not even started studying medicine.

The second question is: is it a true analysis? I believe that it is, but
perhaps it does not give the whole truth. The truth is always a very
complex thing and must be looked for on several levels.

Heidenheimer uses a centre-periphery theory, where he can identify
relationships between actors and institutions, which are positioned at
the centre, middle rings and periphery of three discs — a political disc,
a professional status disc, and a health care resource disc. This is an
interesting model and with the aid of this he can explain many events,
but it is also a dangerous model, which can tempt one to dramatise
events. There is a tendency in his analysis to give persons and
organisations a greater importance than they had in reality. Naturally
I would like to represent a very strong organisation, but in all honesty,
I must admit that I am not sure that the SMA in reality has played such
an important role on all occasions as Heidenheimer would have it.

I personally would especially like to stress the fact that there is a
strong connection between the development of health and medical care
and the development of the rest of Swedish society. The endeavours
towards increased security and equality that have characterised Sweden

since the Second World War have greatly influenced the development of medical care. The same can be said of the demands for decentralisation and co-determination.

Among the events that Heidenheimer has studied, there are a few which I would like to comment on further.

The first is described as 'Doctor Knutson's removal' in 1962. It is true that we were a group of young delegates, who in the beginning of the 1960s conscientiously worked to bring about a change in medical association policy and believed that a change of chairman was a necessary part of that 'modernisation'. It was not, however, a question of direct confrontation or a fight for power. The change did not happen in a particularly dramatic way. The events of the 1950s, which had strained the relations between the association and the government, to some extent prompted our actions. The statutory regulation of specialist competence was one of these, but even more important was the question of medical manpower assessment. Yet there was a basic difference as regards the view of the purpose and role of the medical association in society.

Dag Knutson is a man with high ideals who has performed great services for physicians. He worked untiringly for several years for what he considered to be right for the medical profession and for medical care. To him, perhaps the most important purpose of the medical association was to preserve the high professional and ethical standards of the profession. In a letter to me, he recently described how he looked upon his work in the association:

My main interests were education – further training, specialist training, co-ordination of training of private practitioners and district medical officers and preservation of the freedom of physicians as professionals in their relations with patients, a freedom under the responsibility expressed by the ethical rules. In short, the preserved and constantly improved quality of the medical profession. Of course there were also organizational problems – those of the medical profession and above all those of medical care – within the country and in Scandinavia. Maybe my interests were less connected with questions of money, although I don't want to deny that I, as a young delegate, fought for the improvement of indecently bad conditions and was also very happy to see the results of those efforts. However, I don't want to be described as a pioneer of the general philosophy of to-day – less work, more spare time

and more money – especially considering the increasing lack of
demand for quality in all fields.

For those of us who represented the young physicians at that time, it
was more natural to look upon the medical profession as one qualified
profession among many others, and the medical association as an
organisation, certainly ready to accept its responsibility for the
development of medical care, but with the principal purpose of taking
charge of the interests of its members. We felt no need to preserve a
distinction between 'work' and 'profession', and we wanted to turn the
medical association into something more like a modern trade union.
You can hardly say that we were opposed by Knutson, but because he
was a strong and dominating man it took some time before he
understood what was up. Like many other powerful men, he had by
that time become a little isolated. He was not the only one to blame
for this, as the people surrounding him were also responsible to a great
extent. When Knutson realised that there were many members of the
association who wanted a new chairman, he resigned without
objections.

In this context the transfer of specialty accreditation power in 1960
can be regarded as an event of minor importance. In any event, I don't
think that the discussions about the specialist licensing law weakened
the position of the SMA in relation to the political authorities. At the
time, the question caused quite a row, but it all quietened down very
quickly. Further developments have shown that in reality it has been of
great value for the medical profession that there exist rules, sanctioned
by government, for the education of specialists. It has strengthened the
SMA's position in regard to the question of demanding sufficient
numbers of training posts, resources for guidance during the time of
education and organised course activities.

Concerning the question of the number of physicians, there arose
severe clashes of interests, especially in the 1950s. I believe that these
conflicts of opinion were the primary cause of the serious deterioration
of the relations between the SMA and the government. On the other
hand I don't think that the attitude of the association influenced
medical care policy particularly. The government, on the whole, did
not take any notice of the SMA, but rather brought about one increase
after another in student admissions to the medical faculties.

Another matter I would like to comment on is the proposal about
the so-called Seven Crowns Reform. In order to understand the position

the SMA took on this question it is necessary to take the following circumstances into consideration.

First of all, the fee-for-service system had led to great differences in incomes between different specialists. For example, clinical chemists earned more than twice as much as paediatricians. Another thing was that the working hours for doctors were considerably longer than what was normal for other employees in Sweden. Nor did there exist a positive correlation between long working hours and a high income. On the contrary, those with the highest incomes often worked less. A third factor was that the fee-for-service system influenced the division of work within the clinics in a most unhappy way. As fee-for-service was given only within the ambulatory sector and not for inpatient care, the heads of departments had to devote much of their time to comparatively routine work within the ambulatory sector instead of to qualified inpatient care, guiding their junior doctors or taking care of the administrative side of running the clinics. A fourth factor was that the fee-for-service system had become a nuisance in the eyes of other types of health care personnel. As hospital work developed more and more the concept of team-work it seemed unfair and incorrect that the reward for what the whole team had achieved should go into only the doctor's pocket.

The leadership of the SMA had to take all these things into consideration when the proposal for a uniform fee reform was put forward. This reform meant that the fee-for-service system would be discarded and a fixed salary for all doctors would be established. The demands for changed working conditions were put forward mostly by the young doctors, as they could not themselves influence their working conditions and consequently were hit the hardest by the unregulated working hours. But the fact remains that not all the consultants wanted to preserve the fee-for-service system. On the contrary there were large and rapidly growing groups of consultants — for instance anaesthesiologists, neurosurgeons and psychiatrists — who wanted a fixed salary.

When the leadership of the SMA put together all the different arguments for and against the reform, it was finally decided that the fixed salary system would be accepted, but with the expressed condition that it would be combined with regulation of working hours.

In my opinion further development has shown that this was a correct decision to make. At any rate, doctors achieved considerably improved working conditions after the reform. But I am not at all sure that the reform has been to the advantage of the patients. Many of the problems we have today — growing queues of people waiting for medical care, a lack of continuity, shortcomings in the personal care of the patients — undoubtedly derive at least partially from the Seven Crowns Reform.

Finally, a few words are required about the so-called politicisation of medical care. 'The politicisation of the Swedish health system seemed to remain modest', Heidenheimer says. This is quite true if you mean that there have been no major fights between the different political parties concerning the questions of medical care. On the contrary all the so-called medical reforms during the postwar era have been supported by all the political parties. But if by politicisation you mean that the politicians have increased their influence on medical care, then there has been a politicisation. For instance, so-called county council commissioners have been created (*landstingsråd*) in all the county councils during the 1960s and 1970s. The county council managers (*landstingsdirektörer*), who are unpolitical civil servants, used to have much power and influence and they often had a direct and intimate co-operative relationship with the heads of the hospitals. The board of directors for the hospitals, who were politically appointed, often only had to confirm what in reality had been decided already at the employee level. Now that a direct responsibility for the operation of medical care has been put on the county council commissioners, who are politically elected, the political authorities are much closer to the production of services.

A deplorable side effect of this is that the most influential county council politicians can no longer find the time to be members of the Swedish Parliament. The so-called 'County Council party' (*landstings-partiet*) which earlier had great influence in Parliament — does not exist any more. There are very few people in Parliament today who can handle the questions about health and medical care in a proper way. The debates in Parliament about medical care matters are deplorably meagre.

Part Four:

HEALTH EXPENDITURES AND PUBLIC RESOURCE ALLOCATION

7 WHY IS THE SYSTEM SO COSTLY? PROBLEMS OF POLICY AND MANAGEMENT AT NATIONAL AND REGIONAL LEVELS

Jan-Erik Spek

Introduction

In the advanced industrialised countries of the Western world medical care is now widely recognised to be in a severe economic crisis. Statistical data indicate that the proportion of GNP spent on medical care has been steadily growing in all of these countries (with the exception of Japan and Israel).[1] In all of them, the sustained expansion of expenditures for health and medical care has caused great concern. A large array of measures to curb these expenditures, both voluntary and enforced, has been suggested, and some have been implemented. So far, however, no country claims to have found a satisfactory solution to its problems.

A comparison of the available data for different countries reveals no clear relationship between the rate and level of expenditures for medical care and the general character of socialism/liberalism of the system of medical care delivery. Secondly, the problems and perceived symptoms of the economic crisis of medical care in the different countries seem to be of a similar kind. There would appear to be a set of certain fundamental factors operating in all advanced industrialised countries which account for the similarities of the problems and general tendencies.

Among these factors are the ageing of populations, rising popular demand for medical care in conjunction with the abolition of the price mechanism and various sociological factors, the increase in the GNP, the general mode of operation of modern democracy, the general character and functioning of medical research and technology and the professional status and behaviour of doctors. Some of these factors have to be treated as given and exogenous to the system of medical care, in which case the task is to make the system adapt in a suitable way. Other factors are at least potentially under the influence of the actors in the system, in which case the task may in addition be to adjust these factors favourably. In both cases the problem we have to face, as seen from the point of view of the medical care system, is how to get control and how to get efficiency of operation.

In this chapter I intend first to give an account of the evolution of the economic crisis of medical care in Sweden, in retrospect as well as in prospect. I shall try to sketch what I call the 'trap' we are walking into, i.e. the economic constraints in combination with the demographic trends we must face up to. Finally, I present some current problems of policy and management in Sweden. Some of my data and illustrations refer to Gothenburg and western Sweden. Having studied Swedish medical care in general and communicated with analysts and practitioners in the field for several years, I am firmly convinced that the observations from Gothenburg and western Sweden are on the whole good illustrations of current problems in Swedish medical care in general.

Swedish Medical Care — Some Main Institutional Features

Today one can justifiably say that Sweden has a system of socialised medicine; moreover, it is a system based on the concept of need, in contrast to one based on the purchasing power of the individual. Swedish residents are entitled to medical services at very low out-of-pocket prices.

Two main subsystems within Swedish socialised medicine are the social insurance system and the system of medical care delivery. Whereas the social insurance system is highly centralised, decision-making in the medical care delivery system is decentralised in important respects. Twenty-three county councils and three county boroughs (Gothenburg, Malmö and the island of Gotland) are by law responsible for the planning, operation and financing of the system of medical care. Accordingly, they also are empowered to impose a proportional income tax on their residents. In 1976, nearly 80 per cent of the operating expenses of the counties went to medical care. Patients' out-of-pocket fees covered no more than 3 per cent of the operating expenses of the counties.

While virtually the whole system of medical care delivery is now operated by the counties and county boroughs, the central government, for its part, has at its disposal several different types of instruments for influencing the size, structure and functioning of the system. First of all, the state formulates the basic medical care legislation as well as ancillary statutes stipulating the responsibilities and restricting the action of the counties, their main political and administrative bodies and their key administrative and medical officers. The National Board of Health and Welfare is the main agency of the state for the enforcement of the law and statutes and is responsible for

supervising the counties. A related agency, the Medical Services
Liability Council, is responsible for the central medical audit.

In addition to giving subsidies to the counties, the state fixes
patients' fees as well as the compensation to be disbursed to the
counties from the social insurance. The state has the power to accept or
reject designs for new hospital buildings, and in addition the counties
must seek state authorisation to undertake new buildings. The
counties' access to the capital market is of course under state control.
The National Board of Health and Welfare decides on the number of
appointments of physicians in different medical specialties in the
various counties. The state is responsible for the training of physicians
and dentists as well as for the financing of research in these areas. The
state pays certain of the counties and county boroughs for the right to
use their hospitals and resources for medical training and research.

Further, the state has taken the initiative to introduce a
standardised planning system at the county level, making it possible to
compare and aggregate future medical services in the different counties.
The state issues guidelines on desired future developments. On different
occasions during the last ten to fifteen years the Minister of Finance
has strongly emphasised the importance of curbing the expansion of
expenditures for medical care and limiting county tax increases.

Law- and decision-making by the state is almost always preceded by
varying forms of information-gathering from the counties and mutual
influence between the state and the counties (e.g. *remiss* consultation;
cf. Chapter 3). The Federation of Swedish County Councils is the joint
agency of the counties for negotiating and bargaining with the state.
The chairman and chief executive officer of the Federation are
members of the Delegation on Medical Care, a key body within the
Ministry of Social Affairs with respect to planning, setting investment
priorities and determining the number and distribution of appointments
for physicians. The state and the Federation have jointly established the
Planning and Rationalisation Institute of the Health and Social
Services (SPRI).

To sum up, then, decision-making in the social insurance system is
centralised; the state is the supreme decision-maker. In contrast,
decision-making in the system of medical care delivery is decentralised;
the counties (and county boroughs) make the definitive decisions as to
the size, structure and running of medical care. The state, however, lays
down the rules of the game and is in a position to influence the
development and functioning of medical care, in a restrictive or
expansive way. To attempt a metaphor: the state is equipped with both

bit and bridle and carrots, but it is still up to the horse to decide on its movements.

Historical Development

The Public Sector and Resources for Medical Care

The public sector has undergone rapid expansion during the postwar period. Table 7.1 shows that in terms of resource consumption the share of GNP allotted to the public sector has increased from 22.7 per cent in 1960 to 32.0 per cent in 1975. In contrast to this, the share going to private consumption has decreased from 60.7 per cent to 52.2 per cent during the same period. Local government final consumption (i.e. operating expenditures by municipalities and counties) has grown fastest of all public consumption and investment during this time, increasing from 7.9 per cent to 16.4 per cent of GNP.

The financial counterpart of this development is a very marked increase in taxes and social insurance contributions, from 28.7 per cent of GNP in 1960 to 46.9 per cent of GNP in 1975. In addition to expenditures for consumption and investment, these taxes and contributions also cover pensions and cash benefits from the social insurance system and other transfers. As shown in Table 7.1, the proportional personal income taxes of Swedish municipalities and counties represent a steadily increasing share of total taxes and contributions.

Now it should be recalled that the figures in Table 7.1 are calculated at current prices and therefore show the composite result of price and

Table 7.1: Resources for the Swedish Public Sector, 1960–75. Current Prices

	1960	1965	1970	1975
Private consumption (% of GNP)	60.7	57.6	53.9	52.2
Total public consumption and investment (% of GNP)	22.7	25.5	29.8	32.0
Local government consumption (% of GNP)	7.9	8.9	13.4	16.4
Total taxes and social insurance contributions (% of GNP)	28.7	35.0	40.1	46.9
Local government taxes (% of total taxes and social insurance contributions)	22.1	23.4	26.1	26.2

Sources: National accounts; *Översyn av skattesystemet* (SOU 1977:91, Stockholm, 1977), pp. 346–9; and C. J. Åberg, 'Kommunerna i svensk ekonomi', *Ekonomisk Revy*, årg. 34, nr. 8 (1977), pp. 402–8.

Table 7.2: Price Trends, 1960—75 (Average annual percentage increases)

	1960—5	1965—70	1970—5
GNP	4.1	4.6	8.5
Local govt. consumption	7.3	8.2	11.0

Sources: National accounts and C. J. Åberg, 'Den offentliga sektorns kostnadsutveckling', *Ekonomisk Debatt*, vol. 1, no. 8 (1973), pp. 491—6.

real volume increases. Table 7.2 shows the general price level trend (the implicit GNP price index) and the trend for prices in local government consumption. During all three periods local government consumption prices have increased at a significantly higher rate than the general price level.

The figures in Table 7.3 indicate real volume increases in GNP, private consumption and local government consumption. Private consumption volume has been increasing at a steadily slower rate. The volume of local government consumption has increased considerably faster than private consumption during all three periods, especially during 1965—70.

As Table 7.3 indicates, local government consumption has expanded its share of real GNP since the mid-1960s. Calculated in 1968 prices, this share amounted to 10.3 per cent in 1960, 10.3 per cent in 1965, 13.0 per cent in 1970 and 13.9 per cent in 1975. (These figures may be compared with those of the third row in Table 7.1, which are calculated at current prices.)

Operating expenses for medical care comprise the largest, and one of the most rapidly increasing, items among operating expenditures by municipalities and counties, claiming 32 per cent of these expenditures

Table 7.3: Real Volume Increases in GNP, Private Consumption and Local Government Consumption (Average annual percentage increases)

	1960—5	1965—70	1970—5
GNP	5.1	4.0	2.5
Private consumption	4.1	3.2	2.2
Local govt. consumption	5.0	8.9	3.8

Source: K. Knutsson, 'Kommunalekonomiska utvecklingstendenser' in Kommunförbundet, *Om uppföljning och utvärdering av kommunal verksamhet* (Kommunförbundet, Stockholm, 1978), pp. 6—14.

Table 7.4:   Total Public Expenditure for Medical Care in Sweden, 1928–75 (Current Prices)

Year[a]	Total Public Expenditure (Operation & Investment)			Operating as percentage of Total Expenditures	Net Expenditures of Different Public Bodies as % of Total Public Expenditure			
	Kr. mill	Kr. per capita	% of GNP		State[b]	County[c]	Social Ins. Funds[d]	Total
1928	89	15	1.0	87.9	30.3	62.3	7.4	100
1938/39	197	31	1.5	86.5	25.6	59.8	14.6	100
1946	424	63	1.8	85.9	25.1	58.7	16.2	100
1950	722	103	2.2	86.0	24.6	59.7	15.7	100
1955	1,461	200	2.9	87.1	23.9	61.2	14.9	100
1960	2,391	319	3.3	86.9	24.5	60.9	14.6	100
1961	2,687	356	3.4	86.1	24.1	62.2	13.7	100
1962	3,059	404	3.6	85.4	23.1	63.7	13.2	100
1963	3,487	457	3.8	84.1	24.7	63.8	11.5	100
1964	4,085	531	4.0	84.4	27.9	61.5	10.6	100
1965	4,752	611	4.2	83.1	21.7	65.9	12.4	100
1966	5,881	750	4.8	84.2	21.2	67.0	11.8	100
1967	7,037	892	5.3	84.9	19.4	67.9	12.7	100
1968	8,370	1,054	5.9	87.7	18.1	69.3	12.6	100
1969	9,634	1,204	6.3	89.1	21.1	65.8	13.1	100
1970	11,173	1,383	6.6	90.8	18.0	66.4	15.6	100
1971	12,703	1,565	6.9	91.7	17.9	64.0	18.1	100
1972	13,750	1,691	6.9	91.3	16.9	65.0	18.1	100
1973	14,922	1,832	6.8					
1974	18,119	2,216	7.3					
1975	21,761	2,651	7.6					

a. Data on the expenditures of the state refer throughout to central government budget years (e.g. from 1 July 1975 to 30 June 1976 in the last entry).

b. Net expenditures after deduction of patient fees; including grants and subsidies to the counties.

c. Net expenditures after deduction of patient fees, state grants and subsidies and compensation from the social insurance.

d. Payments to counties and households for medical and dental care (including care administered by private practitioners) and drugs.

Sources: National accounts, official medical care statistics and *Hälsovård och öppen sjukvård i landstingsområdena* (SOU 1958:15, Stockholm, 1958), pp. 152–60.

in 1965 and 36 per cent in 1975 (at current prices). Table 7.4 contains key figures on the financial development of Swedish medical care during the period 1928–75. Medical care is here defined in a broad sense as encompassing all kinds of medical services delivered by the state, the counties and county boroughs, including dental and individual preventive health services. The figures include operating as well as investment expenditures. The four columns to the right in Table 7.4 show the distribution of the financial burden between the state, the counties and county boroughs and the social insurance funds.

The data in the third and fourth columns to the left in Table 7.4 are depicted graphically in Figure 7.1. The curves clearly reveal that public expenditures for medical care were of very minor importance in the Swedish economy until after the Second World War. The real acceleration of expenditures occurred about 1960 and continued throughout the decade. The curves indeed give justification to the expression, 'the Gay 'Sixties of Swedish medical care'.

Two observations should be made in connection with Figure 7.1. The first is that by definition the curves do not depict the development of out-of-pocket expenses of households, and therefore the increase of public expenditures in part reflects the gradual socialisation of Swedish medical care. This socialisation, however, was largely completed by the beginning of the 1960s, the only notable act of socialisation after this time being the dental reform of 1974. It may be added that for the year 1975 net out-of-pocket expenses of households amounted to an estimated Kr. 3,060 millions, equivalent to Kr. 370 per capita, or 1.1 per cent of GNP. Adjusting our data on central government expenditures to correspond to the calendar year 1975, we find that total public and private expenditures for medical care in Sweden that year amounted to Kr. 3,000 per capita, or 8.6 per cent of GNP.

Secondly, the figures in Table 7.4 and the curves in Figure 7.1 express the economic development of Swedish medical care in current prices. Price increases in public medical care, like those in local government consumption in general, have been very marked during the 1960s and the first half of the 1970s. The national accounts permit us to trace the development of prices for medical care from 1963 on. Operating expenses have increased on average by 8 per cent annually during the period 1963–70, and 13 per cent during the period 1970–5. This leaves us with average annual volume increases of 7 per cent and 3.5 per cent, respectively, during the two periods. Given a rising share of operating expenses (falling share of investment expenditure, cf. Table 7.4), we find that a rising proportion of the total

Figure 7.1: Total Public Medical Care Expenditures, 1928-75

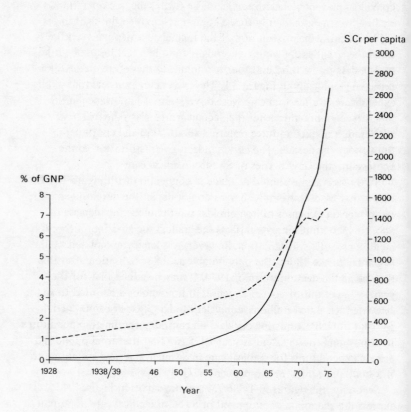

— — — — — Health Expenditures as % of GNP
———— Per Capita Expenditures at Current Prices

expenditures for medical care has had to be devoted to covering price increases in operating expenses.

The rapid growth of medical care expenditures has of course put an increasing financial strain on the counties. County taxes have risen from an average 4.38 per cent of taxable income in 1960 to 12.46 per cent in 1978.

Notes on Morbidity and Mortality

Economic trends are one side of the problem, but any appraisal of the prospects, the 'operating conditions' and the effects of medical care must also take account of data on morbidity and mortality.

There are no regularly published Swedish data which give an unambiguous and comprehensive picture of the trend in morbidity. The social insurance system produces statistics on the number of days of sickness cash benefits and the number of disability pensions paid out. On the basis of these data it is possible to estimate that in 1955 the number of registered days of sickness and disability of individuals aged 16 to 66 years was equivalent to a loss of 7 to 8 per cent of the total number of working hours in Sweden. In 1967 the corresponding figure was 9 to 10 per cent.[2]

Applying the values of the national capital–labour and capital–output ratios in 1955 and 1967, we may infer that in both years the value of GNP loss owing to registered sickness and disability by far exceeded the value of resources allotted to medical care (cf. Table 7.4). Secondly, we note that registered sickness and disability among persons in the 'productive ages' also showed a significant increase (and has continued to increase since then) during a period when the resources for medical care accelerated faster than ever. Several alternative interpretations of these relationships are possible.

Swedish demographic statistics permit the calculation of mortality data as far back as the eighteenth century (Figure 7.2). The most relevant feature of these statistics is the radical decrease in mortality among persons in young and productive ages from the early nineteenth century up to the 1950s. By contrast, during the same period the mortality of elderly persons has remained nearly constant. These two developments show the mechanism of the ageing of populations in the traditional and commonly discussed sense: through decreasing mortality in young and productive age groups a growing proportion of newborn infants live to become 80 years old, but having reached this age, they will have perhaps five years left to live, as has probably been the case for a very long time in the history of mankind.

Figure 7.2: **Mean Life Expectancy at Different Ages from 1751/90 to 1971/75**

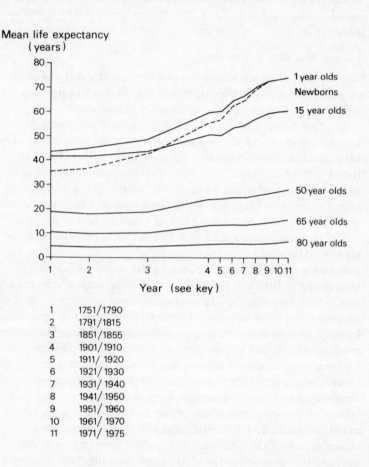

1	1751/1790
2	1791/1815
3	1851/1855
4	1901/1910
5	1911/1920
6	1921/1930
7	1931/1940
8	1941/1950
9	1951/1960
10	1961/1970
11	1971/1975

Source: Official Swedish demographic statistics.

Figure 7.2 reveals that the decrease of mortality among young and 'productive' age groups is slowing down. The figure also shows another very interesting tendency, viz. that for the first time the life-expectancy of octogenarians is increasing. This is a second and quite new kind of ageing of populations. Examining this phenomenon in more detail, we find that the decreasing mortality among the extremely elderly is exclusive to women; Sweden is acquiring a rapidly growing population of aged women.

The significance of a growing number of aged persons for medical care needs is well known. It is clearly documented in data on the number of bed-days per capita in different age groups in Sweden. Several Swedish studies have also noted a very high frequency of serious disease and disability among persons of 80 years and over – again, especially among women. Lindegård, for example, has shown that in Gothenburg during the period 1966–70 persons aged 80 years and over consumed one-third of the total number of bed-days in somatic care. During the same period, terminal care accounted for 25 per cent of the number of bed-days in somatic care.[3]

The facts and developments mentioned here are confirmed in other ways, too. The amount of physical strain required of personnel by the daily care of patients at a somatic nursing home in Gothenburg has been shown to have increased by over 50 per cent between 1968 and 1972.[4] Other nursing homes in Gothenburg have experienced a similar tendency. This development, combined with an increase in the average length of stay at nursing homes, corresponds very well with the pattern of ageing noted above.

The essence of the process described above is a progressive conversion of mortality into morbidity. Meanwhile, the character and composition of morbidity has been changing. In 1920 respiratory and infectious diseases accounted for 32 per cent of the total number of deaths, while circulatory diseases accounted for 19 per cent and malignant tumours 8 per cent. In 1975, only 5 per cent of all deaths were due to respiratory and infectious diseases, whereas 54 per cent died of circulatory diseases and 20 per cent of malignant tumours. As for non-terminal but crippling and disabling disease, the process has resulted in a relative increase in diseases of the nervous and musculo-skeletal systems and psycho-geriatric disease. This changing pattern of morbidity means that medical care to a growing extent has to cope with fatal, chronic and degenerative disease, for which there is rarely any radical therapy, only symptomatic and supportive treatment.

A Note on the Productivity of Medical Care

In Sweden as elsewhere, national accounts contain a certain amount of incommensurability in that data on volumes and prices in the private sector of the economy refer to output (production), whereas the corresponding data for the public sector refer to input (resources). The main reasons for this are that public goods generally have no market prices and that no satisfactory technique for measuring aggregate output of the public sector has been found. Consequently, the data on volumes and prices of local government consumption and medical care presented above refer to inputs.

When discussing the 'cost explosion' of medical care and other branches of the public sector, many authors explicitly or implicitly assume that productivity, i.e. the relation between output volume and input volume, is constant or slowly increasing.[5] With reference to our data, that would mean an average annual increase in output of medical care of at least 7 per cent during the period 1963–70, and at least 3.5 per cent during 1970–5 (cf. p. 187). They also posit that the average cost of output (cost per unit of output) of medical care *at constant (input) prices* has been constant or slowly decreasing during these periods. Assumptions like these are to be seriously questioned. In fact, there is growing evidence that they are false.

One thorough analysis has shown that the cost per case in short-term inpatient somatic care in western Sweden has increased by about 13 per cent per annum during the period 1958–71. The cost per bed-day in long-term somatic care has increased by about 13 per cent per annum, and in inpatient mental care by about 14 per cent per annum during the same period. These rates of increase are measured in current prices. Since the annual rate of increase of input prices can be estimated at about 8 per cent during the same period, this means that the average cost of output at constant prices has increased by about 5 per cent per annum.[6]

The main input factor in medical care is personnel, which accounts for about 70 per cent of full cost. Calculations for Gothenburg show that during the period 1970–5 the number of personnel per case in short-term inpatient somatic care has increased by 4.5 per cent annually. The number of personnel per bed-day in long-term inpatient somatic care has increased by 3 per cent annually, and in inpatient mental care by 8 per cent per annum during the same period.[7] National statistics and data for other parts of Sweden suggest that these figures are quite representative of Swedish medical care.

This suggests a considerable decline in the productivity of Swedish medical care during the 1960s and the first half of the 1970s. A conceivable objection to such a conclusion is that there has been a steady increase in the quality of medical care during this period of time and that our measures — being ratios per case and per bed-day — take no due account of this. Most observers of medical care certainly agree that — in a more strictly clinical and medico-technical sense, at least — there has been a steady increase in quality. It is open to doubt, however, whether the value of this quality increase outweighs the increase in costs and resource-use per unit of output shown here. A final verdict on this must be based on subjective values as well as thorough empirical evaluation and follow-up studies of medical care.

Present and Future Developments

Economic Constraints and Demographic Trends — A Sketch of the 'Trap'

As noted above, the 1960s witnessed a rapid general expansion of the Swedish economy with sharp real increases in GNP. The public sector, particularly local government consumption, has steadily increased its share of GNP, continuing to do so during the first half of the 1970s. Operating expenses for medical care have been the largest and one of the most rapidly increasing items in local government consumption. Meanwhile, the rate of increase of real GNP has slowed down markedly during 1970–5, with private consumption volume increasing at a steadily slower rate during the whole period, 1960–75. Further, we have noted a progressive conversion of mortality into morbidity in connection with the ageing of the population, with consequent increases in the burden on inpatient clinics.

In this section I will discuss the conditions under which Swedish medical care will be operating in terms of economic constraints and demographic trends. First, let us consider the economic constraints.

In the late 1960s, when the expansion of Swedish medical care became a topic of public debate, figures were presented that purported to show that if the rate of expansion of the 1960s were to continue 'forever', the whole of GNP would consist of medical care at about the turn of the century, or half the population would be employed in medical care, and the like. While these extrapolations were based on naïve and simplistic — and sometimes formally incorrect — calculations, they nevertheless pointed out the obvious fact that the rate of increase of the 1960s could not go on forever. In fact, common sense was enough to enable one to see that a turning-point in the rate of increase of resources for medical care must come during the 1970s. Today, the fiscal constraints on medical care as well as other branches of the public sector are quite obvious.

As already indicated, the rate of increase of the Swedish GNP slowed down considerably at the beginning of the 1970s. It can now be estimated that for the whole period 1970—9 the annual rate of increase of the GNP will be about 1.5 per cent, compared to 5.1 per cent during 1960—5 and 4.0 per cent 1965—70. The GNP increase during 1970—9 will also be considerably slower than the 3.4 per cent annual growth rate experienced by the other OECD countries.[8]

The stagnation (combined with inflation = 'stagflation') of the Swedish economy became quite evident from 1974 on. From 1974 to 1977, real GNP did not increase at all, and from 1976 to 1977 the Swedish GNP in fact decreased for the first time in postwar history. The volume of industrial production declined by 7 per cent from 1974 to 1977.

Swedish exports amount to about 30 per cent of GNP. Slackening international demand for various traditionally key Swedish products (e.g. steel, paper and pulp and ship-building) in combination with uncompetitive Swedish export prices in international currency and an economic policy of domestic stimulation gave rise to large deficits in the balance of payments on current account during the period 1975—7.

The reasons for and consequences of the stagnation of the Swedish economy have, of course, been hotly debated.

In 1978, the Ministry of Economic Affairs issued a document on the development of the Swedish economy from 1977 to 1983: *Långtidsutredningen 1978*, here referred to as 'the LU-document'. It also contains a sketch of the long-term development up to the turn of the century.[9]

The main alternative for the medium-term development of the Swedish economy outlined in the LU-document assumes a balanced current account in the balance of payments and full employment of labour and capital in the mid-1980s. This alternative is based on a rapid increase of exports, which in turn presupposes a marked increase in international demand for Swedish products and a considerable improvement in relative export prices for such products. The improvement in relative prices in turn requires that the annual increase in labour productivity in industry will rise from 5.8 per cent in 1970—4 and 0 per cent 1974—7 to 7.2 per cent in 1977—83. Two-thirds of this accelerated rate of increase is assumed to consist of an underlying 'normal' rate of increase in productivity, and one-third is assumed to result from a gradual increase in the use of idle capacity existing in 1977. The assumed expansion of investments and the aim of a balanced current account will leave room for no more than a moderate increase in private as well as public consumption.

Table 7.5 shows the average annual volume increases in GNP, private consumption, public consumption, local government consumption and operating expenses for medical care during 1970–4, 1974–7 and (according to the main alternative of the LU-document) 1977–83 and 1983–90.

Particularly the low and stagnant rate of increase in private consumption indicated in Table 7.5 raises doubts as to the realism and feasibility of the LU-prognosis. Given current commitments to equalising disposable income to the benefit of old-age pensioners, and in view of the fact that the number of old-age pensioners will grow by about 1 per cent per annum, while the number of persons in 'productive ages' will not change, of the 1.8 per cent annual increase in private consumption posited for 1977–83 Swedes in the 'productive ages' will get only a 1.3 per cent annual increase, and they will get less than 1 per cent per annum in 1983–90. Given continued political efforts to equalise disposable incomes among 'productive' age groups, the LU-document expects large groups of income-earners, employers as well as employees, to be content with a constant or declining standard of private consumption.

Will it be possible for Swedish politicians and other leaders of public opinion to persuade large groups of workers and civil servants to be

Table 7.5: Average Annual Volume Increases in GNP, Public and Private Consumption and Medical Care, 1970–90 (Percentage Increases)

	1970–4	1974–7	1977–83	1983–90
GNP	2.2	−0.1	3.7	**2.8**
Private consumption	1.6	2.1	1.8	**1.2**
Public consumption	2.3	4.1	2.2	**1.4**
Local govt. consumption	3.0	5.3	2.8	*1.8*
Medical care	3.0	4.9	2.8	*1.8*

Note: *Bold* figures are derived from figures in the LU-document for the periods 1977–83 and 1977–90.

Italicised figures are not specified in the LU-document but have been calculated on the assumption that the relation between the rates of increase in public consumption, local government consumption and operating expenses for medical care remains unchanged.

Source: *Långtidsutredningen* (1978).

satisfied with constant or declining private consumption for many years to come? I think not. I base this judgement on observations of the behaviour of many Swedish wage-earners during the years of moderate increase in private consumption since about 1970: steadily deteriorating tax-paying morale, a growing tendency towards more part-time work, less overtime and extra work and increasing absenteeism. At the same time there has been a steady trend toward tax-free extra-market barter and do-it-yourself activities, i.e. signs of a beginning disorganisation of the market economy. This behaviour is evidently a response to the very pronounced progression of the direct income tax scale and a very generous income maintenance system in the form of social insurance compensations and other transfers, i.e. precisely the prime instruments for equalising disposable incomes and curbing private consumption.

In my opinion, private consumption must increase faster than the LU-document proposes, and some major changes in the total tax-transfer system may be called for. Otherwise, the tendencies just mentioned will probably continue, and Sweden will face the prospect of chronic deterioration in the incentive to do productive work. Among other things, this would rule out the presumed high rate of increase in labour productivity, one of the main prerequisites for the realisation of the main LU-document alternative.

Other threats to a fast increase in productivity may be discerned, e.g. a growing dislike of geographical and occupational mobility of the labour force, a growing concern for the environment, growing inertia and uncertainty in organisational decision-making in connection with increasing 'corporativist' tendencies.

Considering the necessary increase in investments and the aim of a balanced current account, the only way to get a more rapid increase in private consumption is to lower the rate of increase for the public sector proposed in the LU-document. Barring the unlikely possibility of a radical redistribution of resources within the public sector in favour of medical care, this would also mean a slower rate of increase of resources for medical care during the period 1977–90 – i.e. an even tighter budget constraint – than that assumed in Table 7.5.

Turning now to consider future demographic trends, the total size of the Swedish population is expected to remain constant between 1977 and 1990. This will be the net effect of a decreasing number of births, a constant number of persons in productive ages and an increasing number of aged. The group of very aged (octogenarians and older) will be the fastest increasing subgroup in the population. The significance of this with respect to the frequency of disease and the need for medical care is quite evident. In the LU-document an attempt is made to take account of this in the form of a 'base-index' of medical care consumption.

The index expresses the volume of medical care consumption that must be undertaken *unless* (1) existing political commitments are revised and/or (2) the current standard of services is lowered.[10] In operational terms, the base-index thus indicates the volume of consumption that follows from the realisation of existing plans to expand long-term inpatient somatic care and from future population trends, assuming an unchanged number of bed-days per capita in each age group as regards short-term inpatient somatic care and mental care. The base-index also reflects the number of visits to the doctors' offices.

The authors estimate an annual increase of the base-index of 1.5 per cent during 1977–83. A rough estimate based on the change in the size and composition of the population and the planned expansion of long-term care indicates a slow decline overall in the rate of increase of the base-index throughout the period, 1960–90.

One way to interpret the base-index a little more deeply is to conceive of it as an indicator of a certain level of satisfaction of the need for public medical care. This interpretation demands *inter alia* a certain definition of 'need', a concept essentially based on subjective values. The concept of need I have in mind is a composite of existing need conceptions among politicians, medical experts, patients and the electorate at large in the 1970s, which actually governs the working of the public medical care system.[11] Actually, a certain change in the base-index, judged against this definition, probably contains a certain increase in the level of satisfaction of the need of long-term inpatient somatic care, since the figures for this branch of medical care show a gradual expansion of bed-days in relation to the number of very aged persons. The interpretation also presupposes no significant changes in the effects of medical care, no change in the basic structure of public medical care (the age-specific relation between volume of outpatient and volume of inpatient care, etc.) and no changes in the environment of public medical care (such as the age-specific incidence and prevalence of disease or the possibility and propensity for self-care).

Figure 7.3 attempts to bring together data on operating expenses for public medical care and estimates of the base-index of public medical care. The convergence of the trends of disposable real resources for medical care and the base-index respectively shows the 'trap' that public medical care in Sweden is drifting into. The severity of this trap

Figure 7.3: The 'Trap'. The Trends in Operating Expenses and the Base-index of Public Medical Care, 1963–90

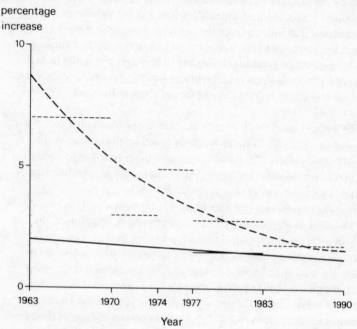

Note: The dashed lines show the annual percentage increases in operating expenses, and the solid lines show the annual percentage increases of the base-index. For the years 1963–77 the lines show the factual *ex post* trend, while for the years 1977–90 the lines indicate the *ex ante* trend according to the main alternative of the LU-document. The horizontal lines show the average annual increases during the respective subperiods. The dashed curve extending over the whole period is a free-hand regression on the average annual increases and is intended to show the long-term trend of real resources for public medical care. Likewise, the solid line extending over the whole period shows the long-term trend of the base-index, i.e. of the level of satisfaction of the need of public medical care that existed about 1977. The base-index, it should be noted, incorporates a certain increase in the level of satisfaction of the need of long-term inpatient somatic care.

is further underlined when we consider (1) that, for the politico-
economic reasons mentioned above, the rate of increase of real
resources for medical care may well be lower than that assumed in
Table 7.5 and Figure 7.3, and (2) that we must reckon with an
observed decline in productivity (measured in volume resources per
unit of output) of as much as 5 per cent in recent years. The latter
factor is to be contrasted with the 1.3 per cent gap between the
annual rates of increase of real resources for medical care and the base-
index posited in the LU-document for 1977–83, not to mention the
still narrower margin assumed for 1983–90. Evidently, very strong
measures to improve the productivity of medical care are a condition
sine qua non for the view of the LU-document to become reality.

Problems of Policy and Management

To recapitulate briefly: the ageing of the Swedish population has
implied a progressive conversion of mortality into morbidity.
Simultaneously, this morbidity has come to be dominated by fatal,
chronic and degenerative disease, for which there is rarely any radical
therapy, only symptomatic, supporting and life-sustaining treatment.
Methodology and technology for diagnosis and treatment are
developing at an accelerating rate as a result of medical research and
development. New advances are very quickly and efficiently
advertised by the mass media, thereby generating demands for more
resources for medical care. These demands are also strengthened by
various socio-economic factors, e.g. the abolition of the price
mechanism, the disintegration of the multi-generation family and an
increasing propensity among women to enter the labour market. All
these factors have put political bodies under strong pressure to expand
medical care.

During the 1960s county council politicians had no serious reasons
to resist this pressure. With a rapidly increasing GNP, medical care
could expand very fast without threatening private consumption or
any other sector of the economy. Rapid expansion of medical care was
also facilitated by the fact that the average county tax amounted to
only 4.38 per cent of taxable income in 1960 and was hardly noticed
by the taxpayer. Consequently, a general generosity and *laisser-aller*
attitude towards spending came to leaven the Swedish system of
medical care during the 1960s. Most county councils approved huge
investments — determining the future production structure of medical
care — without founding the decisions on any long-term strategies or
even simple projections on the consequences of the projects in terms of

operating costs. The first medium-term plans (with planning horizons of about five years) were worked out in the mid-1960s, but most counties had no plan with a planning horizon of ten years or more until the mid-1970s. Work on these, moreover, was initiated by the state.

During the 1960s problems were solved and demands from the medical profession and various pressure groups satisfied by appropriating additional resources and raising county tax rates. Systems for gathering data on inputs and outputs and for continuous control developed only slowly, probably due to lack of interest. Clinical decision-making was not very much influenced by economic considerations, and no serious criticism was raised against superintendent medical officers who showed budgetary deficits in the accounts of their departments. During the 1960s there also developed strong claims for wage increases and shorter working hours among nurses and supporting staff, these claims having formerly been inhibited by a sense of 'calling'. Viewed against this background, the unfavourable development of average costs and productivity discussed here is no surprise. These were the 'Gay 'Sixties of Swedish medical care', and they resulted in an average county council tax rate of 8.06 per cent in 1970.

Swedish medical care entered the 1970s with sustained demands for expansion and more resources. While common sense and simple calculations said there had to be a turning-point in the rate of increase soon, a real understanding of the seriousness of the situation and its ramifications for years to come spread only slowly among the political and administrative bodies of the counties. This was probably partly due to overoptimistic economic calculations in both centrally issued LU-documents and the local plans of the counties themselves.[12] But even when economic stagnation had become a painful reality by mid-decade, there was (and still is) a reluctance among county politicians to grasp the implications of the development and to make the necessary decisions — e.g. to damp external and internal demands for more resources, improve defective instruments for the planning and control of the system, introduce incentives to efficiency — politically unpleasant as they may be.

Many county politicians seem instead to cling to the hope that economic stagnation will be only temporary and that economic expansion, as during the 1960s, is just around the corner. Much time and effort have also been devoted to various attempts to relieve the constraints on county budgets through various forms of state subsidies and grants. The Federation of Swedish County Councils has on several occasions during the 1970s bargained for more money from the state. Obviously, county politicians have preferred seeking financial 'salvation' to the tough job of achieving efficiency and gaining control over the medical care delivery system.

The general attitude of the state towards the growth of medical care expenditures has shifted from indulgence and approval during the greater part of the 1960s to concern and disapproval during the 1970s. The first signs of a dawning concern on the part of the state about the growth of medical care expenditures appeared in 1965. That same year the Minister of Finance publicly criticised the expansive ambitions of the counties, and the Delegation on Medical Care was formed. In 1968 the National Board of Health was reorganised and the Planning and Rationalisation Institute of the Health and Social Services (SPRI) was formed. Also in 1968, the first central guidelines on the structure of medical care (concerning outpatient care) were issued. Through the course of the 1960s, however, these measures by the state had no discernible effect on the actual development of public medical care.[13]

In the early 1970s further central guidelines on the structure of medical care were issued, and it was explicitly declared that long-term somatic care, mental care and outpatient care should be given priority in the planning of medical services. The Delegation on Medical Care made concerted efforts to bring the counties to act in accordance with these guidelines and priorities, among other things by influencing the distribution of positions for physicians. About 1975, a standardised long-term planning system was introduced at the county level on the initiative of the state. The decade has seen a series of centrally instigated projects on the structure of medical care and methods of planning and rationalisation.[14]

Throughout the 1970s the state showed growing concern over the steadily increasing taxes and expenditures of local government (municipalities and counties). Three commissions of inquiry were appointed (in 1971, 1975 and 1976, respectively) and charged to work out proposals on measures to damp local cost and tax increases. The work of these commissions resulted in a 1977 proposal on a system of regular negotiations between the state and the federations of municipalities and county councils with the object of reaching agreements placing ceilings on local tax-rate and expenditure increases. In return, the municipalities and counties are to get a considerable increase in state subsidies and grants from 1980 on.[15] A similar agreement had been made, however, in 1972, when the municipalities and counties pledged not to raise their taxes for the two succeeding years, 1973 and 1974. In return, the counties received increased state subsidies and social insurance compensation. The pledge was largely fulfilled by the counties, but instead, county taxes rose sharply between 1974 and 1975 (from 9.33 per cent to 10.21 per cent of taxable income). A similar pledge for 1976 and 1977 was not very well fulfilled; the average county tax rose to 11.26 per cent in 1977.

Agreements pertaining to 1978 and 1979 include an obligation on the part of the counties to try to limit the annual increase in real expenditure to 3 per cent, while realising their plans to expand long-term inpatient somatic care. In addition to increasing subsidies and compensations to the counties, the state promised to try to avoid making decisions which may be anticipated to give rise to increased county expenditures.

To sum up: consciousness about the future operating conditions of medical care and their implications for the control and efficiency of the system has spread only slowly among county politicians and administrators. Too much energy and interest has instead been devoted to negotiating more favourable financial agreements with the state. The state has been able to restrain county tax increases somewhat and to promote the expansion of outpatient care and long-term inpatient somatic care. Still, county taxes have increased from 8.06 per cent in 1970 to 12.46 per cent in 1978, and so far the agreements have had no obvious effects on productivity in the medical care delivery system. The actual behaviour and mode of operation of the system at the close of the 1970s are fundamentally the same as during the 1960s. Indeed, the outlook is not bright!

Several suggestions have been made on how to manage Swedish medical care problems of the future. Whatever the case, breakthroughs in medical technology and preventive medicine are unlikely to alleviate the situation much in the coming decade. Quite drastic changes in the structure and functioning of medical care may have to be made, such as introducing significant out-of-pocket fees or radically reducing the capacity for hospital-based inpatient and outpatient care. Unless political bodies very soon find ways to improve the efficiency of public medical care, they will have to make painful reconsiderations during the coming decade.

By way of conclusion let us consider some Swedish case-studies and development projects.

Anticipation of the Economic Crisis

As indicated above, the economic crisis in Swedish medical care was foreseeable as early as 1970. In December of 1971 a plan for medical care in 1980 in the western region of Sweden (four counties and the County Borough of Gothenburg) presented elaborate calculations on the economic consequences of realisation of the long-term plans of the counties and Gothenburg. According to these calculations, the tax-rates of the four counties might be expected to practically double: from 8 per cent of taxable income in 1970 to 15 to 16 per cent in 1980.

On the basis of this prognosis and estimates regarding the development of personal incomes, municipal taxes and central government taxes, the authors concluded that an increase in private consumption would be possible during the planning period, but not the annual increase of 3 to 4 per cent assumed in the LU-document of 1970. The regional plan goes on to say that the realisation of the four counties' plans would imply a 'pronounced temperance' as regards an increase in private consumption. The document also stresses the necessity that the counties gain better control of medical care, which in turn demands improved information systems and intensified rationalisation efforts.[16]

Current medium-term plans of the four counties show that the expansion of their medical care systems until 1980 will be rather close to the projected long-term plans of 1971, and thus the calculations of the regional plan document have proved accurate. County taxes in the region will probably amount to 13 per cent of taxable income in 1980 instead of 15 to 16 per cent, but this difference is attributable to increases in state subsidies and social insurance compensation which could not be anticipated in 1971. Again, these subsidies and compensations have had no obvious effect on the productivity of medical care. They have only meant a partial shift from one form of taxation to another.

Modern 'Corporativism' and Traditional Democracy

During the 1970s the power of Swedish trade unions has extended far beyond their traditional wage-bargaining task. New legislation now entitles them to take part directly in the ongoing decision-making processes of various sectors of the economy. An obvious effect of this is that decision-making has become much more time-consuming and complicated. Another effect is that the unions have come to influence not only on-the-job conditions and staffing policy, but also the content and composition of services. A case from Gothenburg illustrates this:[17]

In January of 1978 a major new building at East Hospital, containing some 400 beds, was taken into use. The planning and preparations for this were made in a very comprehensive form of participative management involving, *inter alia*, some 40 consultative working groups. In August of 1977 the Medical Services Board of the county borough submitted its proposals for taking the new building into use to the County Borough Council. A corresponding number of beds was to be closed down at the Sahlgrenska Hospital (also in Gothenburg), the whole affair being a matter of transferring resources from an old hospital for short-term care to a new one. Despite the fact that the net result would imply no change in the capacity for short-term somatic care, a net increase of 309 full-time positions was proposed. This figure included 65 nurses. After having thoroughly examined the proposals, the Council invited representatives of the Medical Services Board to discussions in October.

Council analysts found the proposals to conflict with existing political guidelines for medical care in Gothenburg, which stated: 'Within the bounds of short-term somatic care, demands for more resources must mainly be satisfied by redistributing resources from one discipline to another, by expanding out-patient care and by rationalisation.'[18] Further: 'Long-term care . . . shall be given the highest priority in the plans for 1978–1982.'[19]

The guidelines also stipulate that four new somatic nursing homes should be built during this period. Nurses have been in very short supply for some time, and difficulties in recruiting nurses to the nursing homes have delayed bringing them into operation. The staffing proposals for East Hospital clearly ran counter to these objectives as well.

For these and other reasons Council analysts proposed that the County Borough Council reject the proposal of the Medical Services Board. After lengthy deliberations, however, the Council largely accepted the proposals.

Having studied the facts of the case, I suspect that an important reason for the Council's approval of the proposals was the fact that there was no time to start the process of participative management over again, and that rejecting the proposals would have caused a schism between the trade unions and the ruling Social-Democratic majority of the County Borough.

Medical R & D and Medical Care

The bulk of medical research in Sweden is carried out at the university hospitals, most of which are run by counties and county boroughs with financial contributions from the state. There has been no systematic and regular co-ordination of medical R & D and medical care at the university hospitals to date. Two main factors speak for establishing such co-ordination.

One is the 'resource connection'. Most of the buildings, premises and appliances of the university hospitals are used for medical R & D and medical training as well as for medical care. Most doctors and a lot of other personnel and resources are engaged in all three activities. That is to say, the three activities engage the same pool of real resources. Obviously, rational decisions regarding these activities cannot be made in isolation from one another; co-ordination and information exchange are needed. The other prime reason is the 'result connection'. The results of medical R & D determine planners 'freedom of choice' as regards the possible shape and features of future medical care systems. The results of medical R & D are also vital to increasing the efficiency of medical care.

In response to these needs, in November of 1976 the County Borough of Gothenburg formed a joint committee for the co-ordination and the exchange of information between medical R & D and the medical care delivery system.

Efficiency and Medical Decision-making

The single most important unit of production in the system of medical care is the department for inpatient care and the office for outpatient care. Even though the representatives of nurses and supporting staff may be taking a more active part in decision-making in these units, the doctors still play the key role. Through their medical decision-making they determine not only the effects of medical care, but also — directly and indirectly — medical care costs and resource utilisation. Doctors decide which patients will get medical care as well as the type and volume of diagnostic and therapeutic measures to be applied.

Many factors influence medical decision-making in practice. Among these are ethical considerations, the auditing practices of the Medical Services Liability Council, medical education and scientific ideals. A growing body of empirical evidence suggests, however, that doctors generally do not seem to consider the economic consequences of their therapeutic and diagnostic measures. The economic efficiency of medical care can probably be improved a good deal (cf. p. 192).

There are many ways to go about doing this, such as training doctors in economic and administrative procedures or working out programmes (guidelines) on the efficient diagnosis and treatment of various diseases. In my opinion, one of the best ways to make doctors aware of economic consequences is to introduce a new 'philosophy' and new instruments for pricing and budgeting at the departmental level. The department budget should be regarded as a contract between the superintendent medical officer of the department and the Medical Services Board and specify the minimum output and the maximum costs of the coming budget year. A system of penalties and rewards should be attached to the realisation of the terms of the budget/ contract. If, at the end of the year, it turns out that real costs are below the maximum and/or real output is above the minimum, the department should receive an economic reward for this achievement. In the opposite case the department should be required to pay back some of its deficit within a specified period of time. The present budgetary system operating in Swedish medical care in fact works out the other way around; exceeded budgets have generally resulted in budget increases in succeeding years. Much more might be said about factors outside the control of the superintendent medical officer, factors determining the outcome of the budget and other features and problems of such a budgetary system. It would seem worthwhile to elaborate on a budgetary system along these lines.

Notes

1. B. Abel-Smith, *Paying for Health Services* (WHO Public Health Papers, no. 17, Geneva, 1963); B. Abel-Smith, *An International Study of Health Expenditure and Its Relevance for Health Planning* (WHO Public Health Papers, no. 32, Geneva, 1967); H. E. Klarman, 'The Economic Determinants of Health Care Expenditures' in D. A. Ehrlich (ed.), *The Health Care Cost Explosion — Which Way Now?* (Henry Dunant Institute/Hans Huber Publishers, Bern, 1975), pp. 7–17; R. Maxwell, 'The Case for Intervention' in D. A. Ehrlich (ed.), *The Health Care Cost Explosion — Which Way Now?*, pp. 18–28; R. Maxwell, *Health Care: The Growing Dilemma — Needs vs. Resources in Western Europe, the US and the USSR*, 2nd edn (McKinsey & Co., New York, 1975).

2. J.-E. Spek, 'Sjukvårdsekonomi' in B.-C. Ysander (ed.), *Förvaltnings-ekonomiska problem* (Rätt och samhälle, nr. 7, Jurist- och Samhällsvetareför-bundets Förlags AB, Stockholm, 1972), pp. 178–94.

3. B. Lindegård, 'Sjukvårdskonsumtionens epidemiologi', *Läkartidningen*, vol. 69, nr. 22 (1972), pp. 377–83; B. Lindegård, 'Terminal sjukvård i Göteborg',

Läkartidningen, vol. 69, nr. 22 (1972), pp. 2675–8; J.-E. Spek, 'Att vara åldring i Göteborg på 1980-talet' (Göteborgs stadskontor, stencil, Göteborg, 1976).

4. Community of Gothenburg, Medical Care Administration.

5. W. J. Baumol and W. E. Oates, 'Kostnadssjukan inom tjänstesektorn och levnadsstandarden', *Skandinaviska Enskilda Bankens Kvartalsskrift*, nr. 2 (1972), pp. 42–52; C.-J. Åberg, 'Den offentliga sektorns kostnadsutveckling'; C.-J. Åberg, 'Kommunerna i svensk ekonomi'.

6. J.-E. Spek, 'Sjukvårdens utgiftsutveckling' (Göteborgs stadskontor, stencil, Göteborg, 1975).

7. K.-E. Erickson, I. Svensson and G. Tunerstedt, 'Uppföljning av sjukvård' in Kommunförbundet, *Om uppföljning och utvärdering av kommunal verksamhet* (Kommunförbundet, Stockholm, 1978), pp. 105–20.

8. S. Grassman, E. Lundberg, I. Ståhl and B.-C. Ysander, *Blandekonomi i kris? Konjukturrådets rapport 1978–79* (Studieförbundet Näringsliv och Samhälle, Stockholm, 1978), p. 9.

9. *Långtidsutredningen 1978* (SOU 1978:78, Ekonomidepartementet, Stockholm, 1978).

10. In the field of health and medical care one political commitment is taken into account, viz. the priority assigned long-term somatic care. *Långtidsutredningen* (1978), pp. 178–80.

11. An explication of the 'need' concept is to be found in the following essays: J.-E. Spek, 'On the Economic Analysis of Health and Medical Care in a Swedish Health District' in M. M. Hauser (ed.), *The Economics of Medical Care* (University of York Studies in Economics No. 7, George Allen & Unwin, Oxford, 1972), pp. 261–8; A. Williams, 'Need As a Demand Concept (With Special Reference to Health)' in A. J. Culyer (ed.), *Economic Policies and Social Goals – Aspects of Public Choice* (York Studies in Economics No. 1, Martin Robertson, Bath, 1974), pp. 60–76.

12. *Svensk ekonomi 1971–1975 – med utblick mot 1990*; 1970 års långtidsutredning, Huvudrapport (SOU 1970:71, Finansdepartementet, Sekretariatet för Ekonomisk Planering, Stockholm, 1970); *Svensk ekonomi fram till 1977 – 1970 års långtidsutredning avstämd och framskriven* (SOU 1973:21, Finansdepartementet, Sekretariatet för Ekonomisk Planering, Stockholm, 1973); *Långtidsutredningen 1975, Huvudrapport* (SOU 1975:89, Finansdepartementet, Stockholm, 1975).

13. J.-E. Spek, 'Kommentarer till sjukvårdsdelegationens förslag till ett system med enhetligt uppbyggda sjukvårdsplaner', *Sjukhuset*, årg. 50, nr. 6 (1973), pp. 366–73.

14. Ibid.

15. *Kommunerna. Utbyggnad. Utjämning. Finansiering*, Slutbetänkande av 1976 års kommunalekonomiska utredning (SOU 1977:78, Budgetdepartementet, Stockholm, 1977).

16. *Översiktsplan för hälso- och sjukvården inom den västsvenska sjukvårdsregionen år 1980. Förslag av en arbetsgrupp* (Planeringsnämnden för landstingskommunala angelägenheter i de västsvenska länen, Göteborg, 1972), pp. 145, 147.

17. *Göteborgs Kommunfullmäktiges Handlingar*, nr. 385/1977 (Göteborg, 1977).

18. *Göteborgs Kommunfullmäktiges Handlingar*, nr. 200/1977 (Göteborg, 1977), p. 6.

19. Ibid.

8 THE GROWTH OF HEALTH CARE: TWO MODEL SOLUTIONS

Ingemar Ståhl

During the last few decades all industrialised countries have experienced rapid growth in expenditures for health care. In many countries the rise has been so fast that the problems of the health care sector have become a major issue in political life, and the political arena is full of suggestions on how to cope with what many planners and politicians like to call a health care 'cost explosion'. Sweden is no exception to this general rule.

Health Care Expenditures and Economic Growth

A pure economic analysis tells us, however, that the main determinant of increased health care expenditures is a country's general economic growth. If we compare industrialised countries, the differences in health expenditures can largely be explained by different levels of standard of living (measured by GDP (Gross Domestic Product) per capita). If we apply standard econometric regression techniques to a cross-section of the OECD countries in 1974, the differences in GDP per capita explain about 85 per cent of the variations in outlays on health care per capita, and we turn up with some very simple results.[1] When incomes increase by one dollar, about seven cents will be spent on increased health care. The result can also be reformulated to state that when incomes (GDP per capita) rise by 1 per cent, expenditures on health care will rise by approximately 1.2 per cent. Both these results are compatible with the assumption that in an economic growth process the share spent on health care will also grow. From this rather superficial aspect economic growth is the major explanation, and all the efforts of planners, politicians and different professional groups involved in the health care planning process result in a neat and stable figure (cf. Figure 8.1).

It is also very difficult to draw any far-reaching conclusions about the possible impact of the political system on the level of health expenditures. Sweden, with almost totally nationalised health care, and the USA, with a still large private sector, are both above the regression line, while the UK, with a nationalised system, lies below the trend. (It is of some interest to note that the main explanation of lower health

208

Figure 8.1: Health Care Expenditures and GDP in Nineteen Countries, 1974

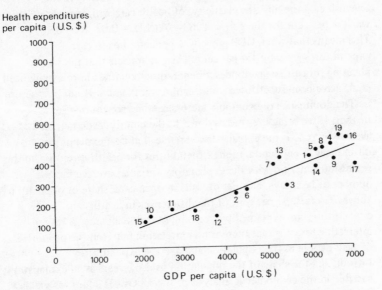

Source: Ingemar Ståhl, 'Health Care and Drug Development' (Department of Economics, University of Lund, memo, 1979).

1. Australia; 2. Austria; 3. Belgium; 4. Canada; 5. Denmark; 6. Finland; 7. France; 8. Germany; 9. Iceland; 10. Ireland; 11. Italy; 12. Japan; 13. The Netherlands; 14. Norway; 15. Spain; 16. Sweden; 17. Switzerland; 18. United Kingdom; 19. United States

expenditures in the UK is the lower per capita income, not any 'planning property' immanent to the National Health Service.)

Very similar results are reached in time-series studies.[2] In the Swedish case the 'income elasticity' of health care with regard to GDP was 1.4 per cent for the period 1963–76 (S.D. = 0.04, R^2 = 0.98). This means that when GDP grew by 1 per cent, health care expenditures grew by 1.4 per cent. Thus, it appears that the whole planning process so vividly described in other chapters in this book could have been substituted with a simple mathematical rule!

The dominance of economic factors can be brought one step further. If we bring the studies down to the county level, taxable average income is the explanatory variable that best explains differences in per capita public expenditures for health care. In a linear regression function with the explanatory variables average income, number of bed/days, number of visits in open care, share of population above 70 years, 37 per cent of the differences in health care expenditures are explained by per capita taxable income. A rather interesting result is that there is no correlation between the proportion of aged people in the population and average expenditures.[3] Introducing the share of the population over 65 years as an explanatory variable in the econometric analysis of the 19 OECD countries yields a similar result: none of the residual can be explained by this variable, although high age still seems to be rather closely related to a concept of need. The main conclusion seems to be that the political process is highly analogous to a market process, with a stable relationship between consumption and income.

The Swedish Financing System

In order better to understand this stable relationship, the rest of the chapter will be devoted to presenting a simple political–economic model that could explain why the political process is in a way analogous to a market process. But, before turning to the model, we should consider some simple data regarding Swedish health expenditures in 1977 (Figure 8.2).

Of total expenditures of 31,611 million Swedish crowns, Swedish consumers paid less than 10 per cent (Kr. 3,042 million) as out-of-pocket costs. Much of these out-of-pocket costs was paid as co-insurance or deductibles; consumers paid full cost only for over-the-counter drugs and some therapeutical equipment (included under 'sundry'). County councils (and to a far lesser extent the central

Figure 8.2: Health Financing in Sweden, 1977 (Millions Kr., Current Prices, excl. Research and Construction)

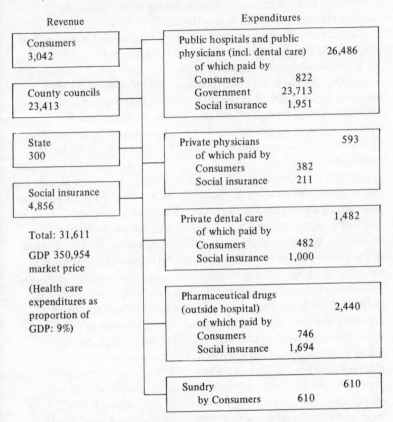

Source: National Accounts, Sweden.

government) and the social security insurance paid 90 per cent of all consumption expenditures, or *in toto* Kr. 28,569 million.

The county council tax is a proportional income tax, and the social security insurance system is financed mainly by a proportional pay-roll tax. Both systems, however, involve transfers from the central government. Before 1972, county council tax was deductible from the taxation of the central government, a fact that may have given the county councils some incentive to expand their activities, since the corresponding tax increases were indirectly borne not only by the population in the county in question, but by all tax-payers. County council taxes are no longer deductible, but some of the rather complicated agreements between the county councils and the central government regarding transfer of central government funds to county councils may still offer similar incentives.

For the sake of simplicity, however, in the following we shall accept proportional income tax as a sufficient description of the tax system for financing health care expenditures.

Through the use of a simple economic—political model we shall
(a) try to explain why an assumed 'perfect' political voting process or a perfect referendum produces a stable income elasticity, and
(b) elucidate why an essentially private commodity or service such as health care is in some countries financed by taxes and not by private insurance.

Economic analysis tells us that a perfect insurance system would lead to an efficient market solution.[4] There will still be some problems, however. Some citizens may try to be 'free riders', counting on the help of a Good Samaritan. This problem can be solved by requiring everybody to have a compulsory minimum insurance. Another problem is that life-long invalidisation and congenital deformities at an early age are difficult to cover by private insurance, unless we require parents to cover unborn children by some minimum insurance.

The arguments in favour of a market solution based on private insurance seem, however, so strong that we may wonder why some countries have preferred tax-financed health service schemes. One reason might be historical: modern health services emerged out of charitable institutions in an era when insurance was technically impracticable. Another reason might be that in earlier periods when infectious diseases predominated, health services were a highly 'public' affair. Today, this *public* health aspect no longer dominates; health statistics tell us that the greater part of the health services produced might be considered typically individual commodities. If a person got tuberculosis, once widespread in Sweden, it was not simply an individual problem, as others' well-being could be directly affected. Problems of high blood pressure or arteriosclerosis, on the other hand, are typically individual problems with no risk of infecting others.

The main reason for tax-financing brought out in this chapter is that tax-financing generally serves to redistribute incomes towards equality. In a political economy with a proportional or progressive tax system, in which the constitution permits the institution of a compulsory, tax-financed health service system, a majority will most likely choose a political solution over a system of private insurance.

One may ask why similar solutions do not apply to all commodities. The answer is probably that it is easier to exert control over and rationing of services offered to individuals than tangible goods, which can be traded in a black market. The use of a licensed 'middleman' like the doctor to administrate the rationing system probably also facilitates the necessary control.

The Market Solution

There are strong arguments for basing the 'market solution' for health services on a market for *insurance contracts*, not direct market procurement of health services. The market may be characterised in terms of the following set of assumptions: We assume that the benefits or utility an individual gets from an insurance contract of volume Q_i is a non-decreasing function $B_i(Q_i)$. The price, P, of one unit of health insurance is assumed to be constant and independent of the volume procured. This means that we assume constant returns to scale in the health-producing sector. For the sake of simplicity we also assume that it is possible to treat health services as a homogeneous and divisible commodity. Increasing the quantity of a contract will thus mean that the quality of the care provided might increase or that an extended contract covers more diseases or longer and more complicated treatments. For example, a 'small' contract may not cover renal dialysis or transplantation, while a 'large' contract might cover extensive dialysis treatment for a long period.

The individual optimum is easily found by maximising the net value of benefits over costs:

$$B_i(Q_i) = PQ_{i\ max} \tag{1}$$

which gives the well-known solution:

$$\frac{dB_i}{dQ_i} - P = 0 \tag{2}$$

i.e. consumption is brought to the point where marginal benefits equal price. In Figure 8.3 the solution is given at the point $Q_i^{\,\circ}$, where the 'marginal willingness to pay' curve intersects the constant price.

It should be observed that this is the solution for the procurement of an insurance contract. Should the person fall ill, we will face an allocation and rationing problem very similar to the one we have in a tax-financed system, with the main difference that a private insurance

Figure 8.3: The Market Solution

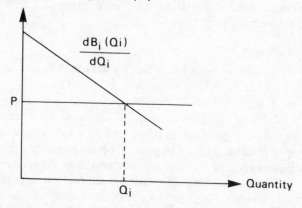

Price, marginal willingness to pay

$$\frac{dB_i(Q_i)}{dQ_i}$$

company, rather than governmental authorities, will act as an intermediary agent between the patient and the providers of health services.

The Political Solution

In the political solution it is assumed that everybody will be treated equally, i.e. that everybody will get the same insurance coverage, $\bar{Q}$. This will generally mean that high income-earners consume less coverage than they would in the market solution, while low income-earners consume more. To simplify, we assume that individuals have roughly the same preferences and that demand for insurance contracts shows a positive income elasticity, i.e. when income increases, the demand for insurance contracts will also increase. (Thus, for the moment we ignore the large differences in consumption related to age.)

Given proportional taxation, the individual with income Y_i will have to pay tY_i for health insurance. The tax rate, t, is simply determined by the equation

$$t\bar{Y} = P\bar{Q} \tag{3}$$

where $\bar{Y}$ is the average income. The meaning of this equation is simply that all social insurance premiums (tax income) will be used for the provision of health services.

The price for increasing health services for the ith individual will then be

$$\frac{dT_i}{d\bar{Q}} = \frac{dtY_i}{d\bar{Q}} = \frac{d\left(P\bar{Q}\dfrac{Y_i}{\bar{Y}}\right)}{d\bar{Q}} = P\frac{Y_i}{\bar{Y}} \tag{4}$$

This means that the 'tax price' the individual pays depends on the size of his income in relation to the average income.

In a perfect referendum economy, in which each individual votes according to his true preferences, the individual optimum for voting will be determined by

$$B_i(\bar{Q}) - \frac{Y_i}{\bar{Y}} P\bar{Q}_{max} \tag{5}$$

with the solution

$$\frac{dB}{d\bar{Q}} - \frac{Y_i}{\bar{Y}} P = 0 \tag{6}$$

In Figure 8.4, $\bar{Q}^1$, $\bar{Q}^2$ and $\bar{Q}^3$ are three different propositions for the

Figure 8.4: The Political Solution

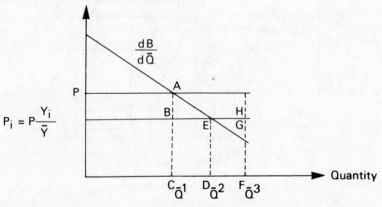

individual with the marginal tax price $PY_i/\overline{Y}$. Proposition $\overline{Q}^1$ will be inferior to proposition $\overline{Q}^2$ because by extending consumption from $\overline{Q}^1$ to $\overline{Q}^2$ the voter/consumer will pay only an amount equal to the area BCDE, while the value of the proposition to the consumer is ACDE. Note that in this case — with a voter with below-average income — the volume preferred in the political process will be larger than the volume demanded in the market solution, which is $\overline{Q}^1$. The opposite will hold true for a voter with above-average income; he will vote for a smaller quantity than he would voluntarily procure in the market. Proposition $\overline{Q}^3$ is also inferior to $\overline{Q}^2$ as the cost to the consumer for this increment will be DEHF while the value of the increment is only DEGF. Proposition $\overline{Q}^2$ will thus be the optimal vote for the voter/consumer paying the marginal tax price, $PY_i/\overline{Y}$.

It is now possible to say something about the quantity of coverage a

Figure 8.5: The Referendum Process

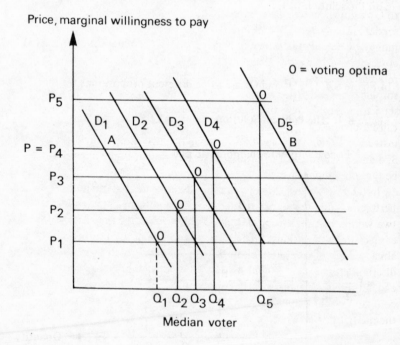

collective will reach under majority rule. The problem is described in Figure 8.5 with five different voters, numbered 1 to 5. The voters have different incomes, and the corresponding marginal willingness-to-pay curves are indicated by D_i (equal to demand curves in the market solution). A tax system based on a proportional tax will, however, function as a price-discrimination system, giving the first consumer/ voter the marginal tax price P_i, etc. ($P_i = PY_i/\overline{Y}$). The optimal solution for voter i is Q_i.

The decision process may be conceived of as a referendum process with continuous voting between alternatives. (The propositions in the referendum will be of the following type: Do you prefer to pay t_1 per cent of your income and receive Q_1 units of health protection or to pay t_2 per cent of your income and receive Q_2 units of health protection? The share t_i is determined by (3) as $PQ_i/\overline{Y}$.) If the first vote involves a choice between Q_1 and Q_2, four voters will support Q_2. Individual 1 will pay P_1Q_1, if Q_1 is the collective decision, and P_1Q_2 if Q_2 wins the referendum. For this person Q_1 is the optimal choice, as an extension to Q_2 will increase his taxes more than the value of the extended services. The individual will simply feel that he could get more for his money by extending his private consumption. Individual 2 will correspondingly pay P_2Q_1 and P_2Q_2 for the alternatives in the referendum. His optimal choice is Q_2 as he will get a consumer's surplus by moving from Q_1 to Q_2 – i.e. the net value of the extended services will be greater than the increase in his tax payments. For the third individual it is also better to pay P_3Q_2 and get Q_2 units of service instead of paying P_3Q_1 and only getting Q_1 units. Thus, individuals 2, 3, 4 and 5 will vote in favour of alternative Q_2, while individual 1 will be the sole supporter of Q_1.

In the next step of the referendum process the choice stands between Q_3 and Q_2. In this referendum three voters will favour Q_3, and two will be against. It is interesting to observe that the low income-earners are voting against further expansion. The political process has already given them more than they would demand voluntarily at the discriminatory tax price, and they will not perceive the extra tax expenditure for financing further expansion as giving enough value, compared to the value they might get by buying other commodities in the market sector.

A vote between Q_4 and Q_3 will end up with a 3-to-2 victory for proposition Q_3. Finally, individual 5 will be alone in favouring Q_5 over Q_4. The result is well known from political theory: the median ('marginal') voter will determine the final result.[5]

The main result of this model is extremely simple: health care expenditures determined in a majority-rule process will over time follow the demand of the median voter. Given stable individual income elasticity for health care consumption (or, rather, the demand for health insurance contracts) and a stable relative income distribution over time, we may expect a political process with tax-financed health care to generate the stable relationships between health care expenditures and GDP per capita presented earlier in the chapter. In a growth process an economy with a political solution of tax-financed health care will show approximately the same growth in health care expenditures as an economy with a market solution with private insurance.

The main difference will be that the political process produces a more equal distribution of health services. This brings us to a final result of the model used: most real world income distributions have a skewness, with average income being higher than the median income (see Figure 8.6). As indicated in (4) the tax price the individual pays for a unit of health services is proportional to the ratio between his own income and the average income. If we return to Figure 8.5 and imagine a referendum between a market process for the provision of health care and a political process based on majority rule, an interesting result emerges.

Assume that individual 4 has the average income (i.e. that the income of individual 5 is high enough to give an average income above the median). In a market process the price of a unit of health services (insurance contract) will be $P = P_4$. The question the voter will ask is

Figure 8.6: Income Distribution

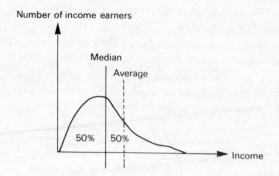

whether it is better to pay P ($= P_4$) and optimise according to this price than pay P_i and get the volume determined by the median voter. Individual 1's optimum in the private market would be at point A. In the political market he is forced to pay $P_1 Q_3$ and to consume Q_3. He will prefer the political solution if the increase in consumer's surplus of consuming Q_1 units at the price P_1 (instead of paying the market price and consuming A units) is larger than the negative consumer's surplus of extending consumption from Q_1 to Q_3. This is very likely to be the case if demand is price-inelastic. Under rather general conditions all individuals with below-average income will prefer the political solution over a market solution. The individual with the average income will be indifferent between the two systems, and the individual with an above-average income will prefer the market solution. For him the market solution (B) will offer a larger quantity at a lower price than the political solution.

The conclusion is that the market solution will lose in a referendum, and a majority will favour the political solution. This result is part of the reason why service sectors, such as education and health care, tend to be tax-financed.

Notes

1. OECD, *Public Expenditure on Health*, Studies in Resource Allocation, no. 4 (OECD, Paris, 1977); I. Ståhl, *Health Care and Drug Development* (Dept. of Economics, Lund University (memo), 1979); B. Jönsson, 'Sjukvårdssektorns expansion – hot eller hopp?' in *Hälso- och sjukvårdsforskning* (Samhällsvetenskapliga Institutionen, Universitetet i Linköping, Linköping, 1979).

2. I. Ståhl, 'Health Care Costs in Sweden' in National Institute of Health, *International Health Costs and Expenditures* (US Government Printing Office, Washington, D.C., 1976); B. Jönsson, 'Sjukvårdssektorns expansion – hot eller hopp?'.

3. R. Granqvist, *Studier i sjukvårdsekonomi* [Studies in the Economics of Medical Care, English summary] (Stockholms universitet, Företagsekonomiska inst., Stockholm, 1978); B. Jönsson, 'Sjukvårdssektorns expansion – hot eller hopp?'.

4. K. J. Arrow, 'Uncertainty and the Welfare Economics of Medical Care'. *American Economic Review*, vol. 53 (1963); A. C. Einthoven, 'Consumer-Centered vs. Job-Centered Health Insurance', *Harvard Business Review*, vol. 57, no. 1 (1979), pp. 141–52.

5. A. Downs, *An Economic Theory of Democracy* (Harper & Row, New York, 1957); J. M. Buchanan and G. Tullock, *The Calculus of Consent* (University of Michigan Press, Ann Arbor, 1962).

Part Five:

THE SWEDISH HEALTH SYSTEM IN COMPARATIVE PERSPECTIVE

9 EQUITY AND HEALTH CARE: SWEDEN, BRITAIN AND THE UNITED STATES

Odin W. Anderson and James Warner Björkman

The Issue of Equity

Nearly a decade ago, it was noted in *Health Care: Can There Be Equity?* that 'problems of equity are inherent in a society's values as to who should get what, when, and where, and for how much – in short, a political issue'.[1] And the book concluded with a prediction that in the United States, Sweden and England, 'the drive toward increasing coordination, integration, and planning will continue'. Since then, all three countries have been striving for ever more clearly articulated structural boundaries; all are attempting ever more stringent budgetary constraints on health expenditures; and all are trying to innovate ways in which patients, administrators and health personnel can reach collective decisions.

These actions are wholly politicised because all efforts to determine 'what is proper' involve value judgements about the distribution of resources and the sharing of scarce benefits. And they are becoming publicly politicised because of the growing insistence that health services be primarily a governmental responsibility. But although equity is an honorific concept which almost everyone favours, individuals rarely agree about what equity means in specific terms or how it should apply in specific situations in society. Dictionaries, as score-cards of common usage, define equity as 'the state, ideal, or quality of being just, impartial, and fair'; and the term itself derives from the Latin word *aequus* meaning 'equal'. Yet individuals frequently disagree over what constitutes justice or fairness, and they likewise disagree about the extent to which equality coincides with justice and fairness.

Many authors have addressed the issue of equity. Some have expounded prescriptive theories as to how society should function. Others have set forth descriptive theories of how an individual or society actually judges the equitableness of a given situation or course of action in terms of specified criteria. In his theory of the moral development of the child, for example, Piaget has identified three sequential stages in distributive justice, or how punishments and rewards should be distributed among members of a group.[2] In the earliest stage, the child tends to accept as 'just' or 'fair' whatever

223

distribution is laid down by the authority figure. In the second stage, the child becomes a strict egalitarian believing that all must be treated absolutely equally. In the most advanced stage, the child tempers equality with equity; his demand for equality is modified by taking into account the circumstances of each individual (age, health, etc.) so as to achieve a higher form of justice. This concept of 'relativistic equality' is employed today by those who favour 'reverse discrimination'; they argue that equal protection under the law may require unequal treatment in order to overcome unequal obstacles.[3]

Similarly, equity in Anglo–American law is a system of principles and remedies which originated about 1500 in the English Court of Chancery. By that time, a large body of laws had grown up which no longer applied in the new and more complex situations constantly developing. Thus, by insisting on the letter of the law, the common law courts often failed to provide real justice. Disappointed litigants then applied to the king for remedy of their grievances, and the lord chancellor was instructed to hear such cases in his court in the chancery. Without the constraints of precedent, he was to provide a higher form of justice than could be obtained through the other courts of the land.[4]

In contemporary Western society, the belief that all men are equal is generally accepted in the realm of law and politics; democracy proclaims equal justice and equal political rights for all citizens, and citizenship is not restricted to the few. The market economy, however, provides an unequal distribution of material goods; differentials in income serve as incentives to make efficient use of resources and thus increase the overall national output. In *Equality and Efficiency: The Big Tradeoff*, Okun addresses this conflict between equal rights and unequal incomes in the United States.[5]

Okun describes the complex interactions between the domains of individual rights and of the market, and notes the unclear and ever changing boundary between the areas where American society says that equality should prevail and those areas where efficiency should reign. Because he views the provision of a certain minimal level of essential material goods as necessary for preserving the dignity of the individual, he calls for certain measures which he says would simultaneously increase both equality and efficiency. These include the elimination of racial and sexual discrimination in job opportunities and the reduction of discriminatory barriers to access to capital. He could easily have also mentioned improved access to good quality health care. Generally, however, Okun gives the American economy high marks as an efficient producer of goods and services.

In addressing the question of the equity of unequal incomes, Okun says that appraisal of the fairness of market-determined incomes is a matter of personal judgement. His ethical preference would be equal incomes reflecting the equal intrinsic worth of each human, and he favours cautious use of taxes and transfer payments to reduce some of the present economic inequality. However, he cannot envisage how to alter the American economy so as to bring about a much greater degree of equality of incomes without either great restrictions on personal freedom or great reduction of the productivity of the society as a whole. Such costs, he contends, are too high to pay for the desirable goal of equalising incomes.

Thus, under certain constraints and with some regrets, Okun accepts inequality of incomes (and, by extension, other services) because the resulting incentives lead to benefits for the vast majority of individuals. Others appraise the inequality of market-determined incomes more harshly. In his detailed philosophical work, *A Theory of Justice*, Rawls maintains that deviation from an equal distribution should be permitted only if every individual benefits.[6] A basic criticism of his theory of justice, however, is that its 'maximin principle' appeals only to persons who are totally averse to risk.

Reward in proportion to contribution, or outcome in proportion to input, is often used as a norm for equity. An allocation norm is a set of criteria used to specify a fair distribution of rewards and resources, and a political actor will usually follow some allocation norm in order to produce order for himself and for other recipients.[7] In any given situation, however, several norms — each representing a different idea of fairness — may be available to the allocator. In addition to equality and equity, these norms include reciprocity, capacity, responsiveness and need. An actor must then choose a norm or combination of norms based on the degree of acceptance each norm has and the pattern of benefits he expects to follow from each norm.

The equity norm (reward in accordance with inputs) is often chosen because it encourages productivity; better performers are attracted to the organisation, their loyalty is strengthened, and their task behaviour is reinforced. In addition, such a norm may encourage poor performers to leave the organisation so that again the overall level of performance improves. However, sometimes the equity norm causes discontent among poor performers which eventually disrupts the entire organisation. If group cohesion and co-operation are very important, then the norm of equal distribution may be chosen since it tends to promote harmony and solidarity among group members. Certainly such development may be true of society as a whole. Often, though, a policy-maker will use a compromise between equity and equality norms in an attempt to minimise discontent while encouraging high performance. But when difficulties in measuring the recipients' inputs frustrate the desire to employ the productivity-generating equity norm, he or she will resort to the equality norm.

The degree of public acceptance of various allocation norms is affected by two opposing ideologies, which Wilensky calls 'economic collectivism' and 'economic individualism'.[8] The ideology of economic collectivism says that society should provide some amount of security to cushion the individual against the risks of modern life, that 'fault' lies with the system and not with the individual. Economic individualism, on the other hand, is based on self-reliance and the belief that effort will necessarily produce success. According to this belief, those who suffer from misfortune deserve their fate. The ideology of economic individualism supports unrestricted competition in the market place with incomes corresponding to contribution, while economic collectivism is more concerned with the needs of individuals.

In summary, equity in a legal context usually invokes a higher form of moral justice. Such justice often modifies claims to absolute equality of treatment by considering the circumstances of the individuals involved. Social equity may therefore permit, if not require, inequalities to exist. Whereas equality as an absolute requires that everyone should have an equal share of services or resources, equity introduces a contextual background of need so that an unequal allocation of services or resources may be essential in order to achieve ultimately a sameness of condition for all. In an economic context, however, equity appears to be used most frequently to refer to the allocation of rewards in proportion to contributions. If efforts are unequal, outcomes will be unequal since some standard of reasonable fairness will be invoked. If these two conclusions about the variable definition of equity are accepted, then the meaning of equity remains problematic in contexts where both social and economic issues overlap. And the task of trying to reconcile these different usages of equity inevitably falls to government.

Comparative Health Performances

Even when there is concurrence on ultimate values or a minimum consensus has been reached on the meaning of equity, there continues to be a paucity of performance indicators by which to determine scientifically what is a proper population ratio of hospital beds and of other facilities, or of physicians, nurses and other health personnel;

likewise, what is the proper number of units of service per person; and what is the proper level of expenditures. During the past decade, the concept of equity in health services and expenditures has clearly shifted towards being equated with the norm of equality but the consequences are ambiguous.

Originally there were only two major objectives for the inauguration of a universal national health insurance or health service scheme: to facilitate access and share costs. Access to personal health services was ensured by eliminating or reducing payment at the time of service, and cost-sharing was achieved through the tax system so that the well-to-do contributed more than the poor. Universal health insurance was simply intended to be a financing mechanism for the established health services delivery system, a financial conduit for an ever expanding system. More was better and big was beautiful. Now, after a few swift years, all countries are redefining and refining the concept of equal access. Because of rapidly rising costs, more attention is being paid to the spatial distribution of services so that, whether measured by time, distance or range, they become more or less accessible to everyone.

These demands for optimal access coincided, of course, with the great advances in technology and with increasing costs due to inflation as well as expanding utilisation. The political response has been predictable. The conventional wisdom is that the demand for personal health services is infinite, although no country has dared to find out. It is asserted that health services create their own demand; a bed built is a bed occupied, and a doctor trained is a doctor whose services must be used. In addition, a physician can create his own demand and therefore influence supply. Personal health services systems are hospital-intensive and correspondingly expensive; therefore payment mechanisms are devised to encourage more ambulatory services. Associated with the service mix is the universal view that the medical profession is overspecialised. Therefore, the standard prescription is to increase the proportion of training posts for primary care physicians and decrease the number of such posts for specialists, particularly surgeons. In any case, personal health services are not a good buy anyway because they have little effect on the usual health indicators. Better health status is more likely to follow changes in personal life-style such as weight reduction, proper nutrition, reduction of tension, elimination of smoking and reduction of consumption of alcoholic beverages. Collectively the public will benefit by the improved health of individuals and, by reducing demand, health services will not cost so much.

The foregoing description of the current status of personal health services is only partly exaggerated. Yet no politicians dare contain the system in any drastic manner. Personal health services are a prime political good among the services and projects by which governments set priorities and justify themselves. With these contemporary trends in mind, how have Sweden, Britain and the United States encountered health services issues since 1970?

The issues in each country — cost, quality, access — are essentially similar but have been handled with quite different political and social problem-solving styles. In order to trace changes over time among these countries, 1950 is an appropriate base-year for comparisons within and between systems. By then the health services in industrialised countries had absorbed the diagnostic and therapeutic technology which accelerated during and after the end of the Second World War. Not until the 1970s did equally spectacular developments take place which have led to equivalent controversies over widespread application. Today renal dialysis and CAT-scans — both of them effective, expensive and popular techniques — are the subject of public debate.

The most politically explosive indicator of performance is, of course, the amount of money spent on the respective systems. By any standard the increase in each country has been phenomenal and by magnitudes unimaginable in the early 1950s. Between 1950 and the latter 1970s the per capita expenditures in the United States on all personal health services increased by fully 500 per cent, with no sign of levelling off yet in sight. In Sweden the increase was fully 2,500 per cent, or 25-fold! In England, as in the United States, the per capita increase was around five-fold. England, however, started from a lower base in 1950 than either the United States or Sweden; and unlike them, England appears to have entered a period of slowed growth through a deliberate public policy of budgetary retrenchment.

In all three countries, expenditures for health services as a percentage of gross national product were under 5 per cent in 1950. Today, health expenditures account for almost 6 per cent of the GNP in England, over 8 per cent in the United States, and almost 10 per cent in Sweden. Informal conversations with Swedish authorities suggest that Sweden's share will exceed 12 per cent before long mainly because of its ageing population. Expenditures for health services have exceeded the growth of the gross national products in all three countries. Between 1961 and 1969, for example, the average annual rate of health expenditure growth was 10.5 per cent in the United States, 9.5 per cent in England, and 14.0 per cent in Sweden. Correcting

Figure 9.1: Percentage of GNP Devoted to Health Care in Sweden, US and UK

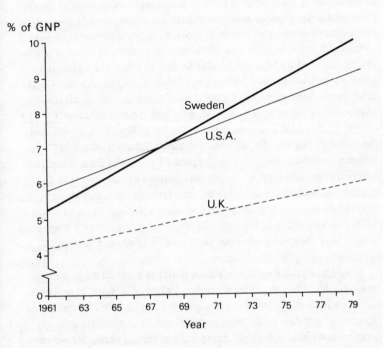

for inflation in the three countries does not essentially change the comparison, as the adjusted rates become 6.9 and 5.6 and 9.2, respectively.[9]

As a crude indicator of possible control over expenditures, it is useful to trace the major sources of funding within the three countries. The patterns indicate the potential ability of each system to direct its resources. The diversity of sources of funding in the United States reveals a multi-nucleated decision-making structure. The private insurance sector itself is extremely diversified among approximately 500 insurance agencies. While the Blue Cross hospital and Blue Shield medical insurance plans exert some influence because they account for roughly half of the insurance payments to hospitals and physicians, even the 'Blues' operate through about 90 independent, mainly state-based, agencies. The major trend towards control is the increasing role of the federal government in financing personal health services. In the 1950s the federal government accounted for 13 per cent of total expenditures whereas currently it provides fully 40 per cent. In contrast, Britain employs a highly centralised source of funding. Since the initiation of its National Health Service in 1948, the national government has provided four-fifths of all health expenditures. On the other hand, Sweden displays a division of fiscal and administrative responsibility between the national level and the county councils. The central government finances about a quarter of health care costs and the counties provide the balance, a relative allocation which has remained quite constant during the past 25 years. All three countries also derive health revenues from contributions by employers and employees, with the proportion of total revenue from this source being highest in the United States and lowest in England. As a result of collective bargaining in the United States and political party bargaining in the other countries, however, the trend everywhere has been to minimise employee contributions.

In all three countries the health system has emphasised acute hospital care at the expense of primary or out-of-hospital care. Often the latter is labelled 'ambulatory care'. In the early 1950s Sweden devoted 47 per cent of its total personal health expenditures to hospital care; England 42 per cent; and the United States 30 per cent. In the latter 1970s the US hospital proportion has gone up to 39 per cent and the English proportion has increased to over 50 per cent, while Sweden remains the same at 48 per cent. Since health services are very labour-intensive, hospitals in all countries have incurred ever increasing costs as non-physician personnel have succeeded in getting incomes commensurate with those in private industry. On the other hand, the variations among the three countries of proportions of expenditures devoted to physicians' services were not marked; at the most, they have ranged between 16 and 18 per cent in recent years.

Comparative data reveal that each country has had 25 years of expanding its personnel, facilities and utilisation. The differences have been mainly ones of pace. In 1950 the United States started with the largest relative supply of physicians, followed in rank-order by England and then Sweden. By international standards, Sweden's supply of physicians was unusually low — being only two-fifths of the US ratio and 70 per cent of that in England. Since then, Sweden has more than doubled its supply of physicians and now begins to approximate the ratio in the United States and to exceed that of England. Significantly, in all three countries the number of nurses has increased dramatically. In 1950 the number of nurses per 100,000 population was 249 in the United States, 182 in Sweden, and 131 in England. By the middle of the 1970s the numbers had increased to 404, 612 and 238, respectively. Turnover and attrition, however, are very high.

On the other hand, while general hospital beds per thousand population have increased markedly in the United States from 3.3 beds in 1950 to 4.5 in the middle of the 1970s, the ratios in England and Sweden have slightly declined. It is difficult to differentiate between general hospital beds and all other types of beds, but clearly Sweden has always had a high bed—population ratio compared to other industrialised countries. In all three countries, however, admissions to general hospitals have been increasing. Since 1950 they grew from 110 per 1,000 to 157 in the United States; from 113 to 156 in Sweden; and from 64 to 104 in England. Paralleling these increases has been a reduction in the average length of stay. The decline in the US has been from slightly over 8 to slightly under 8 days; in Sweden from 16 to 10; and in England from 15 (1960 figure) to 10. Historically the United States has always had a lower average length of stay than other industrialised countries, but for reasons that are unclear. Accordingly, the number of general hospital days per capita continues to vary widely. In the middle 1970s, for example, the United States used 1.2 days per person, Sweden 1.5 and England 1. The differences in the use of mental hospitals are truly staggering and inexplicable with current knowledge. In the United States there is a half-day per capita use of mental hospitals, two days in Sweden, and one day in England. Still, the trend in use of mental hospitals has been downward in all three countries.

Finally, an intriguing difference in health systems — intriguing both theoretically to organisational analysts and practically to hospital administrators — has occurred in the number of personnel (exclusive of physicians) per patient day in general hospitals. In 1950 the United States recorded 1.78 personnel per patient day; Sweden 1.31; and England 1.51. By the early 1970s the United States had climbed to over 3; Sweden almost 2; and England over 3.5. Clearly health care is becoming even more labour-intensive and ever more important as a source of employment in the general economy.

The foregoing selected indicators of performance of health services systems should be regarded as inputs, i.e., the elements necessary to

affect health outcomes like recovery, stabilisation or retarded
deterioration until death. They can also be regarded as outcomes if
the primary intent is to increase access and equalise access to services.
The egalitarian objective is an end in itself. More and more equal use
of services may, therefore, be regarded as output measures. The
increasingly desired measure of output, however, is the effect of
various measures on standard health indicators: life expectancy;
mortality rates by age, sex and cause; and morbidity. Morbidity
continues to be much more difficult to measure than mortality,
although the former is the more relevant and sophisticated measure.
Both measures, however, are difficult to relate directly to personal
health services; and it is now conventional wisdom to give personal
health services no credit at all.

As illustration, let us consider the average length of life. In recent
years life expectancy for both sexes has been estimated at 72 years in
the United States; 75 in Sweden; and 73 in England. In all three,
women live longer than men by as much as five years; but the rank
order by country is again Sweden, England and the United States.
Another very popular health indicator is infant mortality, or the
number of infants per 1,000 live births who die under one year of age.
In the mid-seventies, the United States and England looked rather
similar at 16 to 17 deaths per 1,000, but Sweden's rate is
spectacularly less than 10. The rates are continuing downward in all
three countries, but again for reasons that are not directly apparent.
However, the range among regions in the English-speaking nations is
high — whether given the comprehensive health service in Britain or
the fragmented services in the United States. In contrast, Sweden's
range is very narrow whether a child is born in Gothenburg or
Jämtland. Yet in all three countries, the maternal mortality rate is
exceedingly low. In the 1970s the rate of mothers dying in childbirth
had dropped to 1.5 or less per 10,000 live births in the United States
and to 1.1 in England; in Sweden the rate has become so low that it
approximates zero and has not been considered worth reporting since
1965.

An increasing concern for public policy-makers is that these
foregoing data on vital statistics do not appear to be directly related to
the level of expenditures on health care nor to the delivery system
structures of the respective countries. There is, then, some question
about the value of increasing expenditures in view of the marginal
results that may be achieved. And there is even greater question
whether the pursuit of equality is in any way equitable in either cause

or effect. Perhaps the decade of the 1970s will be regarded as marking the first widespread scepticism by governments and private health insurance agencies alike about the value of marginal returns from increased expenditures for personal health services.

Some Problems and Predictions

This brief review of developments in health services systems in three countries has illuminated the range of performance that is politically and economically possible. All countries currently experience problems when dealing with rapidly rising costs, unequal distribution of services, and more specific controls over the health system. These issues are generic because they represent system responses to the shifting public demands which occur as specialisation increases and hospital-based technology changes. Not many years ago, only about a third of the population saw a physician at least once a year. Now, in all systems at least two-thirds of the population see a physician annually. Furthermore, definition of an emergency has been liberalised considerably so that the primary physician has become physically unable to provide a round-the-clock standby service. Possibly also, the nine-to-five, five-day-week work pattern in the general economy is also being adopted by the caring professions.

All large systems, from health services to automobile manufacturing, strain towards routine. They try to manage spontaneous and seemingly whimsical demands on them by establishing buffers to protect the mainstream of the system and yet to accommodate the demand in some way. In particular, two demands have appeared in the modern health services system which are accommodated by special provisions with special staff arrangements. One set concerns emergency services for traumas such as heart attacks and automobile accidents; the other deals with house-calls when a patient feels unable to go to the physician's office.

Systematic emergency services have been set up rather recently in all health services systems. Each has its own specially trained personnel, equipment, budget and administrative entity — including a widely-publicised telephone number. Immediately the sifting of genuine emergency calls from trivial calls becomes a problem for the emergency service. The other demand — house-calls — is handled in Scandinavia by another separate system through a central switchboard. An agency is set up to hire physicians on a moonlighting basis, and pays them relatively handsomely on a per-call or per-session basis. These physicians are usually younger members of hospital staffs or even engaged primarily in medical research, and are supplied with automobiles and/or drivers. But clearly, the out-of-hospital general practitioners have divested themselves of some traditional responsibilities, and continuity of care is lost.

England has so far succeeded better than any Western country in managing demands on its general practitioners. In 1948 the United Kingdom institutionalised general practice and so maintained general practitioners as virtually one-half of the total physician supply, a proportion not equalled anywhere else. But since the Second World War, even this beneficial institutional arrangement has undergone strain. It was a model seemingly adequate for prewar public demand, but physically unmanageable for a single general practitioner today, even with reciprocal standby arrangements among close colleagues.

The British response, interestingly in a fully governmental system, has been the private initiative of entrepreneurs, some of them physicians. These entrepreneurs have established general practice deputising services in urban areas from which general practitioners can buy standby services for home-calls at any time, regularly or sporadically. These deputising services also hire moonlighting physicians on a per-session basis, provide a car and basic equipment, and contract with the general practitioners. The moonlighting physicians are paid relatively well. In the United States, however, the response thus far has been not to absorb this type of demand at all, or else to do so by calls to the hospital emergency department. The development of systematic emergency services, however, continues apace. And in all three countries, the long-range objective is to establish many health centres with groups of physicians who can set up systematic standby services by rotating the physicians.

In all countries the primary concern is a profoundly political one: how to balance the need and demands of the public, the priorities the countries will give to health services in competition with other national concerns, and the form the organisation of health services will take. In essence, as is true of all health and welfare programmes, the tolerance of the public for politically minimal endeavours is continually being tested. The length of the queue is one such crude but politically real indicator. Another test of tolerance is the willingness of the medical profession to function in what appear to be increasingly constricted circumstances to traditional and powerful professional prerogatives inherent in professional work.

Nevertheless, we may predict that the allocations to health services will continue to increase both relatively and absolutely for the next generation. The desire for health services to cure immediately when possible and to care over the long term when cure is impossible, will continue. What may reverse this trend is a change in the attitudes of the public towards sickness, pain and dying and a turning away from professional service. Such change, however, does not seem likely nor realistic.

The pressures on the system will continue and the response will be as much rationalisation through scientifically established criteria as possible. However, criteria of sufficient depth and scope can probably not be developed to encompass more than a limited range of diagnoses that lend themselves to such specification. A health service which can be managed with as much prior specifications of results as an automobile factory would not be a health service. It would be utterly impersonal. And the ideal patient would be a breathing brick.

Should governments really contain costs through rationalisation, then priority will probably be given to high technology and correspondingly expensive procedures rather than to skilful management of long-term illness. A truly comprehensive health service will be regarded as too expensive for a national economy. But there will be increasing attempts to monitor the decision-making of physicians, as exemplified in the United States by the legally mandated Professional Standards Review Organizations. The efficacy of such attempts has yet to be tested; and the objectives are far ahead of the methodology to implement them.

Countries may be driven to the targeting of problems for special attention. The setting and implementation of priorities within the entire spectrum of health services are still at a crude stage. The tendency is towards comprehensive goals but limited achievements; even achievable benefits are not achieved. For example, there are pockets of infant mortality in the United States and the United Kingdom which have rates twice that of the national average. There are diseases that lend themselves to quite specific cure or prevention, such as venereal disease which continues to be rampant. Others, of course, are chronic and incurable.

Looking ahead to the mid-eighties, the proportions of the GNP the United States, Sweden and England devote to health services will be higher, but in the same rank order. Sweden will reach 15 per cent; the US about 12 per cent; and England over 7 per cent. Nevertheless, the United States will continue to have a more loosely structured system than either Sweden or England, but will be moving towards them in rationalising the system. Britain, on the other hand, will use the 1974 reorganisation of its National Health Service to edge towards equalisation among regions, but will do so slowly in order that no one will feel threatened. Sweden will continue to have a division of responsibilities between county and state, and keep on chipping away at fee-for-service prerogatives for private practitioners.

The respective problem-solving styles will continue undiminished. In the United States, open negotiation and bargaining between interest groups will occur as always. In Britain the moves will be towards structural reorganisation and some continued covert negotiating among interest groups. And in Sweden emphasis will remain on generating consensus through elaborate fact-finding and painstaking public discussion. Likewise, the pace at which sophisticated technology will be adopted will continue to vary. The US will be fastest, followed closely by Sweden, with Britain placing as a distant third. Indeed, given the continuum of economic constraints, Britain might well send patients needing 'heroic' procedures to Sweden and the United States. It would be cheaper than building up its own services.

The proper management of chronic illness will continue to be intractable. The reservoir of need will be vast and larger than today. The capacity of the society and the health services sector to cope adequately with this problem will continue to be limited, not only because of low priority in resource allocation but fundamentally because the kind of care required by patients with long-term and chronic illnesses is beyond price. They need the kind of care that can normally be expected only of families and relatives.

In sum, the health services will continue to be a growth industry and in public demand. The health sector will continue to be labour-intensive. And high technology will continue to develop. All of this will be expensive. There is no cheap way out. Health services cannot be efficient; yet they must be provided. Health services will continue to receive a high priority because they are wanted — regardless of so-called outcome measures.

Notes

1. Odin W. Anderson, *Health Care: Can There Be Equity? The United States, Sweden, and England* (John Wiley and Sons, New York, 1972), p. 189.
2. Jean Piaget, *The Moral Judgment of the Child*, translated by Margorie Gabain (Harcourt, Brace and Company, New York, 1932).
3. David O. Porter, 'Social Equity and Fiscal Federalism', *Public Administration Review*, 34 (1974), pp. 36–43.
4. George H. Sabine, *A History of Political Theory* (Henry Holt and Company, New York, 1950).

5. Arthur M. Okun, *Equality and Efficiency: The Big Tradeoff* (The Brookings Institution, Washington D.C., 1975).

6. John Rawls, *A Theory of Justice* (Belknap Press, Cambridge, Massachusetts, 1971).

7. Gerald S. Leventhal, 'The Distribution of Rewards and Resources in Groups and Organizations', in Leonard Berkowitz and Elaine Walster (eds.), *Equity Theory: Toward a General Theory of Social Interaction* (Academic Press, New York, 1976).

8. Harold L. Wilensky, *The Welfare State and Equality: Structural and Ideological Roots of Public Expenditures* (University of California Press, Berkeley, 1975).

9. J. G. Simanis, 'Medical Care Expenditures in Seven Countries' (Social Security Administration, US Department of Health, Education and Welfare, Washington D.C., 1973).

NOTES ON CONTRIBUTORS

Odin W. Anderson is Professor of Sociology and Director of the Center for Health Administration Studies at the University of Chicago.

Ole Berg is Assistant Professor in the Political Science Department of the University of Oslo.

James Warner Björkman is an Assistant Professor in the Political Science Department of the University of Wisconsin, Madison.

Bo Bjurulf is an Associate Professor of Political Science at the University of Lund, and a Research Fellow of the Swedish Council for Research in the Humanities and Social Sciences.

Mack Carder is a PhD Candidate in the Political Science Department of Washington University, St Louis.

Nils Elvander is Professor of Political Science at the University of Uppsala.

Arnold J. Heidenheimer is Professor of Political Science at Washington University, St Louis.

Bo Hjern is Secretary-General of the Swedish Medical Association.

Hirobumi Ito is a Research Associate of the Institute of Social Medicine at the University of Copenhagen.

Bendix Klingeberg studied sociology and political science at the University of Hamburg and Washington University.

Uncas Serner is a lawyer who has held positions with the Swedish Medical Association and the Swedish Ministry of Social Affairs.

Jan-Erik Spek is a Research Associate of the University of Gothenburg and is also affiliated with the Gothenburg Municipality.

Ingemar Ståhl is Professor of Economics at the University of Lund.

Urban Swahn is Research Associate in the Political Science Department of the University of Lund.

INDEX